SEEING THROUGH WORDS

ELIZABETH COOK

SEEING THROUGH WORDS

The scope of late Renaissance poetry

Yale University Press
New Haven and London
1986

Designed by Gillian Malpass.
Typeset in Compugraphic Garamond by
Boldface Typesetters, London EC1
and printed in Great Britain at
the Bath Press, Avon.

Library of Congress Cataloging in Publication Data

Cook, Elizabeth, 1952–
  Seeing through words.

  Bibliography: p.
  Includes index.
  1. English poetry – Early Modern, 1500–1700—History
and criticism.   I. Title.
PR541.C66 1986   821'.3'09   85–29502
ISBN 0–300–03675–2

For Shirley Chew

Acknowledgements

Much of the material in this book took its first form as a London University Ph D thesis for which I studied at the Warburg Institute. I was supervised by Michael Baxandall and I cannot imagine having written either the thesis or this book without the resource of his judgement and guidance. I sought and obtained his advice throughout and, with immense generosity of time and thought, he has read and helped me through each stage of revision and rethinking. I cannot thank him enough.

J.B. Trapp has been the source of invaluable advice and information and provided a context of encouragement over the years. I am particularly indebted to him for material which appears in chapter 2. Charles Schmidt kindly helped me when I needed to find some bearings in an unfamiliar scientific literature.

I am grateful to Frank Kermode and Michael Podro who examined the thesis and made their comments available to me. Michael Podro generously discussed with me some of the issues that occupy the first chapter and helped me clarify my thoughts.

Alan Wall brought a needed acuity to the manuscript in its penultimate form and has also helped me through many practical difficulties. John Barnard helped me with the Introduction.

The many others who have helped me with points of information and interpretation include: Bridget Anfossy, Vicki Behm, David Fairer, Lucy Gent, Anne Harrison, K.J. Höltgen, Charles Hope, Peter Hulme, Sarah Hutton, Jill Kraye, Fr Donald Lee, David Lindley, Nigel Llewellyn, Elizabeth McGrath, Jonathan Nevitt, Peter Orton and Alistair Stead.

I have had the use of good libraries: the Bodleian library, the British Library, the Brotherton Library at Leeds University, London University Library and, chiefly, the Warburg Institute library. I am grateful to their staffs for much help.

Much of the material in chapter 2 and some of that in chapter 1 has appeared in articles in volumes XLII and XLIV of the *Journal of the Warburg and Courtauld Institutes*. I am grateful to the editors for their permission to use it here. I should also like to thank Roger Nellens and Mme René Magritte for their permission to reproduce René Magritte's *La grande famille* on the book-jacket.

Lastly (chronologically) I should like to thank John Nicoll of Yale University Press for his encouragement over a long period, and Gillian Malpass for her care in preparing the book for press.

PHOTOGRAPHIC ACKNOWLEDGEMENTS

Grateful acknowledgement is made to the following for the supply of photographs and permission to reproduce them: the British Library 2, 11; The Trustees of The National Gallery, London 12, 14; the University of London Library 7, 8.

Contents

The work which this book represents began with the perception that Shakespearean and post-Shakespearean poetry registers a new kind of attentiveness to the material world. Whilst in much of Spenser's poetry it is a question of sight being analogous to the superior sight of understanding, in some of the later poetry it is more a question of proper understanding being dependent upon—a consequence of rather than similar to—proper observation of the physical world.

Writing about the visual art of the period, Svetlana Alpers has argued that 'northern images do not disguise meaning or hide it beneath the surface but rather show that meaning by its very nature is lodged in what the eye can take in—however deceptive that might be'.[1] I too shall be suggesting that meaning was increasingly felt to reside in the world of material particulars, but my subject is poetry and poetic language whose dynamics are other than those of visual art. Francis Bacon's observation that 'the substance of matter is better than the beauty of words'[2] makes a useful and corrective distinction for the experimental scientist but a false one for the poet who knows that the beauty of words is itself a substantial matter.

In the following chapters I shall be looking at some of the ways in which late Renaissance poetry draws on the multiple capacities of language to enlarge our experience of the world which language shows, and to reflect on the kind of showing which language, peculiarly, permits. Aristotle found energy (*energeia*) at the heart of linguistic showing in metaphor.[3] This energy—whether as the tensile energy that holds 'strong-lined' verse in taut compression, or as the more nearly athletic kind which draws upon the imagination's freedom of movement to explore the minutiae of the world's contours—is common to all the works I discuss. My subject is both the range of experience to which language gives access and the compression of that range within language.

I begin by looking at compression: the compression for which 'metaphysical' poetry is known. I ask in what sense this poetry may be called 'compressed' and look at the motivation of the period terms 'strong-lined' and 'far-fetched'. Thomas Hobbes's epistemology provides a possible way of understanding this poetry in terms of a real compression.

In the second chapter I concentrate on what is perhaps the crudest manifestation of an awareness of language's material (in this case graphic) presence: the 'figured poems' whose written contours form representational images. In many of these poems those contours act as foils to language's other, more lively, resources.

The third chapter is on the poetry of George Herbert for whom all individual utterances are partial articulations of a God-given, God-spoken whole. In the course of this book a variety of philosophical positions and narrative occasions will be looked at in terms of the kinds of writing that they enable. Herbert's capacity to refresh the conventional with reference to the world of natural particulars is corroborated by a theology in which eternal and temporal are crucially engaged. Herbert's own poetic energy defines itself in relation to a self-incarnating God for whom good is present and sin an absence.[4]

In the fourth chapter I look at Shakespeare's *Antony and Cleopatra* and Sonnets. In these works Shakespeare shows love as an energising force, illuminating and structuring the world around its loved centre. The condition of 'being in love' is presented as one of heightened imaginative perception and imaginative creativity.

Having examined the kind of mental stamina which enables the lover to hold the world in a state of imaginative clarity, I go on in the fifth chapter to discuss narratives of mobile imaginative energy. The theological tradition by which the soul is described as capable of fast, extensive flight, and the literary, mock-encomiastic tradition by which small objects are celebrated for their ability to invade inaccessible (human) contours, are both discussed in terms of the opportunities they provide for exploring the physical world. The notion of the ubiquity of God and, more loosely, of the pervasiveness of moral states (such as Pride) permits the bringing together of the highly intelligible with the lowly sensible.

Imaginative mobility and attention to the physical world is also the subject of chapter six which examines the relation between plot and poetry in *A Midsummer Night's Dream* and *The Tempest*. The narratives of each of these works contain the idea that the socially low may be morally valuable: that the lowly are beloved. This cherishing of the, metaphorically, low coincides with a poetry which is extraordinarily and freshly attentive to what is, literally, at ground or sea level.

The book begins by looking at linguistic compression and it concludes with a study of the work of Andrew Marvell where that compression is a governing principle. The wit of his language is to suggest the absorption of meaning into a material world and to point to a pre-linguistic world of radiant significance.

Chapter I

STRONG LINES

The poetry of the late Renaissance which we, following Dryden and Johnson, call 'metaphysical', is often characterised in terms of its linguistic and conceptual compression. In style and narrative this poetry evinces a movement which is compressing, compacting and unifying. Subject matter and philosophical orientation often corroborate the virtue of a compression which takes place on the level of style. The Christian search for atonement and the Stoic advocacy of retreat might both be seen to require a formal compression. Ben Jonson and Andrew Marvell, poets who often take positions of Christian Stoicism, identify the moral virtues of retreat and economy with an aesthetic of compactness:

> In small proportions, we just beautie see:
> And in short measures, life may perfect bee.
> ('To the immortal memorie, and
> friendship of that noble paire, Sir Lucius
> Cary, and Sir H. Morison, ll. 73–4)

> *Humility* alone designs
> Those short but admirable Lines,
> By which, ungirt and unconstrain'd,
> Things greater are in less contain'd.
> ('Upon Appleton House, to my
> Lord Fairfax', ll. 41–4)[1]

There is all the difference in the world between the tight rope of the Stoic *via media*, pulled taut between the extremes it knows, and a flaccid mediocrity. Similarly there is a difference between something which is compressed, and something which is merely small. If the juxtaposition of disparate objects in a metaphysical conceit, or the poles of signification in a pun or paradox do not register, in contracted form, a real span of mental experience, they cannot be described as examples of compression. There are those who would argue that the wit of this poetry is a record of logical affinities which can only be grasped if an imaginative sensory response to the words is suppressed. This is not my view.

STRONG LINES

The literary critical vocabulary of the late Renaissance includes several
terms that revolve around the idea of *strength*. This strength is spoken of
as if it derived from some substantial compression: like the strength of
three-ply cable. Francis Bacon commends the use of 'a good digest of
common-places' to aid and order the memory:

> I hold the entry of common-places to be a matter of great use and
> essence in studying; as that which assureth copie of invention, and con-
> tracteth judgment to a strength.[2]

The 'strength' of 'strong-lined' poetry seems also to have been thought
of as the product of contraction. Henry Reynolds suggested that poets
who lacked 'closeness' lacked mysteries worth concealing.[3] Others might
describe such 'closeness' as an unappetising fibrous density. Francis
Osborn tells his son to:

> spend no time in reading, much less writing, *strong lines*; which like
> tough meat, aske more paines and time in chewing, then can be recom-
> pensed by all the nourishment they bring.[4]

But Carew (in his elegy on Donne) and Bacon both commended a 'mascu-
line expression'. Muscular compactness is not self-evidently bad, but
there is a danger of becoming linguistically muscle-bound, in the way that
Shakespeare's Antony becomes as he punningly describes a strength that
thwarts itself:

> All length is torture: since the torch is out,
> Lie down and stray no farther. Now all labour
> Mars what it does: yea, very force entangles
> Itself with strength:
>
> (IV.xiv.46–9)[5]

Succinctness of style deriving from a lack of superfluity was a classical
ideal. Ben Jonson paraphrases Horace (and Alberti) when he recommends
'A strict and succinct style ... where you can take away nothing without
losse, and that losse to be manifest'.[6] But Jonson thought that some
concision did involve a manifest loss:

> Whatsoever looseth the grace, and clearenesse, converts into a Riddle;
> the obscurity is mark'd, but not the valew ... Our style should be like a
> skeine of silke, to be carried, and found by the right thred, not ravel'd,
> and perplex'd; then all is a knot, a heape.[7]

Thomas Hobbes suggests a distinction between true and spurious strength
of lines. In his 'Answer' to his friend Davenant's 'Epistle' he censures:

> ... the ambitious obscurity of expressing more than is perfectly con-
> ceived; or perfect conception in fewer words than it requires. Which

expressions, though they have had the honour to be called strong lines, are indeed no better than riddles, and not only to the reader, but also after a little time to the writer himself, dark and troublesome.[8]

But besides such a pretence of strength in which 'perfect conception' is expressed 'in fewer words than it requires' is the true strength of apt expression. In the preface to his translation of Thucydides Hobbes approvingly cites Cicero's opinion of his author:

> For he is so full of matter, that the number of his sentences doth almost reach to the number of his words; and in his words he is so apt and so close, that it is hard to say whether his words do more illustrate his sentences, or his sentences his words.[9]

Hobbes adds, 'There is for the pithiness and strength of his style.' The distinction Hobbes would have us make is between tough, close thinking expressed in tough close language, and the void obscurity of an empty language with only the appearance of strength. He defends Thucydides against the charge of obscurity:

> ...the obscurity that is, proceedeth from the profoundness of the sentences; containing contemplations of those human passions, which either dissembled or not commonly discoursed of, do yet carry the greatest sway with men in their public conversation. If then one cannot penetrate into them without much meditation, we are not to expect a man should understand them at the first speaking...If therefore Thudydides in his orations, or in the description of a sedition, or other thing of that kind, be not easily understood; it is of those only that cannot penetrate into the nature of such things, and proceedeth not from any intricacy of expression.[10]

THE FAR-FETCHED

Another term which began to be applied to language in this period was *far-fetched* (or far-fet). Philip Sidney uses it, in *Astrophil and Stella*, 15, to refer to an idiom which had come all the way from Tuscany:

> You that do search for everie purling spring,
>   Which from the ribs of old *Parnassus* flowes,
>
>   .   .   .   .
>
>   You that poore *Petrarch's* long deceased woes,
> With new-borne sighes and denisend wit do sing;
>   You take wrong waies, those far-fet helpes be such,
>   As do bewray a want of inward tuch.[11]

George Puttenham seems to have a different kind of journey in mind when he describes the figure of *Metalepsis*:

> ...the sence is much altered & the hearers conceit strangly entangled
> by the figure *Metalepsis*, which I call the *farfet*, as when we had rather
> fetch a word a great way off then to vse one nerer hand to expresse the
> matter aswel & plainer. And it seemeth the deuiser of this figure, had a
> desire to please women rather then men: for we vse to say by manner of
> Prouerbe: things farrefet and deare bought are good for Ladies: so in
> this manner of speach we vse it, leaping ouer the heads of a great many
> words, we take one that is furdest off, to vtter our matter by.[12]

Puttenham's own metaphor suggests that a language user's lexical reper-
toire is stored in some kind of finite space in which some words are contig-
uous and near, others not.

Jonson uses the term to express the Aristotelian judgement that '*Meta-
phors* farfet hinder to be understood, and affected, lose their grace.'[13]
Hobbes, in his free translation of Aristotle's *Rhetoric*, writes that 'A met-
aphor ought not to be so far-fetched, as that the similitude may not easily
appear.'[14] It is apparent from the account of mental processes which he
gives elsewhere that Hobbes's own metaphor of far-fetching may be moti-
vated by a conception of some kind of space in which journeys of varying
lengths can take place.

HOBBES AND MENTAL ENDEAVOUR

Hobbes accounts for all thought as the interactive play of the images (or
phantasms, for they are not all visual) which derive from direct sensory
confrontation with the material world of which the perceiving individual
is part. For Hobbes the imagination is entirely adequate as a means of rep-
resenting, though not of duplicating, the external world. To underline
this he conceived of a hypothetical situation in which the entire universe
is annihilated with the exception of one man who conserves in his
memory all the phantasms of the bodies which he had perceived in their
presences before they were destroyed:

> For the understanding of what I mean by the power cognitive, we must
> remember and acknowledge that there be in our minds continually cer-
> tain images or conceptions of the things without us, insomuch that if a
> man could be alive, and all the rest of the world annihilated, he should
> nevertheless retain the image thereof, and of all those things which he
> had before seen and perceived in it; every man by his own experience
> knowing that the absence or destruction of things once imagined, doth
> not cause the absence or destruction of the imagination itself.[15]

This is not an utterance of terrified scepticism. (The apocalyptic suggestion is
not the point.) Unlike Descartes' idea of a *malin génie*, this hypothetical
situation has no ontological implications. Its function is to illustrate how
thoroughly and adequately representative the imagination is. Thus:

... if we do but observe diligently what it is we do when we consider and reason, we shall find, that though all things be still remaining in the world, yet we compute nothing but our own phantasms. For when we calculate the magnitude and motions of heaven or earth, we do not ascend into heaven that we may divide it into parts, or measure the motions thereof, but we do it sitting still in our closets or in the dark.[16]

Henry Peacham had described the art of 'Cosmographie' as that which gives us 'the world in a string, in our owne chamber'.[17] In this art, 'at once both feeding the eye and the mind', agreed and visible symbols represent and make accessible to the understanding a universe otherwise beyond man's grasp. In Hobbes's system the phantasms which constitute the imagination have a similar representative function, contracting the sensed and sensible world into the circumference of a man's mind so that he could be 'bounded in a nutshell and count [him] self king of infinite space.'

It is this emphasis on the sufficiency of the imagination's representative powers which is at the root of Hobbes's description of imaginative range:

For memory is the world, though not really, yet so as in a looking-glass, in which the judgment, the severer sister, busieth herself in a grave and rigid examination of all the parts of nature, and in registering by letters their order, causes, uses, differences and resemblances; whereby the fancy when any work of art is to be performed, finds her materials at hand and prepared for use and needs no more than a swift motion over them, that what she wants, and is there to be had, may not lie too long unespied. So that when she seemeth to fly from one Indies to the other, and from heaven to earth, and to penetrate into the hardest matter and obscurest places, into the future, and into herself, and all this in a point of time, the voyage is not very great, herself being all she seeks. And her wonderful celerity, consisteth not so much in motion as in copious imagery discreetly ordered, and perfectly registered in the memory.[18]

Hobbes describes the journey which the fancy undertakes with its 'swift motion' in terms which derive from patristic descriptions of the soul sent out in flight. But the journey is an internal one. The speed of thought is accounted for by the contiguity of the phantasms with which thought works.

More immediately than the Church Fathers, Hobbes's description of the mind's repertoire of phantasms recalls his mentor Galileo's celebration of alphabetical writing (I am using Thomas Salusbury's late seventeenth-century translation):

what sublimity of mind must have been his who conceived how to communicate his most secret thoughts to any other person, though very far distant either in time or place, speaking with those who are in the

Indies, speaking to those who are not yet born, nor shall be this thousand, or ten thousand years? And with no greater difficulty than the various collocation of twenty-four little characters upon a paper?[19]

Both Galileo and Hobbes celebrate the enormous range which the finite repertoires of the alphabet or 'copious imagery' allow. The images which Hobbes describes, 'discretely ordered and perfectly registered in the memory', are like the letters in a fount, capable of almost infinitely various combinations, but in the meantime compactly stored. The mind as Hobbes describes it is one in which no conception—and consequently no metaphor—can be 'farfet'. No voyage within such a mind can be 'very great' since none of the variously collocated images can need fetching very far.

Yet the model of mind which Hobbes was to develop does allow for distinctions of speed and distance to be made. His most influential contribution to the poetic theory of the next generation was his distinction between 'wit' and 'judgement'. In *Leviathan* he describes judgement as the faculty which isolates and dissects; 'wit' or 'fancy' as the one that observes relations and creates syntheses:

> NATURAL WIT, consisteth principally in two things; *celerity of imagining*, that is swift succession of one thought to another; and *steady direction* to some approved end . . . those that observe their similitudes, in case they be such as are but rarely observed by others, are said to have a *good wit*; by which, in this occasion, is meant a *good fancy*. But they that observe their differences, and dissimilitudes; which is called *distinguishing*, and *discerning*, and *judging* between thing and thing; in case, such discerning be not easy, are said to have a good *judgement*.[20]

In the later *De Homine* Hobbes makes more explicit the distinctions between wit and judgement and suggests that natural wit can be employed in different ways:

> Dispositions differ in two ways due to the mobility of the animal spirits (that is, from the swiftness of imagining things): first, because some dispositions are more acute; whence some people are of a lively disposition, and others of a slow one; secondly, of those that are of a quick disposition, because some let their thoughts wander over vast spaces, and some let them revolve around only one thing; whence fancy is praiseworthy in some, while judgment is commendable in others. And so the disposition of the latter people is suitable for resolving controversies, and for philosophy of all kinds (that is, for reasoning); of the former, for poetry and invention; both alike are suitable for oratory. And indeed, judgment subtly distinguisheth among similar objects while fancy pleasingly confounds dissimilar objects.[21]

The 'spaces' over which those of a 'quick disposition' let their thoughts wander are, though hardly 'vast', not entirely figures of speech. Though no 'voyage' within the mind as mapped by Hobbes can be 'very great', there are incalculably small distinctions to be made between the various speeds and distances which the animal spirits cover as they range in thought between phantasm and phantasm.

Hobbes, following Galileo, saw the world as consisting of bodies in motion. In order to describe the motions of bodies he developed the concept of *conatus*, or endeavour, which he defined as instantaneous motion through minimal space: 'motion made through the length of a point, and in an instant or point of time'.[22] Hobbes's pre-calculus mathematics were not up to the task of measuring infinitesimals but the notion of *conatus* is perhaps more useful in its application to psychic motions in that it allows a description of 'mental discourse' to adhere to a system of causality without reducing the mind to a crude and lumbering machine.

In chapter vi of *Leviathan* Hobbes describes the transition between volition and activity in these terms:

> ...because *going, speaking*, and the like voluntary motions, depend always upon a precedent thought of *whither*, *which way* and *what*; it is evident, that the imagination is the first internal beginning of all voluntary motion. And although unstudied men do not conceive any motion at all to be there, where the thing moved is invisible; or the space it is moved in is, for the shortness of it, insensible; yet that doth not hinder, but that such motions are. For let a space be never so little, that which is moved over a greater space, whereof that little one is part, must first be moved over that. These small beginnings of motion, within the body of man, before they appear in walking, speaking, striking and other visible actions, are commonly called ENDEAVOUR.[23]

Similarly imperceptible but extant motions must be implicit in Hobbes's description, in his 'Answer' to Davenant, of the fancy's activity when

> ...she seemeth to flie from one Indies to the other, and from heaven to earth, and to penetrate into the hardest matter and obscurest places... all...in a point of time...[24]

The voyage here is not 'very great'—it is in fact immeasurably small— but it is a voyage of sorts. And, as the distinction between 'wit' or 'fancy' and 'judgement' suggests, these minute distances are traversed by animal spirits which vary in their capacity for range and speed.

Hobbes's description of consecutive thinking conforms to the determinism of his system. He divides 'mental discourse' (so called to distinguish it from verbal) into two categories:

> ...unguided...in which case the thoughts are said to wander, and seem impertinent one to another, as in a dream...[and in the other] *regulated* by some desire, and design.[25]

His description of the former is of something very close to psychoanalytic 'free association'—and Hobbes appreciated as much as Freud was to how little freedom is really involved in this incalculably determined process:

> When a man thinketh on any thing whatsoever, his next thought after, is not altogether so casual as it seems to be. Not every thought to every thought succeeds indifferently. But as we have no imagination whereof we have not formerly had sense . . . so we have no transition from one imagination to another, whereof we never had the like before in our senses.[26]

Hobbes gives us two examples of seemingly random 'non sequiturs' and teases them out to reveal a sequence of mutually connected ideas which had been compressed out of sight and yet which govern and fill the 'gap' between apparent incongruities. The first example appears in *The Elements of Law* where he analyses the association between St Andrew and a tumult:

> . . . from St. Andrew the mind runneth to St. Peter, because their names are read together; from St. Peter to a stone, for the same cause; from stone to foundation, because we see them together; and for the same cause, from foundation to church, from church to people, and from people to tumult. And according to this example, the mind may run almost from any thing to any thing. But as to the sense the conception of cause and effect succeed one another; so may they after sense in the imagination.[27]

Eleven years later in *Leviathan* he gives a more complex example:

> in a discourse of our present civil war, what could seem more impertinent, than to ask, as one did, what was the value of a Roman penny? Yet the coherence to me was manifest enough. For the thought of the war, introduced the thought of the delivering up the king to his enemies; the thought of that, brought in the thought of the delivering up of Christ; and that again the thought of the thirty pence, which was the price of that treason; and thence easily followed that malicious question, and all this in a moment of time; for thought is quick.[28]

In these descriptions, in which instantaneous and surprising associations are teased into intelligibility, Hobbes demonstrates how 'the mind may run almost from anything to anything', speeding through, rather than (in Puttenham's phrase) 'leaping over' the intermediary links in a universe which is continuous and in which all metaphor (if 'perfect conception' lies behind the words) is a form of metonymy. The resonating mesh of interdependence potentially cast out by trains of thought may thus be as intricate and exhaustive, though not as consoling, as any grid of divine intentionality. Hobbes's account is one in which the conjunction of apparently incongruous verbal images may be achieved by means of an imperceptibly quick mental journey through an intervening continuum. It is an account in which the 'strength' of strong lines can be derived from their compression of real, if incalculable, space.

* * *

In Hobbes's account language is subsequent to, and should subserve, 'mental discourse'. He would have the significations of words settled in the manner of geometric definitions:

> Seeing then that truth consisteth in the right ordering of names in our affirmations, a man that seeketh precise truth, had need to remember what every name he uses stands for, and to place it accordingly, or else he will find himself entangled in words, as a bird in lime twigs, the more he struggles the more belimed. And therefore in geometry, which is the only science that it hath pleased God hitherto to bestow on mankind, men begin at settling the significations of their words; which settling of significations they call definitions and place them in the beginning of their reckoning.[29]

In another, irrepressibly metaphorical, passage Hobbes writes that:

> the light of human minds is perspicuous words, but by exact definitions first snuffed, and purged from ambiguity . . . metaphors, and senseless and ambiguous words, are like *ignes fatui*; and reasoning upon them is wandering amongst innumerable absurdities.[30]

The resistance of words to the kind of strong government which Hobbes would impose on them belies his geometric analogy.

Hobbes does allow words a graphic and an acoustic substantiality. As graphic phenomena words may be associated by contiguity—a contiguity which is probably, though not necessarily, semantically determined: 'from St. Andrew the mind runneth to St. Peter, because their names are read together'. But the graphic or acoustic substantiality of written or spoken language can only, in Hobbes's view, undermine its contractual, semantic function. Words are contracted to signify conceptions (or phantasms). The conception of the words themselves as material beings which create auditory or visual phantasms can only undermine this contractual function:

> When a man, upon the hearing of any speech, hath those thoughts which the words of that speech and their connexion were ordained and constituted to signify, then he is said to understand it; *understanding* being nothing else but conception caused by speech . . . And therefore of absurd and false affirmations, in case they be universal, there can be no understanding; though many think they understand then, when they do but repeat the words softly, or con them in their mind.[31]

A sense that words inhabit the sensible and conceivable world—that they cannot be reduced to their signifying function—preys on Hobbes's thought. The power of words can only distract from the kind of power with which he was primarily concerned. The place he allows words in his system is one of subjugation.

Hobbes's epistemology provides an approximately contemporaneous way of understanding the compression of strong lines as the product of a real compression—the compression of the sensed and sensible world into the mind that inhabits and perceives it. As a nominalist, Hobbes was acutely aware of words' perilous creativity. Universals are the creations of language alone; they have no existence outside it. For Hobbes, whose duty is to the extra-linguistic world where universals have no being, such creativity is misleading and distracting. For a more positive sense of what language's various and contradictory resources can peculiarly do, it is necessary to look at other kinds of practice.

*   *   *

Jeremy Taylor, in his contribution to the protracted debate over the permissibility of religious images, shows an unusually keen understanding of the difference between verbal and pictorial representation. He does not fall for the argument that biblical metaphor—verbal 'imagery'—constitutes a divine sanction for pictorial representation:

> For it is said, that it is true God's essence cannot be depicted or engraven; but such representations by which He hath been pleased to communicate notices of Himself can as well be described with a pencil as with a pen, and as well set down so that idiots may read and understand as well as the learned clerks. Now because God was pleased to appear to Daniel like the Ancient of days, and the Holy Ghost in the shape of a dove, and Christ in the form of a man, these representations may be depicted and described by images without disparagement to the divinity of God.[32]

Taylor sees a very firm distinction between the incarnation of the Word as Christ in his humanity—an act on God's part which permits the representation of Christ as man—and the metaphorical bodying forth in language of the invisible which makes the other two parts of the Trinity accessible to the understanding. In rejecting the use of scriptural metaphor as the justifying basis for representing God the Father and God the Holy Ghost, Taylor shows an understanding of the difference between visual images and verbal imagery—a knowledge that the latter is not reducible to the former:

> If because mention is made of 'the Ancient of days' in Daniel, it were lawful to picture God like an old man, we might as well make a door and say it is Christ, or a vine and call it our master, or a thief and call it

the day of judgment: a metaphorical or mystical expression may be the veil of a mysterious truth, but cannot pass into a sign and signification of it; itself may become an hieroglyphic when it is painted, but not an image which is μοϱφὴ εἰδικὸς [sic], and the most proper representation of any thing that can be seen and is not present.[33]

By 'hieroglyphic' Taylor presumably means some kind of representation that, by its evidently unnatural configuration, signals the need for a mental translation into significance. Of Daniel's vision he writes:

> . . . if it were expressed in picture as it is set down, [it] would be the most strange production of art, and a horrid representation of nature; and unless something were supposed which is not expressed, it would be a strange new nothing. For 'the Ancient of days' does by no violence signify an old man; for it being a representment of eternity, is the worst of all expressed by an old man; for that which is old is ready to vanish away, and nothing is more contrary to eternity. Again, here is no mention of the appearance of a man. There is indeed mention of a head, but neither of man nor beast, bird nor fly expressed; and hair like pure wool, but in what it is like excepting only the purity is not told, nor can be imagined: after this there is nothing but 'a throne of flames' and 'wheels of fire', and all this together would make a strange image, a metaphor to express eternity, a head of I know not what light without substance, visibility without a figure, a top without a bottom, the whiteness of wool instead of the substance of hair, and a seat upon wheels, and all in flames and fire: that it should ever enter into the head or heart of an instructed man to think that the great, the immense, the invisible, the infinite God of heaven, that fills heaven and earth and hell, should be represented in image or picture by such a thing, by such a nothing, is as strange and prodigious as the combination of all the daughters of fear and sleep and ignorance.[34]

Implicit in this passage is Taylor's understanding of the way in which verbal metaphor can refer without identifying—the way in which 'is unlike' underwrites every statement of 'is like'.

Taylor's discussion of the difference between the realised images of visual representations and the not-to-be-realised references of verbal metaphor, would seem to support Rosemond Tuve's thesis in *Elizabethan and Metaphysical Imagery*, that consideration of the effects of language, in both Elizabethan and later Renaissance England, revolved more around the strictly logical function of images chosen on the basis of logically applicable predicaments, than around the referents' integrity as sensible objects:

> The didactic theory operates to lessen the emphasis upon the sensuous function of images and to subtilize and multiply the logical functions they are capable of performing. Both these habits of thinking run

counter to what Romantic criticism and Symbolist poetic have taught
us to expect of poetic imagery.[35]

Thus, in certain kinds of simile, once the logical applicability of the image
has been grasped, other qualities of the 'vehicle' may be discarded as
irrelevant. Predicaments of 'quality' and 'manner of doing' inform the
images in which Daniel's vision is described; other predicaments of snow,
wool, fire and flame, are intrusive and should not be entertained.

But Tuve's own readings unnecessarily limit the ways in which late
Renaissance poetry can work. The poetry of this period shows an extra-
ordinary alertness to the resources of language and to what it is possible to
do with words alone. Different capacities, different facets may be brought
into play (and conflict) at different times. On each occasion some capaci-
ties will be masked off, others culled. Sonnet 9 of Sidney's *Astrophil and
Stella* works in a way that Tuve would recognise. It demands that the
reader suppress irrelevant predicaments:

> Queen *Vertue's* court, which some call *Stella's* face,
>   Prepar'd by Nature's chiefest furniture,
>   Hath his front built of Alablaster pure;
> Gold is the covering of that stately place.
> The doore by which sometimes comes forth her Grace,
>   Red Porphir is, which locke of pearle makes sure:
>   Whose porches rich (which name of cheekes endure)
> Marble mixt red and white to enterlace.
>   The windowes now through which this heav'nly guest
> Looks over the world, and can find nothing such,
> Which dare claime from those lights the name of best,
> Of touch they are that without touch doth touch,
>   Which *Cupid's* selfe from Beautie's myne did draw:
>   Of touch they are, and poore I am their straw.

This sonnet turns on the notion of the body as the house of the soul, but it
works only if we limit our imagination of the referents to considerations of
colour, beauty and, above all, value. We must suppress images of size, shape
and texture. If we did not suppress these, irrelevant, aspects of the refer-
ents the result would be as grotesque and 'horrid a representation of
nature' as a literalistic rendering of Daniel's vision. Indeed the conspic-
uous grotesqueness of Arcimbaldo's paintings and those of his followers,
in which analogues are visually forced beyond the tangent at which they
are logically and decorously appropriate, testifies to the delicacy and res-
traint of Sidney's verbal method. By assuming in his readers an ability to
mask off so many aspects of his chosen image, Sidney is able to evaluate
by a reference which never hardens into identity.

But if this poem works in a way which Tuve would recognise, others do
not. John Donne's poem about *metempsychosis*, 'The Progresse of the

Soule', also turns on the idea of the body as the house of the soul. But in this poem energy is directed towards particularising the concept so that the soul's various corporeal homes can be explored as they are inhabited. In this poem Donne uses the traditionally mobile soul as an imaginative vehicle which enables a poetry of extraordinary particularity:

> To an unfettered soules quick nimble hast
> Are falling stars, and hearts thoughts, but slow pac'd:
> Thinner then burnt aire flies this soule, and she
> Whom foure new comming, and foure parting Suns
> Had found, and left the Mandrakes tenant, runnes
> Thoughtlesse of change, when her firme destiny
> Confin'd, and enjayld her, that seem'd so free,
> Into a small blew shell, the which a poore
> Warme bird orespread, and sat still evermore,
>   Till her inclos'd child kickt, and pick'd it self a dore.
>
> Outcrept a sparrow, this soules moving Inne,
> On whose raw armes stiffe feathers now begin,
> As childrens teeth through gummes, to breake with paine,
> His flesh is jelly yet, and his bones threds,
> All a new downy mantle overspreads,
> A mouth he opes, which would as much containe
> As his late house, and the first houre speaks plaine,
> And chirps alowd for meat...
>
> (ll.171−88)[36]

Language universalises and predicates. Sidney draws upon these capacities in *Astrophil and Stella* 9. But language also refers and particularises, and Donne, in 'The Progresse of the Soule', draws upon these capacities to a far greater extent than does Sidney in the sonnet. Imagination of *sensibilia* is not impertinent on the part of Donne's reader.

The poles of universal and particular may be drawn out and made more evident by certain narrative situations. In such cases the narrative might be said to illustrate by the exaggeration of caricature potentialities which are, in the first instance, linguistic. Shakespeare's Venus—'She's love, she loves and yet she is not lov'd' (*Venus and Adonis*, 1.610)[37]—is both a universal principle, and a particular embodied instance, and as such a victim, of that principle. In her dual nature she is a type—almost an explanatory caricature—of the language which bestows such duality upon her. Marvell's mower, emblem of the Great Reaper but also, in his individuality, its potential victim ('By his own Sythe, the Mower mown', 'Damon the Mower', l.80) has a similar doubleness productive of poetry at once emblematic and particular. In this case the individuality of Damon the mower invigorates the traditional emblem of Death the Reaper, while the authority of the emblem works to rescue the poem from mere circumstantiality.

Words are held taut between the contrary pulls of particular and universal; meaning would be lost if either surrendered its claims. But different occasions call for different emphases and Sidney, in *Astrophil and Stella* 9, draws principally on language's universalising movement. It is this that Petrarch, and writers in the Petrarchan tradition, tend to draw out. The unparticularised images employed in this poetry show the beloved to have a more than local significance. Laura's loveliness and the poet's response to it are presented as part of a universal principle of love.

But if Petrarchan poetry exploits and turns uppermost the universalising face of language, 'anti-Petrarchan' poetry, written in response to numbly formulaic Petrarchan travesties, deliberately ignores the expressive possibilities of such universalising. It pretends to take the Petrarchan idiom as one which tries, and fails, to particularise. Shakespeare, in sonnet 130, works by a method of negative definition which asks us to imagine with inappropriate fulness the kinds of referents employed in the traditional *blazon*:

> My mistress' eyes are nothing like the sun—
> Coral is far more red than her lips' red—
> If snow be white, why then her breasts are dun—
> If hairs be wires, black wires grow on her head:
> I have seen roses damasked, red and white,
> But no such roses see I in her cheeks,
> And in some perfumes is there more delight
> Than in the breath that from my mistress reeks.
> I love to hear her speak, yet well I know
> That music hath a far more pleasing sound.
> I grant I never saw a goddess go;
> My mistress when she walks treads on the ground.
>   And yet by heav'n I think my love as rare
>   As any she belied with false compare.[38]

The effect of this sonnet is oddly to reaffirm the validity of the sort of false comparison it exposes since, in spite of the muted and ambiguous affirmation of the couplet, the first eight lines have an air of insult: a mistress with lips less red than coral and breasts less white than snow is a poor thing. It is not until 'I love to hear her speak' that we realise that it is the idiom of comparison, not the mistress, that is being scrutinised and found wanting. Spenser, uncharacteristically, takes the 'Petrarchan' idiom at its word when he uses its materials to assemble the zombie false Florimell in Book III of *The Faerie Queene*:

> The substance, whereof she the bodie made,
>   Was purest snow in massie mould congeald
>   .   .   .   .

> In stead of eyes two burning lampes she set
>   In siluer sockets, shyning like the skyes,
>   And a quicke mouing Spirit did arret
> To stirre and roll them, like a womans eyes:
>   In stead of yellow lockes she did deuise,
>   With golden wyre to weaue her curled head.
>   (Canto viii. verses 6 and 7)[39]

There is a deliberate, comic perversity in the way in which Shakespeare and Spenser, in these last instances, insist on recovering the sensible, referential aspect of verbal images which were intended to evaluate in an intelligible way. Both poets draw upon, and often focus upon the difference between, the sensible and the intelligible directions of language. But it is characteristic of late Renaissance poetry that the referential, particularising aspect of language be given greater attention than before.

The word 'rare', suggesting the inappropriateness of all comparison, is the most significant in Shakespeare's sonnet 130. It also occurs in the less ambiguously loving 'anti-Petrarchan' sonnet 21:

> So is it not with me as with that muse,
> Stirred by a painted beauty to his verse,
> Who heav'n itself for ornament doth use,
> And every fair with his fair doth rehearse—
> Making a couplement of proud compare
> With sun and moon, with earth and sea's rich gems,
> With April's first-born flow'rs, and all things rare
> That heaven's air in this huge rondure hems.
> O let me true in love but truly write,
> And then believe me, my love is as fair
> As any mother's child, though not so bright
> As those gold candles fixed in heaven's air.
>   Let them say more that like of hearsay well;
>   I will not praise that purpose not to sell.

This sonnet is much more than an artful expression of ingenuousness. It is a poem that thinks about, rather than merely plays with, the question of how to invent sincere expression about a unique object in a genre which is conventional and a language which is analogical. The conventionality of the genre—the conventionality of the sonnet itself—is a more graspable form of the conventionality of language. If one is turning towards the particular then, as legislators know, the formulations of language contain an inevitable injustice. The finite lexicon of necessity rounds off and simplifies the infinity of instances which it names. This injustice is the price of our sanity.

It nevertheless remains true that the resources of mobilised language extend our experience of the world far more than they are felt to limit it.

If we feel that language is capable of particularising adequately, it is because language has shown us those particulars. Shakespeare's sonnet 21 insists on the referentiality of language and assumes that the two referents involved in a metaphorical comparison exist in a mutually affecting relationship. Those 'rare' objects usually referred to in elevating comparisons are here thought of as degraded and debased by the 'couplements' that poet-pimps enforce between them and their painted beauties. The word 'use', with its connotations of profit and usury, communicates the acquisitive conversion of all lovely diversity into commodity: the opportunism of poets. This surely implies a very different conception of 'imagery' from that of which Rosemond Tuve writes and with which Sidney was working in *Astrophil and Stella*. According to the argument of Shakespeare's sonnet 21, the 'couplements' of metaphor involve a mutual relationship in which objects distinct and 'rare' affect each other.

Elsewhere in the Sonnets Shakespeare uses images in a way which sets their logical function in the argument at odds with their expressive function:

> Shall I compare thee to a summer's day?
> Thou art more lovely and more temperate:
> Rough winds do shake the darling buds of May,
> And summer's lease hath all too short a date;
> Sometime too hot the eye of heaven shines,
> And often is his gold complexion dimmed;
> And every fair from fair sometime declines,
> By chance or nature's changing course untrimmed:
> But thy eternal summer shall not fade,
> Nor lose possession of that fair thou ow'st,
> Nor shall death brag thou wand'rest in his shade,
> When in eternal lines to time thou grow'st.
> > So long as men can breathe or eyes can see,
> > So long lives this, and this gives life to thee.
>
> (18)

The poem's implicit answer to the question of the first line is, 'No. The comparison would be inappropriate for the following reasons...' Nevertheless, and in a way which is different from the sophistical backtrackings of 'inexpressibility topoi', Shakespeare does use the image of a summer's day to provide us with an image of threatened and transient beauty of the kind which gives the loved boy his value and which inspired the desire to perpetuate that beauty in a sonnet which pretends to have satisfied that desire. The beauties of the summer's day are both compared to and contrasted with the loveliness of the boy. The boy is both included in the fate which awaits every fair thing (1.7) and avoids this common destiny by his 'preservation' in the sonnet. 'Rough winds do shake the darling buds of May': 'darling' hints at the mutual applicability of the image: that which is being apparently contrasted with the boy is in fact evocative of the same anxious cherishing. But Shakespeare is not merely doing what he says he is not doing. The 'darling buds of May' do not exist, as they might in an overt simile, only to subserve the notion of the boy's threatened beauty. They are themselves objects of concern and grief: they do not exist in an allegorical relation to a prior subject.

What language denies, it also presents. To name—even for the purposes of refutation, denial, contrast or exclusion—is to give some measure of presence:

> I was neither at the hot gates
> Nor fought in the warm rain
> Nor knee deep in the salt marsh, heaving a cutlass,
> Bitten by flies, fought.
> (T.S. Eliot 'Gerontion' ll.3–6)

Those things that were not are summoned into presence. What is named as absent has more presence than all unnamed absences. This is why 'reckoning' in language is such a perilous business. For Hobbes 'words are wise men's counters, they do but reckon by them; but they are the money of fools.'[40] But these 'counters' have a momentum of their own which can work against their logical function. In language it is possible to affirm and deny, compare and contrast, at the same time and in the same words:

> Dull sublunary lovers love
> (Whose soule is sense) cannot admit
> Absence, because it doth remove
> Those things which elemented it.
>
> But we by a love, so much refin'd,
> That our selves know not what it is,
> Inter-assured of the mind,
> Care lesse, eyes, lips, and hands to misse.
> ('A Valediction: forbidding mourning',
> ll.13–20)

Donne, by a careful placing of the words which demands a careful articulation on our part as we read, has drawn upon this quality of affirmation latent in all naming to charge the bare nouns—'eyes, lips, and hands'— with a lingering tenderness which belies the unregretful surface argument of the stanzas.

In Shakespeare's sonnet 65 the logic of the syntax would tell us that 'Brass,...stone,...earth,...[and] boundless sea' are all vulnerable to 'sad mortality'. But the words themselves argue in a different direction. As images of power they are associated with, and become specific images of, that 'sad mortality' to which they are, we are told, subject:

> Since brass, nor stone, nor earth, nor boundless sea,
> But sad mortality o'ersways their power,
> How with this rage shall beauty hold a plea,
> Whose action is no stronger than a flower?
> O how shall summer's honey breath hold out
> Against the wrackful siege of batt'ring days,
> When rocks impregnable are not so stout,
> Nor gates of steel so strong but time decays?

The 'rocks impregnable', the 'gates of steel', are alike susceptible to time, but they work against this argument by seeming to detail and bring into closer focus 'the wrackful siege of batt'ring days'. This detailing, though contrary to the logic of the argument which tells us these things are vulnerable, adds to the imaginative weight of the argument. In language such serene contradictions are possible.

*   *   *

For Hobbes the mind's fount of phantasms, derived in a calculable way from the larger world which it inhabits and represents, is compression enough. In his view, the further compression of these unique confrontations into equivalents from a finite lexical repertoire, marks a danger area for all but the most rigorous thinker who will remember that 'there [is] nothing in the world universal but names'.[41]

But while the plenitude of language with its synchronically finite lexicon is necessarily more limited than the plenitude of the non-linguistic world, the intimation and experience of that world's plenitude is, for individual language users, predominantly derived from linguistic experience. We experience more of the world through language than through any other means of confrontation. The synchronically finite lexicon, like the twenty-six letters it breaks down to, is, in its 'various collocations', capable of a reach that can seem almost adequate to the world it articulates (though only insofar as the lexicon is felt to fall short of the world are thought, and the lexicon, extended).

The compression and reach of the lexicon is the compression and reach of its constituent words. The compression which distinguishes so much late Renaissance poetry derives from, and draws attention to, the compression of the word. The stylistic features of this poetry, far from being period idiosyncrasies, draw out and make evident the multiplicity of ways in which words function.

Chapter 2

FIGURED POETRY

The convention of the sonnet form may be used in a way which draws attention to the conventionality of language: Shakespeare uses the form in this way in his sonnet 21. The 'figured poems' which enjoyed a vogue in the late sixteenth and early seventeenth centuries throw the conceptual subtleties of language into relief by taking its graphic materiality to an extreme which might be called caricature. In these works, the shape of the poem on the page is not the generated product and reflection of the poem's audible and conceptual structure so much as its preimposed determinant. Addison was to see in this mode of writing a cautionary example of 'false wit'[1] and Hobbes writes slightingly of those who 'vary [their] measures, and seek glory from a needless difficulty; as he that contrived verses into the forms of an organ, a hatchet, an egg, an altar, and a pair of wings'.[2] But such works commanded serious admiration from others. In England, George Herbert produced at least two poems in this mode; poems which are not aberrant from, but which carry to more demonstrative extremes, and which may thereby make more evident, the linguistic consciousness shown in the rest of his work.

'No object', said Magritte,' is so attached to its name that another cannot be found which suits it better.'[3] But Magritte's power to disturb whilst exposing the apparent randomness of our designations, in a painting such as *La Clef des Songes*, derives from the way in which something of the object actually does rub off onto the word with which it has long been associated. The maker of a figured poem would seem to be straightening the attachment between word and object to as near an identity as is possible whilst using a non-iconic script.

However specious this man-forged link may be, the finished figured or acrostic poem (for many of the more complex figured poems involve the technique of acrostic coincidence) achieves a seemingly neutral fittingness which put it on a par with a page from Nature's Book, in which sage medieval and Renaissance readers could perceive a tightly structured design. In this book Galileo read the language of mathematics,[4] perceiving divine intentionality in the geometric forms of the universe. The mathematics on which he relied were, in the course of the seventeenth century, to become the model and touchstone of all enquiry. It was to geometric certainty that Hobbes, Descartes and Pascal appealed: lexical language had to conform to a geometric paradigm in order to make sense.

Prior to this access of scientific empiricism (and for such as Sir Thomas Browne, considerably after),[5] it had been possible to discern words as well as forms and numbers inscribed in Nature's Book. The moment of inscription is described by Ovid in the passage where the mourning Phoebus tattoos the flower that sprang from the dead Hyacinthus' lips with the words of his own grief:

> Ipse suos gemitus foliis inscribit et AI AI
> Flos habet inscriptum, funestaque littera ducta est.

(...in the flower he weau'd/The sad impression of his sighes: which beares/*Ai*! *Ai*! displaid in funerall Characters.)[6]

(Metamorphoses, x. 215–16)

Such inscriptions may, as in this last example, form a commentary on their objects, or they may have the confirmatory effect of tautology. This latter is true of the custom which Dante recalls when he sees the shrunken faces of the penitents, so starved 'that the skin took its form from the bones', ('che dall'ossa la pelle s'informava'):

> Parean l'occhiaie anella sanza gemme:
>   chi nel viso delli uomini legge 'omo'
>   ben avria quivi conosciuta l'emme

(Their eye-sockets were like rings without stones: he who finds 'omo' written in men's faces, might easily there have made out the M.)

(Purgatorio, xxiii. 31–3)[7]

The analogy between the reader of a figured poem and the reader of Nature's Book is made by the seventeenth-century Spanish Jesuit, Juan Eusebio Nieremberg, in a chapter entitled 'The world is a poetic labyrinth':

> Plotinus called the world the Poetry of God. I add, that this Poem is like a labyrinth, which is read in every direction, and gives intimation of, and points to its Author.[8]

He then proceeds to mention some of the Hellenic figured poems from about 300 BC, known to us through the Greek Anthology: Theocritus' 'Pipe', the 'Wings', the 'Egg', and the 'Axe' of Simmias. But the work which he deems 'most cunning and incomparable' is that of Optatianus Porfyrius in his panegyric to Constantine.

Porfyrius' panegyric poems (for which Constantine made him *praefectus urbi* in 329) are of great acrostic complexity. They occupy a full rectangle within which, without disturbing the continuity of the rectangularly framed poems, other inscribed forms appear. The letters of these individual

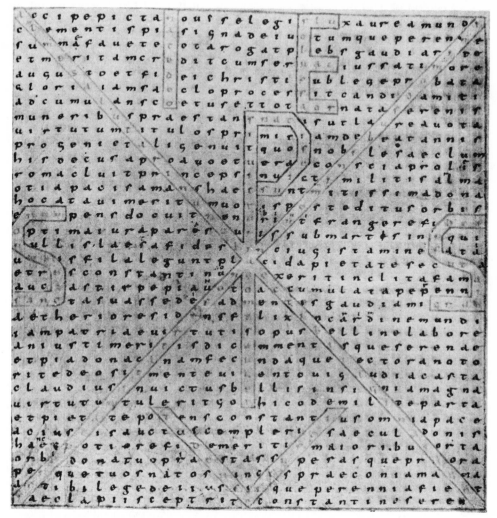

1. Porfyrius, Panegyric of Constantine (Bern, Burgerbibliotek, MS 212, III, fol.119v).

inscriptions coincide with those of the primary, horizontally-read verse (Fig. 1).[9] It is this intricate knitting of a multiplicity of statements which Juan Eusebio so admired in Porfyrius' work. Each poem was to him a labyrinth in whose every direction could be read a message of praise: 'So do I imagine the world to be a panegyric of God.' The literal congruences of an acrostically figured poem imitate the well-considered intricacy of a providentially structured world.

Porfyrius' work was known and consciously imitated by the Carolingian abbot, Hrabanus Maurus, in his *De Laudibus Sanctae Crucis*.[10] This work, available to Renaissance readers through Jakob Wimpheling's edition of 1503, comprises a variety of cruciform arrangements within pages which can be read horizontally as wholes, and acrostically, according to the parts. The twenty-three figurations of the cross, with their glosses on the facing pages, demonstrate the comprehensiveness of the cross's reach. The glosses include numerological explications[11] and suggest that while, on a contingent level, Hrabanus is the 'opifex' of the volume, he is ultimately fulfilling the more humble role of copyist and interpreter. The unraveller of numerological significance perceives a structure which is already there to be read.

Wimpheling's edition of *De Laudibus* was republished in 1605. The preface to this edition reveals the late-Renaissance reader's sympathy with the 'originality' and 'wit' (*novitas* and *ingenium*) that Hrabanus' work displays. In a century in which God could be thought to take a particular delight in the creation of a 'witty fabulist',[12] *novitas* and *ingenium* can be seen to lead to and derive from a passionate understanding of Christian mysteries:

> I beseech you, fair reader, whoever is a true Christian, to make this unique book your own: so that you will see its originality, and praise its ingenuity, and you will marvel at its extraordinary nature and be inflamed with love for the cross.[13]

Launcelot Andrewes is known to have possessed a copy of this book, and Henry Reynolds mentions Hrabanus' work with admiration in his heavily Cabbalistic *Mythomystes*.[14] But the only seventeenth-century poet whose work I have found to include acrostically lettered figures which coincide with the words of a larger whole, in the manner of Porfyrius' and Hrabanus' works, is the much maligned Edward Benlowes, who concludes his *Theophila* with a beautiful and intricate poem around the three crosses at Calvary (Fig 2).[15] The thieves' crosses on either side of the larger, central cross bear the words: MEICUM UENERIS IN REGNUM TUUM and ES CHRISTUS SERUATE IPSUM ET NOS. On Christ's cross in the centre is written: DEUS MEUS DEUS MEUS CUR ME DESERUISTI. The letters of these vertical inscriptions coincide with the horizontally read Passion meditation of the whole.

Many Christian figured poems can be understood in relation to meditative practice. The very composition of a figured poem provides a paradigm for the meditative act: the simple visual form exists as the unifying focus for the meditator's gaze while the reading of the text constitutes the enactment of the meditation, an enactment which transforms and goes beyond the anchoring material focus. The final illustration to Hrabanus' work, 'De adoratione crucis ab opifice', portrays the kneeling figure of Hrabanus beneath a rudimentary cross. Hrabanus' work as 'opifex' has been that of reverent interpreter and meditator, whose devout concentration upon the single and simple form of the cross has transformed that form into one rich with significance. The previous illustrations have

Alleluia alma dies INCHRI sti sacra triumphu

M
O
R
T
V
A
L
T
A
M
E
A
E
S
t
a
r
d
e
o
a
m
o
r
e
t
u
l

R E D E O A M O R E T U I M U N D I S A L U A T O R I E S U

MEICUMVENERISINREGNUMTUUM

CHRISTUSSERUATEIPSUMETNOS

2. The crosses at Calvary, Edward Benlowes, *Theophila*, 1652, p.268.

opened out that significance so that the form to which we are returned is now dense with meaning, a motivated sign.

Figured poems, drawing attention to their graphic and literal materiality tend to move either in the direction of compounding that materiality or of refuting it. Those which work in the way of meditations refute it, using their representational contours for analogical demonstration of less localised congruences and as the provisional focus which the text transcends as it becomes audible and intelligible. The method of acrostic coincidence, so beautifully employed by Hrabanus and Edward Benlowes in their meditations, can provide an analogical demonstration of the happy congruences of divine intentionality. But the acrostic technique could serve a more mundane practicality: the inclusion of the author's name in an acrostic form can act as a device against plagiarism, the work becoming inseparable from evidence of authorship. Dionysius of Herakleia (*c*. 328– 248 BC) claims to have passed off one of his dramas as the work of Sophocles and then to have revealed his authorship by identifying an acrostic of his lover's name which he had inserted into the work.[16] Acrostics of Virgil's name have been found in the *Georgics*,[17] And the description of Misenus' tomb in *Aeneid* vi (232–5) clearly shows that Virgil identified the preservation of the *nomen* with a form of immortality. Such a notion extends naturally to the use of acrostics in tomb inscriptions: the name is locked perpetually in place.[18]

The Renaissance concern with personal fame made classical funerary monuments and their inscriptions objects of particular interest.[19] In the sixteenth century, collections of classical and contemporary inscriptions began to appear in print and the 'lapidary' inscription, no longer truly lapidary, began to develop a paper life of its own.[20] Apianus and Amantius, authors of one of the finest collections of inscriptions, *Inscriptiones Sacrosanctae Vetustatis*,[21] proclaim themselves on the title page as 'Mathematicus' and 'Poeta'—perhaps suggesting that the lapidary style demands a combination of scientific measurement with poetic talent. Many of the inscriptions in this volume are framed within imaginary architectural settings—often appropriately ruinous. The appearance of substantial and ruinous monuments on paper—a substance not subject to the same elemental ravages as stone—emphasises the difference of materials which the writers of poems with the contours of stoney monuments knowingly exploited (Fig. 3). Their monuments, unlike those of bronze or stone, cannot be eaten away by weather and time.

The literal, graphic or typographic composition of a poem is something which poets in a written culture cannot ignore, though those who subdue every other aspect of language than its visible presence do so at their poetry's cost. The graphic or typographic presence of the poem on the page is the most obvious and least haunting form of its presence.[22] The coherence and integrity of its outline are both analogous to and promising indices of the profound coherence which a good poem has.[23] The interest

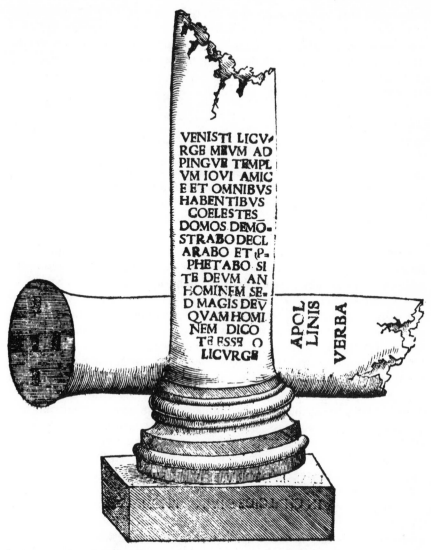

3. Broken column, Apianus and Amantius, *Inscriptiones Sacrosanctae Vetustasis*, 1534, p.497.

which so many poets have shown in the physical processes of writing, printing and engraving must derive from a desire to appropriate and motivate with meaning the conventional forms of writing. It is as if the arbitrariness of the graphic forms can be overcome by the care involved in inscribing, cutting and inking.

When the lapidary inscription left its stone origins and moved onto paper, the acuteness of the stone-cutters' tools (which preferred concise and symmetrical inscriptions) left its trace in the stylistic sharpness of the new lapidary writing. Emanuele Tesauro, in his *Cannocchiale Aristotelico*, describes the lapidary style as 'a composite half-way between poetry and oratory', a lesser art than poetry but higher than oratory. He finds the ancient Romans lacking in this skill:

> The ancient Romans composed their inscriptions with a clear gravity but without any life or pointedness ... later, great stylistic elegance is combined with a certain tenderness of affect; but neither the eye nor the ear had distinguished the lapidary period.[24]

He then attempts to correct the imperfection of ancient Rome by rewriting a passage of Cicero in the lapidary mode, lineating it so that the rhetorical structure is visibly pointed (Fig. 4). This done he asks, 'Do you not see how, with a slight alteration, an elegy which was audible has become one that is readable?'

Lapidary writing, calculated to display the virtuosity of Renaissance typesetters, had become a recognised genre by the middle of the seventeenth century.[25] (It was thought particularly suitable for panegyrics of dynasties.) Printed books of *elogia* were common. Though these lapidary works were not shaped into any recognisable forms, their careful display and symmetry suggest that the look of words upon a page, and not only their sound and meaning, had become increasingly important. Father Ong, writing about the quantifying, spatialising thought processes that became predominant during the Renaissance, considers the invention of the printing-press to have been the 'central strategic operation in the procedure of visualising knowledge.'[26] This seems incompatible with the number of illuminated manuscripts that preceded the printing-press, but the Renaissance printers were certainly keen to demonstrate their skills in the display of uniform type in clearly contoured diagrammatic forms. The tapering or urn-shaped chapter endings of countless Renaissance books remind one, even more strongly than the lapidary inscriptions, of the forms of figured poems (Fig. 5).

George Puttenham, who devotes a whole chapter of his *Arte of English Poesie* (1589) to figured poems under the heading 'Proportion in Figure', anticipates Tesauro in his account of the affinity between eye and ear. Aural values dominate the treatise: while the good 'maker' will not 'wrench his words to helpe his rime', either by falsifying his accent or by 'vntrue orthographie', it is nevertheless 'somewhat more tollerable to help the rime by false orthographie, then to leaue an vnpleasant dissonance to the eare, by keeping trewe orthographie and loosing the rime'.[27]

This is good poetic sense; but, while Puttenham concedes that it is better to interfere with the written and visible form of a poem than to disrupt its audible harmonies, it is his firm belief that the need to do so will seldom arise because of the congruity between the audible and the visible. The diagrams with which he demonstrates to his readers his notions of proportion and concord are given in this faith:

Fortunata Mors,
Natura debita; Patriæ reddita.
Legio verè Martia,
A Patrio Numine Nomen adepta.
Vt idem Armorum Deus
Vrbem hanc Gentibus: vos huic Vrbi genuerit.
In fugâ, fœda Mors: in Victoriâ, gloriosa.
Mars enim fortissimòs pigneratur.
Vos victi victores,
Pÿ impios occidistis, occisi.
Itaque, dum impios mulctant Inferi;
Vos Superas inter sedes, triumphatis.
Breuis Vita, Memoria sempiterna.
Quæ nisi Vitâ longior essset,
Quis gloriam quæreret per Mortes?
Actum igitur præclarè vobiscum,
Fortissimi olìm Milites, nunc Sanctissimi.
Quorum Virtus,
Ne vel obliuione vel reticentiâ insepulta sit;
Immortali Sepulcro Senatus cauit.
Ingentes Exercitus Punicis, Gallicis; Italicis bellis,
Maiorem felicitatem habuere, non præmium.
Atque vtinam maiora possemus, qui maxima accepimus.
Vos Hostem Antonium
Furentem auertisse, redeuntem repulisse,
Æterna hac Moles, æternitati testabitur.
Hanc quamdiu spectabunt oculi, vos lingua loquentur,
Pro mortali conditione, immortalitatem consecutos.

4. Cicero 'alla maniera lapidaria', Emanuele Tesauro, *Il Cannocchiale Aristotelico*, 1670, p.597.

beutified and adorned, as the matter requireth. I haue cho=
sen out in these Orations soche questions , as are right ne=
cessarie to be knowen and redde of all those, whose cogitaciō
pondereth vertue and Godlines. I doubte not,but seyng my
trauaile toucheth vertuous preceptes, and vttereth to light,
many famous Histories , the order of arte obserued also,but
that herein the matter it self, shall defende my purpose aga=
inste the enuious, whiche seketh to depraue any good enter=
prise, begon of any one persone. The enuious manne
though learned,readeth to depraue that,which he
readeth,the ignoraunt is no worthie Iudge,
the learned and godlie pondereth vp=
rightly & sincerely,that which
he iudgeth, the order of
these Orations
followeth afterward,and
the names of thē.

5. Conclusion of preface, R. Rainolde, *Foundation of Rhetoric*, 1563, p.7.

I set you downe an occular example: because ye may the better con-
ceiue it. Likewise it so falleth out most times your occular proportion
doeth declare the nature of the audible: for if it please the eare well, the
same represented by delineation to the view pleaseth the eye well and *è
converso* : and this is by a naturall *simpathie* betweene the eare and the
eye, and between tunes & colours.[28]

As Wittkower has demonstrated, the sympathy between the ear and the
eye was more than a synaesthetic conceit in the Renaissance—music and
painting both convey harmonies, and they are the same harmonies.[29]

Another 'occular example' is given to illustrate Puttenham's notion
of 'entertangling' to make 'band' (Fig. 6).[30] This is nothing more compli-
cated than an *ababab* rhyme scheme as opposed to what he calls 'Plaine
compasse'—an *abba* scheme. But his terms of 'entertangling' and 'band'
suggests the technique of a weaver.[31] An interdependence is set up which
binds the whole structure and preserves it from fragmentation. The ear
perceives the consonances as they are heard in sequence and, by relating
those consonances to each other, the finished, a-temporal structure of the
'occular example' is revealed.

The belief that visible symmetry and audible harmony are one and the

ligh,of all which I will giue you ocular examples;a
Concord in

Plaine compaſſe ⟹　⟸ Entertangle.

firſt in a *Quadreine* there are but two proportions,

6. Rhyme scheme, George Puttenham, *Arte of English Poesie*, 1589, p.72.

same is implicit in Puttenham's recommendation of 'Proportion in Figure' —'so called for that it yelds an ocular representation, your meeters being by good symmetrie reduced into certaine Geometricall figures, whereby the maker is restrained to keepe him within his bounds, and sheweth not onely more art, but serueth also much better for briefenesse and subtiltie of deuice'.[32] Surprisingly, Puttenham was not acquainted with the Hellenic examples from the Planudean Anthology (printed in 1494): 'I find not of this proportion vsed by any of the Greeke or Latine Poets, or in any vulgar writer, sauing of that one forme which they cal *Anacreons egge*.' (This latter is almost certainly a confused reference to the 'egg' of Simmias, of which J.C. Scaliger gives two imitations in his *Poetices*.)[33]

According to Puttenham, this method of shaping poems is an oriental device to which he was introduced by a traveller he met in Italy.[34] This traveller observed that the Orientals

> are in all their inuentions most wittie, and haue the vse of Poesie or riming, but do not delight so much as we do in long tedious descriptions, and therefore when they will vtter any pretie conceit, they reduce it into metricall feet and put it in forme of a *Lozange* or square, or such other figure, and so engrauen in gold, siluer or iuorie, and sometimes with letters of ametist, rubie, emeralde or topas curiousely cemented and peeced together, they sende them in chaines, bracelets, collars and girdles to their mistresses to weare for a remembrance.[35]

This is a serious and admiring description, for 'wit' and 'conceitedness' with their concomitant demands of compression and restraint, are valued qualities in the sixteenth- and seventeenth-century poetic and have their place as much in 'long tedious descriptions' as in brief lyrics.[36]

The value of the oriental examples which Puttenham describes lies as much in their materials as in their wit. Precious and beautifully ornate gifts, they play upon the interaction of real and metaphorical values, the precious stones acting both as metaphors for love and as materially generous expressions of it. The material value (an arbitrary derived monetary value) is a grosser and more evident example of the true value which language can more closely convey. It is both its travesty and demonstration.

Puns upon the convergence and disparity of literal and metaphorical levels are implicit in the nature of a figured poem which, with its recognisable shape, declares itself an object, unlike an ordinary poem. Yet, in its wordy content, it denies the object it seems to be, proclaiming itself more subtle, less local, than any thing. These separate levels of meaning may set up a tension by which the one may seem to complement the other, the visible form acting as a specious proof of the verbal content.

Puttenham's ignorance of Hellenic examples demonstrates that the renewed popularity of this mode in the late Renaissance cannot simply be put down to the availability of, and interest in, the poems in the Planudean Anthology. But there were some self-consciously scholarly imitations which can be accounted for in this way. Amongst these are Jean Crispin's pipe-shaped notes to Theocritus' 'Syrinx'[37] and the various 'eggs' of Pierius Valerianus,[38] the elder Scaliger[39] and Richard Wills[40]—all in reverent imitation of Simmias' Greek original. The figured poems in Richard Wills's *Poematum Liber* carry on the serious task he set himself in his theoretical *De Re Poetica*[41] of defending the respectability of poetry—it would seem by demonstrating that it can be hard work, the overcoming of what Hobbes considered 'needlesse difficulty.'

It is these scholarly imitators of the early Greek figured poems whose frivolity was particularly castigated by Spenser's friend, Gabriel Harvey, in his *Letter Book*. Simmias he deems a

folishe idle, phantasticall poett [and deviser of] ridiculous madd gugawes and crockchettes, . . . of late foolishely reuiuid by sum, otherwise not-vnlernid, as Pierus, Scaliger, Crispin, and the rest of that crue. Nothinge so absurde and fruteles but beinge once taken vpp shall haue sume imitatoures.[42]

The renewed popularity of figured versifying must have been as surely stimulated by humanist studies of Egyptian hieroglyphs as was the development of the emblem. The emblem, despite its pictorial form, is a very literary device, for its pictorial language is dependent upon verbal decoding. Whilst the hieroglyph and Chinese ideogram are their own texts, the emblem is dependent upon a conjoint text in order that its metaphorical intention be understood.[43]

Thomas Fuller, in *The Worthies of England*, particularly admired the conjunction of poetic text with emblem which he found in Quarles's work:

His *visible Poetry* (I mean his *Emblemes*) is excellent, catching therein the eye and fancy at one draught, so that he hath *out-Alciated* therein, in some men's judgement.[44]

It was Edward Benlowes who encouraged his friend Quarles to illustrate his poetic *Emblemes* and *Hieroglyphikes* with emblems copied from the

Pia Desideria and the *Typus Mundi*, and it was probably also Benlowes who provided a large and necessary sum of over £120 to finance the plates.[45] But despite Benlowes' evident interest in the emblematic mode it was not one which he chose to adopt himself, preferring to straighten the links between words and (other) things in the forms of figured poems. In a figured poem one is closer to the compact ideal of the Chinese ideogram which, in Bacon's words, makes use of 'Characters Real, which express neither letters nor words in gross, but Things or Notions'.[46]

The assertion which Bacon makes earlier in *The Advancement of Learning* that 'the substance of matter is better than the beauty of words'[47] typifies the nausea of anxiety which abstractions induced in many seventeenth-century minds. It is a characteristic of metaphysical poetry that sophistry and fallacy are often obscured by an appeal to the incontrovertible (though often irrelevantly applied) laws of geometry and physics. The makers of figured poems exploited the specious authentication and seeming reification with which the forms of 'things' imbued their words.

The relation between a figured poem's words and the 'thing' suggested by its shape may be one of confirmation or refutation (or the pun's easy combination of both). On the simplest level these poems are characteristic of a wider tendency of the Baroque towards over-presentation in which all means are endorsed towards a composite end. As in the over-determination of a pun, the various layers of communication in baroque art tend to work cumulatively to achieve a collaborative intensity. The skeletons that border and the black pages that interleave Sylvester's elegy on the death of Prince Henry are simple visual intensifications of the funereal tone of the verse.[48]

This mournful presentation may have been the printer's idea, but Sylvester's own propensity for giving visual emphasis to his words is evident in his translation of Du Bartas. The poem 'Spectacles' is headed by an illustration (Fig. 7)[49] which, for all its jokey appearance, precedes a long and serious meditation upon vanity. The significance of the drawn spectacles consists in their difference from the ordinary spectacles which they resemble, for these spectacles are able to see beyond the corporeal and into the moral nature of things.

The *Corona Dedicatoria* of this volume is figured, with a lot of help from the printer, into a series of pillars, and this is followed by a pyramid shaped elegy on the death of Sidney (Fig. 8). The pictorial form of the poem seems to contradict Sylvester's claim that he is 'in wit and art so shallow' that he cannot follow Sidney's masterly pencil strokes. But Sidney's pencil is a metaphorical one, his beauty the 'Divine pure Beauties of the Minde'. Sylvester's poem is a homage to what it is not—a rare and invisible moral beauty.

The theme of Horace's Ode III.xxx was rehearsed with an almost obsessive frequency during the late Renaissance:

Exegi monumentum aere perennius
regalique situ pyramidum altius,
quod non imber edax, non Aquilo impotens
possit diruere aut innumerabilis
annorum series et fuga temporum.
non omnis moriar multaque pars mei
vitabit Libitinam: usque ego postera
crescam laude recens, dum Capitolium
scandet cum tacita virgine pontifex,
dicar, qua violens obstrepit Aufidus
et qua pauper aquae Daunus agrestium
regnavit populorum, ex humili potens
princeps Aeolium carmen ad Italos
deduxisse modos. sume superbiam
quaesitam meritis et mihi Delphica
lauro cinge volens, Melpomene, comam.

(I have finished a monument more lasting than bronze and loftier than the Pyramids' royal pile, one that no wasting rain, no furious north wind can destroy, or the countless chain of years and the ages' flight. I shall not altogether die, but a mighty part of me shall escape the death-goddess. On and on shall I grow, ever fresh with the glory of after time. So long as the Pontiff climbs the Capitol with the silent Vestal, I, risen high from low estate, where wild Aufidus thunders and where Daunus in a parched land once ruled o'er a peasant folk, shall be famed for having been the first to adapt Aeolian song to Italian verse. Accept the proud honour won by thy merits, Melpomene, and graciously crown my locks with Delphic bays.)[50]

Whilst brass, stone, earth and boundless sea are all subject to 'sad mortality', only the immaterial can evade material ruin. Thus Shakespeare can confer an immortality upon his lover:

The earth can yield me but a common grave,
When you entombed in men's eyes shall lie.
Your monument shall be my gentle verse,
Which eyes not yet created shall o'er-read,
And tongues to be, your being shall rehearse,
When all the breathers of this world are dead,
    You still shall live—such virtue hath my pen—
    Where breath most breathes, ev'n in the mouths of men.
                                                              (81)

It is in this way that Horace's beautifully crafted monument will evade the destruction of wind and rain for, being neither material nor local, it is not subject to their attacks. It is of course the taut structure—the good 'band'

7. Spectacles, Joshua Sylvester, *Du Bartas, His Divine Weekes and Workes*, 1621, p.1176.

—of Horace's verse which preserves its integrity from dissolution. But this quality is a formal one, not graspable substance.

The fairy who speaks up for poetry against the fairies of architecture, painting and gardening in La Fontaine's *Le Songe de Vaux*, argues that poetry is composed of a uniquely durable matter:

> Mes mains ont fait des ouvrages
> Qui verront les derniers âges
> Sans jamais se ruiner:
> Le temps a beau les combattre,
> L'eau ne les saurait miner,
> Le vent ne peut les abattre.
>
> Sans moi tant d'oeuvres fameux,
> Ignorés de nos neveux,
> Périraient sous la poussière:
> Au Parnasse seulement
> On emploie une matière
> Qui dure éternellement.[51]

(My hands have produced works which will witness the end of ages without themselves being ruined. Time cannot combat them; water cannot

ENGLAND's
Apelles (rather
OVR APOLLO)
WORLD's-wonder
SYDNEY,
that rare more-thá-man,
This LOVELY VENVS
first to LIMNE beganne,
With such a PENCILL
as no PENNE dares follow:
How thē shold I, in wit & art so shalow,
Attēpt the *Task* which yet none other can?
Far be the thought, that mine vnlearned hand
His heavenly Labor should so much vnhallow:
Yet, left (that Holy-RELIQVE being shrin'd
In som High-Place, close lockt from cõmon light)
My Countrey-men should bee debarr'd the fight
Of thefe DVINE pure Beauties of the Minde;
Not daring meddle with APELLES TABLE,
This haue I muddled, as my MVSE was able.

undermine them; wind cannot beat them down. Without me countless famous works would perish under the dust, unknown by posterity. On Parnassus only, one employs a substance which endures forever.)

Given that the strength of this enduring 'matter' derives from its immateriality, the literalism with which some writers took Horace's metaphor of 'monument' to shape their commemorative writings into the forms of stoney monuments—pyramids and pillars—seems rather self-defeating. In practice, and by the cumulative illogic of over-determination, they have it both ways. The visible pyramid of words which William Gager constructed as a memorial to Sidney gains a specious sense of solidity and durability through its resemblance to a substantial model. But we are told that it is precisely because it is not constructed of such crude stuff as marble or brass, but of something more elusive and enduring, that this pyramid is inviolable. Its strength is the fame of Sidney's virtue 'which cannot be matched by the strength of marble, iron or bronze'.[52]

An awareness that 'Putrefaction is the end/ Of all that Nature doth intend' ('Putrefaction')[53] threads through all the poetry of Robert Herrick: it is the theme of his meditations and the context of his celebrations. His pursuit of immortality is almost obsessional and, in line with Ovid, Horace, Shakespeare and many forgotten poets, he hopes to win it through the fame of his verse:

> A FUNERALL stone,
>   Or Verse I covet none;
>   But only crave
>   Of you, that I may have
> A sacred Laurel springing from my grave:
>   Which being seen,
>   Blest with perpetuall greene,
>   May grow to be
>   Not so much called a tree,
> As the eternall monument of me.
>
> ('To Laurels')

'Blest with perpetuall greene' these laurels are more than the conventional poetic crown. They are, like Elizabeth Herrick's 'living epitaph' of roses, objects of perpetual regeneration.

Herrick apostrophises *Hesperides*, his secular volume, with a (slightly misquoted) line from Ovid, celebrating the power of poetry to cheat mortality: 'Effugient avidos Carmina nostra Rogos' ('Our songs will flee the hungry funeral pyres'). This is the central theme of the volume. His renowned 'delight in disorder', his love of incidental, transient beauty has its obverse in the careful shaping of his volume as he builds his eternal monument. In 'His Poetrie his Pillar' he rejoices in the 'living', quicksilver quality of his stone which gives Time no forms to grasp:

8. Pyramid, Joshua Sylvester, *Du Bartas, His Divine Weekes and Workes*, 1621, n.p.

Onely a little more
  I have to write
   Then Ile give o're
And bid the world Good-night.

'Tis but a flying minute,
  That I must stay,
   Or linger in it;
And then I must away.

O time that cut'st down all!
  And scarce leav'st here
   Memoriall
Of any men that were.

How many lie forgot
  In Vaults beneath?
   And piece-meale rot
Without a fame in death?

Behold this living stone,
  I reare for me,
   Ne'r to be thrown
Downe, envious Time by thee.

Pillars let some set up,
  (If so they please)
   Here is my hope,
And my *Pyramides*.

Like Gager's pyramid to Sidney (though a better poem) it is the incorpor-
eality of Herrick's verse which makes it invulnerable. The effortless shift
of metaphor from 'pillar' to 'pyramides' in the last verse flaunts the Ariel
agility of his poetic monument in contrast to its inert, stoney coun-
terpart.

It is surprising, after this teasing celebration of poetry's inability to be
grasped and bound, to find that the last poem in the volume 'The Pillar of
Fame', assumes the shape of its titular metaphor though its subject is, as
before, poetry's immunity to the shocks which real pillars must suffer.
Yet the visible structure of this poem does serve a more positive purpose
than that of reminding us of what poetry is not. In its key position as last
poem of the book it calls attention to the making of that book. The evi-
dent, visible shaping of the poem exemplifies, by the simplification of cari-
cature, the care which has been lavished on the volume as a whole. The
architectural metaphor expressed by the poem's shape refers back to the
preceding volume and the poem epitomises the finish and polish which
Herrick wishes us to see in his completed work.[54]

Fames pillar here, at last, we set,
Out—during *Marble*, *Brasse*, or *Jet*,
Charm'd and enchanted so,
As to withstand the blow
Of   overthrow:
Nor shall the seas,
Or   OUTRAGES
Of storms orebear
What we up-rear,
Tho Kingdoms fal,
This   pillar   never   shall
Decline   or   waste   at   all;
But stand for ever by his owne
Firme and well fixt foundation.

Seventeenth-century literary theorists repeatedly turned to analogies with building to convey their ideals of poetic crafting. Alberti's definition of beauty in *De Re Aedificatoria* as 'the harmony and concord of all the parts achieved in such a manner that nothing could be added or taken away or altered except for the worse'[55] is almost a paraphrase of the precepts laid down by Horace in the *Ars Poetica*. Ben Jonson, who is truly Horatian in his censure of those who 'thinke rude things greater then polish'd; and scatter'd more numerous, then compos'd',[56] echoes Alberti in his definition of a 'strict and succinct style [as] that, where you can take away nothing without losse, and that losse to be manifest'. Jonson, who knew about bricklaying, goes on to make the architectural analogy explicit:

The congruent, and harmonious fitting of parts in a sentence, hath almost the fastning and force of knitting, and connexion: As in stones well squar'd, which will rise strong a great way without mortar.[57]

In 'An Execration upon *Vulcan*' Jonson expresses nothing but scorn for the forms of figured verse, but the adoption of architectural forms for the shape of a poem might be seen as the, mistakenly, literal fulfilment of precepts such as his.

Whilst secular figured poems, often involved with the commemoration of individuals, gesture beyond the material world to whose logic and stability their forms appeal, expressing both desire and fear of corporeal perpetuity, a Christian context demands a suppression of the concerns of individual egoism. Herrick dedicates his *Noble Numbers or His Pious Pieces* to God:

For every sentence, clause and word,
That's not inlaid with Thee, (my Lord)
Forgive me God, and blot each Line
Out of my Book, that is not Thine.

A couplet towards the end of the volume acknowledges God as the author of everything, including Herrick's book:

> God is *all-present* to what e're we do,
> And as all-present, so *all-filling* too.

Finally, God is the only content. He is 'in' Herrick's book because his name is included (in the way that God has Donne when he has done), but beyond that he is in the book because he is everywhere, included and inclusive.

'The Cross', the figured poem in *Noble Numbers*, is quite unlike its predecessor in *Hesperides*. There, Herrick used the pillar as a metaphor for construction whilst emphasising that if it were more than metaphor, and the pillar were of stone, his hopes of fame and survival would be less well-founded. The contradictions involved were those of sophistry and ambivalence. The contradictions involved in religious figured verse are the mysterious contradictions compatible with and endorsed by religious thought—the mystery of three in one and one in three, of infinite variety coexisting with perfect unity. The unity is expressed in the single form of the verse's shape; the complexity embraced by that unity is the subject of the meditation, the verse inscribed within the shape. Hrabanus' *De Laudibus Sanctae Crucis* repeats the single form of the cross whilst exploring the scope of its implications in the designs and the glosses.

Herrick's 'Cross' is placed as the culmination of a series of meditations upon Calvary—a *Homo vide* lyric and an address by the meditator to the Crucified, which are more medieval than Renaissance in tone. The 'I' of these lyrics is not the individual identifying 'I' of Herrick's secular poems, but the 'ethopoeic I' of medieval meditations. The form of 'The Cross' imitates the gold or silver crucifix upon which worshippers gaze during meditation, to the extent that the word JESUS is placed where it would be affixed to a material cross. The words of the poem describe the imaginative participation induced by meditation. The meditator imaginatively assists at the embalming of Christ's body; the wounds are probed and the emotion intensified. Like the cross in *The Dream of the Rood*, this cross realises its symbolic nature and yields to its gazer a climactic rehearsal of affective piety. The act of reading this cross contributes to its meaning: it brings us, worshipping, to its feet.

The architectural metaphor which Herbert takes for his volume *The Temple*, looks at first as if it is going to be consistent. The volume begins with 'The Church Porch' and 'Superliminare' which prepare the reader spiritually and topographically for entrance into the church itself. The first poem in *The Church* is 'The Altar', not adjacent to the west or south door of a church, but clearly the point to which all eyes, and the structure of the church itself, are directed. The metaphor seems now to be working in the order of things seen, rather than ground covered, and the emphasis upon sight is furthered by the shaping of this poem into the form of an altar. But it is at this moment, when the titular metaphor seems to be most fully realised, that consistency breaks down. 'The Altar' is not followed by 'The Church-floore' or 'The Windows', thus continuing our tour of the church, but by 'The Sacrifice', a long and meticulous *homo vide* lyric.

Yet it is 'The Altar' which reveals that the apparent breakdown of the titular metaphor is in fact a breakthrough into realising that metaphor's fullest meaning: that the 'Temple' of God is not confined within the walls of a particular building but exists within each Christian heart, and comprises the whole Christian communion. 'We say amisse/ This or that is' ('The Flower')—God does not go in for topographical segregation.[58]

Puttenham's home-made examples of figured poems had included two pyramids (Fig. 9):[59] one, dedicated to Queen Elizabeth, was to be read from the bottom to the top to express the heavenly aspirations of her terrestrial self; the other, on the subject of God as the source of all goodness, was to be read, appropriately, from the apex down—a pyramid which only God could construct. Herbert, in his far superior 'Altar' similarly capitalises upon the usual direction in which a poem is read—from top to bottom—to reveal that the creator of this altar, which is recreated by us as we read it, is not Herbert but God. 'Thine', the last word and 'corner stone' of the poem, surrenders all claims by Herbert to the construction of the form. The 'broken altar' of which the poem speaks, at first perplexingly, is not the symmetrical form we admire on the page but the inadequate and broken heart of the servant-poet which seeks to perfect itself through emulation. Two biblical references, implied in the poem, clarify its meaning. The first is 2 Corinthians iii.3:

> In that ye are manifest, to be the epistle of Christ, ministered by vs, and written, not with yncke, but with the Spirit of the liuing God, not in tables of stone, but in fleshlie tables of the heart.

The second is Exodus xx.25:

> But if thou wilt make me an altar of stone, thou shalt not buylde it of hewen stones: for if thou lift vp thy tole vpon them, thou hast polluted them.

The New Testament passage, which undercuts our admiration for Herbert's inky act of creation, presents us with the recalcitrant material of the Christian heart; the passage from Exodus further takes away from the claims of the human artificer and suggests that the perfect (not 'broken') altar we see on the page is God's structure upon which the servant's broken heart is seeking to perfect itself through emulation. The structure's independence of the poet is confirmed by the lines 13−14:

> That, if I chance to hold my peace,
> These stones to praise thee may not cease.

```
          Skie. 1
          ___
          Azurd 1
          in the
          assurde,
          ___
        And better,
        And richer,
        Much greter,
        ___
      Crown & empir
      After an hier
      For  to aspire  4
      Like flame of fire
      In forme of spire
        ___
      To mount on hie,
      Con ti nu al ly
      With trauel & teen
      Most gratious queen
      Ye haue made a vow  5
      Shews vs plainly here
      Not fained but true,
      To euery mans vew,
      Shining cleere in you
      Of so bright an hewe,
      Euen thus vertewe
        ___
    Vanish out of our sight
    Till his fine top be quite
    To Taper in the ayre  6
    Endeuors soft and faire
    By his kindly nature
    Of tall comely stature
    Like as this faire figure
```

```
          1 God
            On
            Hie
          2 From
            Aboue
            Sends loue,
            Wisedome,
            Iu stice
            Cou rage,
            Boun tie,
          And doth geue
          Al that liue,
          Life & breath
          Harts ese helth
          Childrẽ, welth
          Beauty strẽgth
          Restfull  age,
          And at length
          A mild death,
        4 He doeth bestow
          All mens fortunes
          Both high & low
          And the best things
          That earth cã haue
          Or mankind craue,
          Good queens & kings
          Fi nally is the same
          Who gaue you (madã)
          Seyson of this Crowne
          With poure soueraigne
        5 Impug noble right,
          Redoubtable  might,
          Most prosperous raigne
          Eternall  re nowme,
          And that your chiefest is
          Sure hope of heauens blis.
```

9. Pyramids, George Puttenham, *Arte of English Poesie*, 1589, p.79.

The poet's action has not been a creation but an imitation, and the poem concludes with a request that this imitation be perfected:

A broken ALTAR, Lord, thy servant reares,

Made of a heart, and cemented with teares:

Whose parts are as thy hand did frame;

No workmans tool hath touch'd the same.

A   HEART   alone

Is   such   a   stone,

As .   nothing   but

Thy pow'r doth cut.

Wherefore each part

Of my hard heart

Meets in this frame,

To praise thy Name:

That, if I chance to hold my peace,

These stones to praise thee may not cease.

O let thy blessed SACRIFICE be mine,

And sanctifie this ALTAR to be thine. [60]

'Easter Wings' (Fig 10), the other specifically figured poem in *The Temple*,[61] is a less complicated articulation of the same theme. The form is not Herbert's (nor is it Simmias's), but God's. The poet, 'imp'-ing his own upon it, requests strength and perfection. It is a demonstrably self-fulfilling request, for the poem is mimetic in its action as well as in its completed whole. The tapering movement towards the centre of each verse enacts the poverty of Godless man ('Most poore', 'most thinne'): and in each verse it is the phrase 'with thee' which visibly initiates the regenerative consequences of 'combining' with God.

Though figured verses appear as idiosyncratic oddities within the history of literature, their forms give the impression of neutrality and impersonality—an impression congenial both to the Christian poet subduing the wayward ego, and to the poet concerned with perpetuating the individual by association with permanent forms. The shapes of these poems are not organic productions of the poet's individuality, but forms borrowed from a common pool (and it took a Mallarmé and an Apollinaire to extend a rather limited repertoire of shapes). As shapes, the poems are finished before they have been read; the sequential sounding of the poem's words is resolved into the silence of the a-temporal form.

This silence possessed by figured poems is a feature of Herbert's poetry as a whole. His poems seem to achieve silence as if words and emotion existed in inverse proportion. The verse empties as the heart fills: 'Ah! no more; thou break'st my heart!' Several of his poems ('Redemption', 'The Collar', and 'Love (iii)', for example) cease into a tongue-tied articulateness. As a poet and as a preacher Herbert's energies and business are invested in words. But as a Christian his role is as reader rather than writer. 'Love (iii)' turns upon an unspoken pun on the word 'Host'—it is as if the individual articulation did not matter. The Christian who wishes to silence the strident voice of individuality fights with the poet, but the two are reconciled in those poems which seem not so much to invent (except in the true sense) as to 'spell' out the divine, pre-existing Word.

Though all particularity is dissolved in God, the mortal must necessarily act, speak and think within the framework of particularities. Only through, and in relation to, a sequential, temporal structure can the unchanging eternal nature be revealed. Herbert's 'Our Life is hid with Christ in God' enacts this mutually confirming 'double motion' by an elaborate extension of the acrostic method:

> *My* words and thoughts do both expresse this notion,
> That *Life* hath with the sun a double motion.
> The first *Is* straight, and our diurnall friend,
> The   other   *Hid* and doth obliquely bend.
> One life is wrapt *In* flesh, and tends to earth:
> The other winds towards *Him*, whose happie birth
> Taught me to live here so, *That* still one eye
> Should aim and shoot at that which *Is* on high:
> Quitting   with   daily   labour   all   *My* pleasure,
> To   gain   at   harvest   an   eternall   *Treasure*.

As we read this poem our eyes follow the 'straight' linear sequence of the argument, completing it in time as one word follows another. The other, 'obliquely bend'-ing message is revealed only when the poem is completed and we have been released from the sequential tyranny of time. This message is, literally, a revelation, but one not independent of the sequential argument with which it, obliquely, coincides. The effect of this is to reveal the correctness and fittingness of the temporal structure as one which will, though not straightforwardly, reveal the eternal. It is a poem which fuses and reconciles the alternative acts of writing and reading, revealing that the end of writing—to be read—can only be a confirmation of what was legible before. Herbert's figured poems take as their subject the urge towards identity—an identity which, if achieved, would silence all poetry. The near-match of emulation which these poems do describe, and the visible symmetry of their forms, hint at that silence whilst reconciling poetic skill with Christian humility. In Herbert's work the anonymity, the sense of already created fittingness, and the mimetic endorsement of content which a figured poem can achieve, are most perfectly exploited, and an otherwise 'needelesse difficulty' is the source of expressive form.

The vogue for this kind of writing dwindled in the later part of the seventeenth century. Dryden, who was to create new orthodoxies for English poetry, scorned the 'acrostick land' of his predecessors, seeing in it nothing but absurdity. But its appeal to the pious continued. In 1668, nearly forty years after the publication of *The Temple*, a Carmelite monk

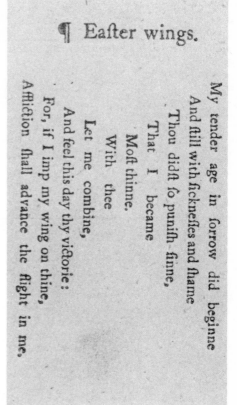

¶ Easter wings.

Lord, who createdst man in wealth and store,
Though foolishly he lost the same,
Decaying more and more,
Till he became
Most poore:
With thee
O let me rise
As larks, harmoniously,
And sing this day thy victories:
Then shall the fall further the flight in me.

¶ Easter wings.

My tender age in sorrow did beginne
And still with sicknesses and shame
Thou didst so punish sinne,
That I became
Most thinne.
With thee
Let me combine,
And feel this day thy victorie:
For, if I imp my wing on thine,
Affliction shall advance the flight in me.

10. *Easter Wings*, George Herbert, *The Temple*, 1633.

and professor of literature in Ravensburg produced a work which contains instructions for the making of every conceivable ingenious type of poem.[62] The descriptions that the monk Paschasius gives of these forms are practical and remarkably lacking in indications as to why, whether or when they should be used. In effect the book is a very beautifully illustrated manual to aid the aspirant 'poeta ingeniosus'. The examples he gives are predominantly religious in content, conceived and executed with a devotion which far exceeds the necessity in a book of instruction. The loving humility with which this book is presented—the humility of a medieval craftsman rather than the bravado of the Renaissance artist—suggests that Paschasius felt no need to vindicate the seriousness of these extraordinary poems which, in their strange symmetry, could be seen as beautiful analogies and demonstrations of holy mysteries (Fig. 11).

Though figured poems initially present images to the corporeal eye which give us an immediate sense of reference and meaning, these poems imply an acute consciousness of what is involved in reading or hearing the

11. Rose poem, Pascahsius, *Poesis Artificiosa*, 1668.

words which make them up. The corporeal eye is bribed by the immediate gratification provided by the image on the page, to perform the more menial accessory task of scanning the words which stimulate a more subtle understanding, and suggest images less complete, but also less inert and more various than any dumb outline.

Chapter 3

GEORGE HERBERT

In love, more than in bed

The images which the contours of George Herbert's figured poems suggest are of an integrity which the poems claim to seek. But these images, like Herbert's verbal 'imagery', have a provisional, as opposed to an absolute function. Though there is an obvious and traditional association between figured poems and lapidary writing, the movement of Herbert's poetry is consistently away from the reifying aspirations of the lapidary mode. The biblical pairing and opposition between bread and stone suggest the extreme states to which language may aspire. The stone tablets of Mosaic law contrast with the oral communication of the New Testament: the Gospel is spread by word of mouth and the body of Christ is received orally in the form of broken bread. But the Law may itself be thought of as wholesome and nourishing: its stone may be turned into bread, as Milton suggests with his play on 'tabl'd' when he writes that when God 'himself tabl'd the Jews from heaven, that Omer which was every man's daily portion of Manna, is computed to have bin more then might have well suffic'd the heartiest feeder thrice as many meals'.[1] Many poets—the makers of figured poems amongst them—have claimed for their works the dense inviolability of stone. In contrast to these, Herbert's poems seek the condition of bread: not so much 'self-consuming artefacts' as artefacts to be consumed.

Typically, Herbert's poems structure and semantically motivate the silence that follows them. The silence that concludes *The Temple* is one in which speaking has been replaced by eating. The mouth's two apparently distinct capacities of speaking and eating—externalising and internalising functions—are found to be only temporarily distinct. One form of communication yields to the other in which the participating communicant's individuality is subsumed into the one body of faith. The metonymic contiguity of attributes (in this case the capacities of speaking and eting) is transformed by the divine subsumation which places all predicates in a relation of synecdoche. Speaking and eating are both eventually absorbed into the silence of immediate communication when God will speak, as he did to Moses, 'mouth to mouth, and by vision, & not in darke wordes' (Numbers xii.8).

Reference to a whole of which all that is conceivable and nameable is part, both undermines and justifies all Herbert's poetic utterance. The partiality of an understanding which proceeds through discrete particulars and individual words, is corrected by the idea that God's 'word is all, if we could spell' ('The Flower'). Galileo, in the *Dialogue on the Great World Systems*, distinguishes between the simultaneity and totality of divine knowledge, and the sequential partiality of human knowledge. Whilst human knowledge is infinitely surpassed by the 'Divine Wisdom ... the knowledge of those few [propositions] comprehended by human understanding equals the Divine'. To know at all is to know part of what God knows:

> For example, we, to attain the knowledge of some property of the circle, which has infinitely many, begin from one of the most simple and, taking that for its definition, do proceed with argumentation to another, and from that to a third, and then to a fourth, and so on. The Divine Wisdom by the simple apprehension of its essence comprehends, without temporal ratiocination, all these infinite properties which are also, in effect, virtually comprised in the definitions of all things; and, to conclude, being infinite, are perhaps but one alone in their nature and in the Divine Mind ... these inferences, which our intellect apprehends with time and gradual motion, the Divine Wisdom, like light, penetrates in an instant, which is the same as to say has them always all present.[2]

Not being able to take in the 'all' of God's word in the silence of simultaneity, we have to make it out piece by piece, word by word, irradiating the parts of this whole with our momentary understanding.

The spiritual argument of Herbert's poems is determined by the relation between creator and creation, and by the knowledge that apparent distinctions—of substance, mood, property—are only conditional:

> From thee all pitie flows.
> Mothers are kinde, because thou art,
> > And dost dispose
> > To them a part:
> Their infants, them; and they suck thee
> > More free.
>
> Bowels of pitie, heare!
> Lord of my soul, love of my minde,
> > Bow down thine eare!
> > Let not the winde
> Scatter my words, and in the same
> > Thy name!

> Look on my sorrows round!
> Mark well my furnace! O what flames,
>> What heats abound!
>> What griefs, what shames!
> Consider, Lord; Lord, bow thine eare
>> And heare!
>
> Lord Jesu, thou didst bow
> Thy dying head upon the tree:
>> O be not now
>> More dead to me!
> Lord heare! *Shall he that made the eare,*
>> *Not heare?*
>> ('Longing', ll.13–36)

The knowledge that God did make the ear and the inclusion of the word *ear* in *heare*, guarantees that the separation between man and God is only apparent and temporary.[3] Comparably, God's hospitable acceptance in 'Love (iii)', an acceptance that annihilates distinctions, is presented in the homophony of 'Who made the eyes but I?' (1.12).

The silence of absorption both fulfils and threatens Herbert's poetry. The idea that 'Thy word is all, if we could spell' suggests that the opportunities for writing and for vocalisation derive from misprision, bad spelling. When the speaker's marred eyes are taken into the 'I' of God ('I AM THAT I AM'), when the words are spoken mouth to mouth, the poetry is silenced. God's forgiving acceptance promises to dissolve the boundaries and differentiations through which we live and speak.

But Herbert's priestly duty and poetic effort are to 'convey' God to man:

> ...th' holy men of God such vessels are,
> As serve him up, who all the world commands:
> When God vouchsafeth to become our fare,
> Their hands convey him, who conveys their hands.
>> ('The Priesthood', ll.25–8)

The paradox here, shockingly anticipated in 'serve him up', represents a poetic as well as a spiritual crisis. The poetic impulse is to show, to speak out (*eloquor*); the priestly duty is to bring God to man. The fact of divine omnipresence works quietly against both these endeavours by dissolving the distinctions through which priest and poet must work. The eternity and ubiquity of God promise to dissolve grammatical distinctions:

> Yet if thou shunnest, I am thine:
> I must be so, if I am mine.
> There is no articling with thee:
> I am but finite, yet thine infinitely.
>> ('Artillerie', ll.29–32)

Herbert's puns image simultaneously an impulse towards identity and indistinction, and a semantic resistance to such merging. The semantic distinctions and our own perception of alternative meanings exist in opposition to a divine will which annihilates difference in homophony. Even antonyms can be brought together by divine omnipotence; reconciled in a pun: 'Some said, that I the Temple to the floore/ In three dayes raz'd, and raised as before' ('The Sacrifice', ll.65–6). The legal pun in 'Artillerie' brings together the priestly habit of presenting the divine in a familiar terminology with the recognition that the clear contours of allegory and parable are themselves about to dissolve: 'There is no articling with thee.'

In 'Obedience' Herbert again puns on the idea of 'conveyance'. The legal use of the word is called upon from the start and the less specialised sense of 'communicate' appears to be secondary:

> My God, if writings may
> Convey a Lordship any way
> Whither the buyer and the seller please;
> Let it not thee displease,
> If this poore paper do as much as they.

But here, as so often elsewhere, Herbert employs the businesslike terminology of a flourishing bourgeoisie in a way which finally undermines those terms and the values they imply. The legal image of 'conveyancing' has been employed only to 'convey' to others a spiritual condition which is entirely in opposition to the 'articling' of the law:

> He that will passe his land
> As I have mine, may set his hand
> And heart unto this Deed, when he hath read;
> And make the purchase spread
> To both our goods, if he to it will stand.
>
> How happie were my part,
> If some kinde man would thrust his heart
> Into these lines; till in heav'ns Court of Rolls
> They were by winged souls
> Entred for both, farre above their desert!
> (ll.36–45)

Our sense of 'goods' (l.40) as 'chattels' seems increasingly misguided as we realise what kind of good is really being conveyed. But a poem has been constructed and this good conveyed on the basis of a misprision.

A poem conveys and shows ('Loving in truth, and faine in verse my love to show', *Astrophil and Stella*, 1, l.1). While the poems towards the end of *The Temple* prepare their readers for the silent reception of and by their heavenly host, many of the poems at the beginning of the volume address problems of conception and comprehension which are only secondarily matters of poetic showing:

> I have consider'd it, and finde
> There is no dealing with thy mighty passion:
> > ('The Reprisall', ll.1−2)

And it is the attempt to come to terms and 'deal with' the Passion which is the poetic and spiritual centre of 'Good Friday'.

The first stanza of 'Good Friday' poses the question of how to comprehend the central event of the Crucifixion:

> O my chief good,
> How shall I measure out thy bloud?
> How shall I count what thee befell,
> And each grief tell?

The infinite implications of this single event place it beyond the scope of a language that refers, quantifies and enumerates. The conversion of Christ's infinitely redemptive blood into poetic quantities ('measure') seems to be an inevitably trivialising process. As in the later 'Grief', poetic measures are both compulsive and intrusive, 'parcelling out' the infinite ('How hath man parcel'd out thy glorious name' 'Love (i)', l.3). The event which 'Good Friday' addresses seems to be beyond the scope of poetry.

In the second and third stanzas various principles of decorum are suggested for finding a suitable way of telling and imaging the unspeakable event:

> Shall I thy woes
> Number according to thy foes?
> Or, since one starre show'd thy first breath,
> Shall all thy death?

> Or shall each leaf,
> Which falls in Autumne, score a grief?
> Or can not leaves, but fruit, be signe
> Of the true vine?
> > (ll.5−12)

The suggestion of lines 5−6—'Shall I thy woes/ Number according to thy foes?'—does not solve the problem of quantifying the innumerable; Christ's foes are numberless and that is his woe. To think otherwise is to behave as one of those foes ('according to thy foes'). The next suggestion seems more promising: 'Or, since one starre show'd thy first breath,/ Shall all thy death?' Here is a natural sign with a divine precedent. For all Jeremy Taylor's reluctance to concede that the Holy Ghost might be represented by a dove,[4] few iconoclasts would have denied that the Magi saw a star (not something with qualitative similarities to a star) and that this was a sign to them of where Christ was to be found (Matthew ii.9, 10). With a single star as a God-chosen sign of Christ's birth, might not all stars adequately and decorously signify his death? I think there is a sense in which Herbert would have felt that all stars do signify Christ's death but not in a way that is accessible to creatures with marred eyes. We cannot spell so that, even though God's word is all, we can only be brought to understanding by means of partial and selective manifestations. Could we read this all, and not just partial anagrams of it, we should not have to read. 'Starres are poore books' ('The H. Scriptures (ii)', l.13). We need to have things spelt out more clearly. The image suggested in the next stanza implies another reason for rejecting all the stars as means to show Christ's death:

> Or shall each leaf,
> Which falls in Autumne, score a grief?
>
> (ll.9–10)

The mournfulness of autumn leaves suggests that stars were rejected as too celebratory to signify the Crucifixion (an event which God did not illuminate: 'there was a darknes ouer all the land, vntil the ninth houre' Luke xxiii.44). But autumn leaves are even less appropriate: as dead things they cannot signify the life-giving death of Christ. The fallen leaves of Vallombrosa may decorously image Satan's beautiful legions of rebel angels since they are involved with spiritual death and falling from grace (*Paradise Lost*, i. 301–4). But autumn leaves won't do for a death that generates life and resurrection. Natural, sensible appropriateness needs to be corroborated by an intelligible, interpretative aptitude.

This poem, like so many of Herbert's, moves in a self-correcting way that demands a cooperative understanding on the part of the reader. By this point in the poem we have become involved in the speaker's difficulties and the movement, in the following lines, from leaves to fruit, enforces the understanding that Christ's death was a generative act:

> Or can not leaves, but fruit, be signe
> Of the true vine?
>
> (ll.11–12)

At this point in the poem a traditional image is 'discovered'. Of course every Christian poet must sometimes resort to the store of typological and parabolic images which tradition offers; not to do so would imply an inappropriate individualism. The images within this traditional iconography—Christ as the 'true vine' is an example—work rather more on the level of *intelligibilia* than of *sensibilia*. And it is this central aspect of Herbert's imagery that Rosemond Tuve concentrates on. She calls this use of a traditional and typological iconography 'symbolical writing' and warns against an impertinent response:

Symbolical writing (including Herbert's) is confusing only when we read symbol as picture, when we allow the concrete particulars of garden and tree to carry us, by connotation, into alien contexts dependent on our individual fancies. There is an element of the irrevocable in symbols; they have meanings, and limitations of meaning, by virtue of a kind of social compact, and are not ours to do as we like with.[5]

Tuve has done Herbert's poetry an enormous service by alerting today's more secular readers to the conventional nature of many of his images, but she seems at times unaware of the variousness of their modes. She is at pains to exonerate Herbert from charges of audacity or indecorum:

The images of 'The Agonie', for example, are radical and to us surprising; but they are not audacious, they are conventional—and when we read Herbert's poems without knowing this we take away from them the quietness which is part of their power.[6]

But Christianity, in spite of the churches, has audacity and indecorum at its heart. It is part of typological convention to see Samson as a type of Christ. But the way in which Herbert makes the connection shows us the shocking paradoxes of a self-incarnating, self-immolating God:

As Sampson bore the doores away,
Christ's hands, though nail'd, wrought our salvation,
('Sunday', ll.47−9)

Tuve's opposition of audacity and convention is a false one. The quietness of Herbert's images often contains an audacity which may well be authorised by convention. The movement from shock to recollection of the authority is one source of their power. Stanza 4 of 'Home' is an example:

There lay thy sonne: and must he leave that nest,
    That hive of sweetnesse, to remove
Thraldome from those, who would not at a feast
    Leave one poore apple for thy love?

That 'one poore apple', gobbled up with the rest of the feast, initially seems to be an individual, natural apple. As such its triviality surprises in a stanza about the Incarnation. Only after the apparent indecorum of the image has shocked us into attentiveness do we find its justification in the original *malum malum*. It is a conventional image, but it is deliberately used as if it were not so. The effect of this stanza depends upon the almost punning conjunction of the conventional and the audaciously natural. Divine typology feeds into and informs the world of natural particulars.

The conjunction of eternal significance and ephemeral particular is also revealed in 'The Collar'. There, the rebellious speaker utters as if he were operating in a world of only natural and local significance:

> Sure there was wine
> Before my sighs did drie it: there was corn
> Before my tears did drown it.
> (ll.10–12)

But the submission with which the poem concludes is written into these images of the Eucharist. The speaker, who sees only the natural world, complains of the lack of bread and wine but, as readers, we are required to supply the knowledge that the gifts of bread and wine are available within the limits of Christian obedience. These images, like the 'poore apple' of 'Home', work poetically by combining two apparently antagonistic functions: the natural and local with the conventional and traditional.

Herbert's use of imagery that is conventional and traditional is not simply an inevitable feature of his Christian inheritance: he uses this iconography to signify his acceptance of this inheritance. In 'Good Friday' the typologically traditional image of Christ as the 'true vine' is presented as the discovery of the speaker who has, until this moment, been casting around for the appropriate, expressive image. The familiar and the conventional have been made strange and, in this way, thrown into relief and reauthenticated. 'Good Friday' (like 'Jordan (ii)' and *Astrophil and Stella* 1 and 3) makes the etymologically correct discovery that true invention is an act of uncovering what is already there. The 'fruit' of line 11 occupies the boundary between natural and conventional imagery. It may have the same status as the autumn leaves which they follow as a more lively alternative. Line 12 discloses the decorum of the image by relating it to the typological motif of 'the true vine'.

The image which 'Good Friday' achieves in its third stanza is a conventional one, but it has been achieved in such a way as to make us reflect on its appropriateness. The conventional image is effectively remotivated when we have been alerted to its difference from other, rejected, images. We are made to feel that this image has been imbued with more significance by tradition than could be found by any single poet working independently. Herbert has contrived to present the traditional image as, not stiffer, but richer than natural images, and he has done so in a way which invests the intelligible traditional image with the sensible vitality it might otherwise lack. A visual analogue to Herbert's reanimation of the conventional can be seen in Crivelli's *Annunciation* in the National Gallery, London (Fig. 12). Hovering over the head of Mary is an entirely conventional, formalised representation of the Holy Ghost in the form of a dove. But in the top left of the painting, and linked to the Holy Ghost by a diagonal line, is a group of naturalistic, fluttering doves. The effect here, as with Herbert, is of reinvigorating the traditional with the energy of the natural whilst reciprocally suggesting the permeation of ordinary life with spiritual realities.

'Good Friday', like so many of Herbert's poems, dedicates the resources

of the individual poet to the deprecation of those resources. The problem
with which the poem began was both a spiritual and an artistic one: how
to find a language adequate to the crucial moment. The solution to this
problem is presented as a wholly spiritual one: forget about finding apt
images and concentrate on your spiritual state. The tree is known by its
fruit (Matthew xii.33). The quality of the individual Christian life is the
most apt signifier of the true vine of Christ. A conventional iconography
is arrived at when independent poetic resourcefulness has been found
inadequate. The remainder of the poem describes a state of spiritual sub-
mission in which individual images are replaced by an overwhelming
empathy. The spiritual solution—anticipated in the previous stanza's sub-
mission to the typological—presents a poetic solution. The son of God,
being also the sun of the world, is both imageable and the source of illumi-
nation:

> Then let each houre
> Of my whole life one grief devoure;
> That thy distresse through all may runne,
> And be my sunne.
> (ll.13–16)

The stanza which follows and concludes this part of the poem, breaks this
'one grief' into the parts which make up the whole: a partiality which has
been justified by the whole:

> Or rather let
> My severall sinnes their sorrows get;
> That as each beast his cure doth know,
> Each sinne may so.
> (ll.17–20)

The issue now is more a matter of apt contrition than of poetic decorum.
     In the second (and originally separate) part of the poem the writer
whose writings are requested is not the faltering poet, but God. God's self-
expression depends upon willing materials. Image and medium are united
in the superlative decorum of blood:

> Since bloud is fittest, Lord, to write
> Thy sorrows in, and bloudie fight;
> My heart hath store, write there, where in
> One box doth lie both ink and sinne:
> (ll.21–24)

To a less profoundly religious nature than Herbert's, a Christian poetic
might seem exclusive and limiting. But Herbert's God comprehends all
and the result is a poetic which is permissive in its reference and which
authenticates its metaphors in a way of which secular poets can only
dream:

12. Carlo Crivelli, *Annunciation* (London, National Gallery).

> The wanton lover in a curious strain
>   Can praise his fairest fair;
> And with quaint metaphors her curled hair
>   Curl o're again.
>
> Thou art my lovelinesse, my life, my light,
>   Beautie alone to me:
> Thy bloudy death and undeserv'd, makes thee
>   Pure red and white.
>   ('Dulnesse', ll.5–12)

Secular poetry, re-curling the curled, is twice removed from the straightness of truth. 'Jordan (i)' implicitly contrasts secular poetry's indirect access to truth by means of a spiral staircase with the straight ladder which connects devotional poetry with the realm it addresses. No living mistress is as truly 'red and white' as Christ's blood-drained, blood-stained body. And the intelligible connotations of 'pure red and white' are wholly true when the object is Christ rather than some more or less innocent woman.[7]

In 1536 *Il Petrarcha Spirituale* ('The Spiritual Petrarch') was published in Venice. It was the work of a Minorite friar, Girolamo Maripiero, who presents the volume as a response to a plea from Petrarch's wandering ghost to rewrite the *Canzoniere* as celebrations of divine, and no longer mortal, love and beauty. Maripiero, who tells Petrarch that 'all your verses and love songs are allegorical and have spiritual meanings',[8] is happy to oblige and speed his master's ghost to bliss. The result is a volume which retains, to the best of Maripiero's abilities, Petrarch's vocabulary and rhyme schemes in poems which, rather woodenly, express the human soul's longings for God.

Maripiero's officiousness ignores the resonance of metaphorical description which does not assume the possibility of identity. The poignancy of Petrarch's metaphors derives from the knowledge that they are only metaphor; that Laura 'aspettata al regno delli dei/ cosa bella mortal passa e non dura' (that she 'awaited in the realm of the gods, this beautiful mortal thing passes and will not stay') (248). In their precarious extravagance the status of Petrarch's metaphors is very different from that of Dante's. The divine context of the *Commedia* works to authenticate metaphor, to make metaphor true. Paolo and Francesca, 'Quali colombe, dal disio chiamate' ('like doves, summoned by desire'), drift for eternity on the winds that once imaged their desire (*Inferno*, v.82).

The density of linguistic reference varies: language is not always trying to get out of itself. But the nature of the extra-linguistic referents may change the status of the linguistic expression. Herbert understands the way in which God can motivate language and claims this support. 'A Parodie' (which has a specific original in a poem by Edward Herbert) is a kind of anti-parody: it reappropriates the paradoxical language of secular love poetry into a context where it can be motivated by truth. Herbert's relation to secular poetry is self-confident. His enormous and experimental range of verse forms evince a fascination with poetic technique at least as great as that of the overtly theorising technician, Philip Sidney. Literary self-confidence allows Herbert to refer to the works of other poets by means of parody or near-quotation. In every such case Herbert is claiming that this language makes more sense when it is addressed to God. The precarious self-importance of erotic love which can make 'one little roome, an every where' (Donne, 'The good-morrow')[9] becomes authentic and irrefutable paradox in the context of Herbert's 'Temper (i)':

> Thy power and love, my love and trust
> Make one place ev'ry where.
> (ll.27–8)

A similar process of authenticating reappropriation of secularised language—in this case Sidney's in *Astrophil and Stella* 1 and 2—is involved in the conclusion of 'Jordan (ii)':

> ...while I bustled, I might heare a friend
> Whisper, *How wide is all this long pretence!*
> *There is in love a sweetnesse readie penn'd:*
> *Copie out onely that, and save expense.*
> (ll.15–18)

The similarity between this conclusion and that of *Astrophil and Stella* 3 —'In *Stella*'s face I reed/ What Love and Beautie be, then all my deed/ But Copying is, what in her Nature writes'—is close enough to say that Herbert is making a literary reference. But the language which Sidney is employing—the conceit of the Book of Nature—is properly part of a religious discourse. Herbert takes it back into the context where it is no longer loving hyperbole but true.

Figurative truths, pretty 'Petrarchan' paradoxes, become literal truths when God is their reference. Lovers are all too painfully not together when they are apart. Jacobean dramatists could only motivate the paradox of 'My love hath my heart and I have his' by an act of murder that leaves the beloved heartless. But God and the individual soul cannot be separated:

> Souls joy, when thou art gone,
> And I alone,
> Which cannot be,
> Because thou dost abide with me,
> And I depend on thee;
> ('A Parodie', ll.1–5)

Herbert frequently refers to his endeavours to 'wash' a secularised language (the two 'Jordan' poems; 'The Forerunners'). He sees himself as cleansing the language into a transparency to be coloured and motivated by God's meaning. He describes the Holy Scriptures as 'the well/ That washes what it shows' ('The H. Scriptures (i)', ll.9–10) and, in pointing out his choice of scriptural metaphor (like the true vine) he turns the cleansing of his own language into a source of revelation. But he also works in another direction: that of himself remotivating the dead or moribund metaphors of Christian iconography. The Holy Ghost is traditionally represented as a dove. Herbert's dove in 'Whitsunday' has warm down with which to hatch the egg of the human soul:

> Listen sweet Dove unto my song,
> And spread thy golden wings in me;
> Hatching my tender heart so long,
> Till it get wing, and flie away with thee.
>
> (ll.1–4)

The dead, conventional equation, Dove = Holy Ghost, has been reanimated by the verb 'hatching' as effectively as by the lively doves in Crivelli's *Annunciation*. In 'The Agonie' it is again a verb—'hunt'—which has the effect of reanimating an image which Rosemond Tuve rightly sees as conventional:

> Sinne is that presse and vice, which forceth pain
> To hunt his cruell food through ev'ry vein.
>
> (ll.11–12)

The verb 'hunt' brings the intelligible and conventional image of Christ as the wine press quite startlingly into the realm of the sensible.

Herbert's verbs work very hard. The verb 'hatching' in the example from 'Whitsunday' has the power to make specific and palpable both the dove of the Holy Ghost and the vulnerable unfledged heart. By investing so much animating power in his verbs Herbert achieves an effect much more quietly than by adjectival qualification of substantives. It is, nevertheless, an effect, and it would be a mistake to confuse this quiet reanimation of the traditional with its mute repetition. Herbert conceives of the theological universe in spatial terms with heaven above, earth below, and hell in the depths ('The heav'ns are not too high,/ His praise may thither flie:/ The earth is not too low,/ His praises there may grow' ('Antiphon (i)'); 'Although there were some fourtie heav'ns, or more,/ Sometimes I peere above them all;/ Sometimes I hardly reach a score,/ Sometimes to hell I fall' ('The Temper' (i)). The business of the individual Christian and the justification for his poetry is the bridging of the gap between high heaven and low earth. Spiritual energy, enabled by 'suppling grace' ('Grace', l.19), is needed to bridge that gap. Sundays are presented as the springy stepping-stones to heaven:

> Thou art a day of mirth:
> And where the week-dayes trail on ground,

Thy flight is higher, as thy birth.
O let me take thee at the bound,
Leaping with thee from sev'n to sev'n,
Till that we both, being toss'd from earth,
    Flie hand in hand to heav'n!
        ('Sunday', ll.57–63)

That verb 'toss', conveying the anti-gravitational movement from earth to heaven, is used again in 'The Pulley', where the movement finds its rhetorical embodiment in the *antistasis* (or *antanaclasis*) of 'rest':

Yet let him keep the rest,
But keep them with repining restlesnesse;
Let him be rich and wearie, that at least,
If goodnesse leade him not, yet wearinesse
    May tosse him to my breast.
        (ll.16–20)

The way in which Herbert concentrates so much metaphorical force into his verbs answers his conception of a gap between heaven and earth which can only be traversed with considerable spiritual energy. That energy comes across in his choice of verbs:

We are the earth; and they,*
Like moles within us, *heave*, and *cast about*:
   And till they *foot* and *clutch* their prey,
They never cool, much lesse give out.
       ('Confession', ll.13–16)

If I say, Thou shalt be mine;
   Finger not my treasure.
       ('Dialogue', ll.11–12)

But when I thus dispute and grieve,
   I do resume my sight,
And *pilfring* what I once did give,
   Disseize thee of thy right.
       ('Submission', ll.9–12)

Go search this thing,
Tumble thy breast, and turn thy book.
       ('The Method', ll.9–10)

In each of these examples fairly commonplace metaphors are brought to life by the particularity of the verbs.

The forcefulness of Herbert's verbs—'doing words' as every schoolchild knows—connects with his spatial conception of the theological

---

* afflictions

universe and with his dread of a spiritual inertia that might strand him down here. Meister Eckhart writes:

> If I were asked to say to what end the Creator has created all creatures, I would say: rest. If I were asked secondly what the Holy Trinity sought altogether in all its works, I would answer: rest. If I were asked thirdly what the soul sought in all her agitations, I would answer: rest. If I were asked fourthly what all creatures sought in their natural desires and motions, I would answer: rest.[10]

But rest experienced on earth is premature—the stasis of spiritual lethargy which rests 'in Nature, not the God of Nature' ('The Pulley', l.14). The only desirable stasis is the stasis of perfection:

> O that I once past changing were,
> Fast in thy Paradise, where no flower can wither!
> ('The Flower', ll.22–3)

C.S. Lewis has observed that, whereas Marlowe, Shakespeare and Milton present evil as 'abounding and upsurging', Spenser presents good as essentially active, and evil as deathly and inert.[11] The power of virtue in *The Faerie Queene* is built into the word. Virtue prevails clad in the armour of God, because that is what virtue does. But the inevitable power of virtue must have slipped for Milton to need to recuperate it at the end of *Comus*: 'Or if Virtue feeble were,/ Heaven itself would stoop to her'. Herbert is not operating on the same allegorical level as Spenser. For Herbert, spiritual good is not so much analogous to the goodness of tangible experience as present within it. He presents virtue as intrinsically energising. Virtue is active and it is present and is involved in the principle of being in its impulse towards incarnation. Sin has none of these qualities which are so conducive to representation:

> O that I could a sinne once see!
> We paint the devil foul, yet he
> Hath some good in him, all agree.
> Sinne is flat opposite to th'Almighty, seeing
> It wants the good of *vertue*, and of *being*.
>
> But God more care of us hath had:
> If apparitions make us sad,
> By sight of sinne we should grow mad.
> Yet as in sleep we see foul death, and live:
> So devils are our sinnes in perspective.
> ('Sinne (ii)')

Herbert, following Augustine, presents sin as a lack, a state of deprivation. It is this fact, and not the fact that sin is an abstract noun, which makes sin so unimaginable. (Though, as the play on 'seeing' in the first

stanza suggests, language is able to paint sin by means of negative definition.)
This poem suggests that only goodness—virtue—is impelled towards realis-
ation and incarnation. The same concept of virtue and heavenly pleasures
being endowed with greater presence than their opposites, is suggested in
'Vanitie (ii)':

> Poore silly soul, whose hope and head lies low;
> Whose flat delights on earth do creep and grow;
> To whom the starres shine not so fair, as eyes;
> Nor solid work, as false embroyderies;
> Heark and beware, lest what you now do measure
> And write for sweet, prove a most sowre displeasure.
>
> (ll.1–6)

The urge towards epiphany and incarnation, rather than any disembodied
spirituality, is the aspect of the divinity which most helpfully colludes
with the representational endeavours of preacher and poet:

> God hath made starres the foil
> To set off vertues; griefs to set off sinning:
> Yet in this wretched world we toil,
> As if grief were not foul, nor vertue winning.
>
> ('The Foil', ll.5–8)

Herbert presents his God as making spiritual qualities sensibly accessible,
and places his own poetic demonstrations within this framework. That
Herbert's verbs should carry so much metaphorical freight is in keeping
with his sense of a divine movement outwards: a perpetual process of
manifestation. Poetic energy, the energy which is at the heart of meta-
phor, thus participates in the divine.[12]

The didactic impulse of the preacher is to make spiritual truths manifest
and accessible. Biblical parables provide good precedent for preacherly
exemplification and Herbert frequently uses this method of domesticating
spiritual truths. Yet he tends to do so with a self-mocking edge which
acknowledges that the necessity for such terms is the product of inade-
quacy. I have already said something about 'Obedience'. 'Redemption' is
another example of a poem that finally works against its clarifying, worldly
imagery. There the last line undermines the poem's bustling persona at
the very moment that it gratifies his quest. The absurdity of self-important
temporal business, and even the affectation of rational manipulation as
imaged in the logical form of the Shakespearean sonnet, are annihilated in
the last lines:

> Having been tenant long to a rich Lord,
>   Not thriving, I resolved to be bold,
>   And make a suit unto him, to afford
> A new small-rented lease, and cancell th' old.
> In heaven at his manour I him sought:

> They told me there, that he was lately gone
> About some land, which he had dearly bought
> Long since on earth, to take possession.
> I straight return'd, and knowing his great birth,
> Sought him accordingly in great resorts;
> In cities, theatres, gardens, parks, and courts:
> At length I heard a ragged noise and mirth
> Of theeves and murderers: there I him espied,
> Who straight, *Your suit is granted*, said, & died.

The fitting of the narrative to the first three quatrains images the control of the persona who knows his way around. But this knowing persona cannot himself understand figurative language: the spiritual resonances of 'rich Lord' and 'dearly bought' are lost on him and his incomprehension illustrates the perils of parabolic translation which, like nature, may offer a false repose. The speaker's inadequacy—of which he seems to have no intuition—is made obvious in the way that the couplet which should complete his leisurely narrative is wrested away from him and interrupted so that it seems no couplet. The final line and a half are discontinuous with the preceding narrative and replace its circumlocutions with chastening directness. This 'straight' saying makes the 'straight' of line 10 seem the most arrant self-ignorance. And this 'straight' saying silences the poem. The errant circumlocutions of the first twelve and a half lines foil the silence of the conclusion, ensuring that the silence is a full one. If God has made stars the 'foil/ To set off vertues', Herbert ascribes to his own linguistic images a task both momentous and modest: that of foiling and illuminating the unspeakable.[13]

Theologically speaking, any image which Herbert presents, any experience which his poetry illuminates, stands in a relation of synecdoche to the whole of God's Word. The whole is only dimly accessible to human understanding through 'temporal ratiocination' and through the enumeration of some of the infinite properties which comprise that whole. The distinctions of properties, or grammatical classes, which enable human ratiocination to proceed, do not exist in the unity of divine knowledge. 'Gather vp the broken meat which remaineth, that nothing be lost' (John vi.12): This verse was glossed by Bede and Alcuin as an injunction to gather together in exegesis the prophecies and allegories scattered in the Bible. The different modes of scriptural writing are themselves symptomatic of the fragmentary and partial nature of our understanding which works through different forms of mediation. The expression 'literal truth' is itself a metaphor. The scriptural letters of God's word are the mediating residue of his letterless Word. To have gathered up all the fragments, pieced them together, would be to know the Word made flesh, the living bread.

The partiality, the fragmentary nature of human knowledge, is something which Herbert consciously works with. A partial understanding is better able to appreciate a variety and fullness of experience, since the perception of variety derives from the perception of limits—the kinds of distinctions which a divine knowledge would dissolve.[14] There is a delight in beginning to piece the whole together:

> Waters united are our navigation;
> Distinguished, our habitation;
> Below, our drink; above, our meat;
> Both are our cleanlinesse. Hath one such beautie?
> Then how are all things neat?
>
> ('Man', ll.38–42)

Sidney seems to have found the English language fortunately lacking in grammar: 'for grammar it might have, but it needs it not, being so easy in itself, and so void of those cumbersome differences of cases, genders, moods, and tenses, which I think was a piece of the Tower of Babylon's curse, that a man should be put to school to learn his mother-tongue'.[15] This jest suggests that Adam's language lacked grammatical distinctions. Distinctions of case, mood, class, the locations and conjunctions of syntax, are all part of 'temporal ratiocination'. The shock of zeugma derives from our capacity to distinguish between concrete and abstract nouns, figurative and literal uses. Herbert's work contains many startling zeugmas:

> Onely do thou lend me a hand,
> Since thou hast both mine eyes.
>
> ('Submission', ll.19–20)

> When blessed Marie wip'd her Saviours feet,
> (Whose precepts she had trampled on before)
>
> . . . .
>
> Why kept she not her tears for her own faults,
> And not his feet? . . .
>
> ('Marie Magdalene', ll.1–2, 9–10)

> Both frosts and thoughts do nip,
> And bite his lip;
>
> ('Mans medley', ll.28–9)

> And in this love, more then in bed, I rest.
>
> ('Even-song', l.32)

> Thy clothes being fast, but thy soul loose about thee.
>
> ('The Church Porch', l.414)

Zeugma, whether it is intentional or not, is always striking. The most grotesque example I know of is in Marlowe's description of the sack of Troy when Priam 'would have grappled with Achilles' son/ Forgetting both his want of strength and hands' (*Dido Queen of Carthage*, II.i.251).

The effect of zeugma can be to shock us into attention, offend us into thought. The effect is similar to that of the apparently indecorous low naturalism of images which consideration reveals to be traditional (the 'one poore apple' of 'Home'). The application of a single verb to apparently incommensurable nouns—a concrete and an abstract—or the startling juxtaposition of idioms—one a colloquial dead metaphor and the other a passionately felt figure for spiritual blindness ('Submission', ll.19–20)—offend only from a restricted viewpoint. A language dualistic for convenience of explication could say that God straddles the two worlds of spiritual and physical existence. But that distinction is only temporary and would be collapsed by perfect understanding—just as the graphic and apparently semantic distinction between 'eye' and the 'I' which is the I AM of God, collapses in the assimilation of divine hospitality. Herbert's zeugmas alert us to the partiality of our own understanding.

But the shock of these zeugmas is as important as the resolution of that shock in understanding. The indecorum of Herbert's conjunctions is not tamed by the recollection of their theological propriety. It is more a case of Herbert's language releasing again the mercifully terrible impropriety of the Incarnation:

> *My God, my God, why dost thou part from me?*
>   Was such a grief as cannot be.
> Shall I then sing, skipping thy dolefull storie,
>   And side with thy triumphant glorie?
> Shall thy strokes be my stroking? . . .
>   ('The Thanksgiving', ll.9–13)

The horror of these lines should belie the commonly held image of Herbert as bobbish celebrant.

What is for Sidney a perplexing matter of aesthetics—why 'cruel fights well pictured forth do please' (*Astrophil and Stella* 34), how it can be that a poetic representation of sorrow can be the source of aesthetic pleasure ('mine annoyes/ Are metamorphosd straight to tunes of joyes')[16]—is for Herbert the crux of faith. The recognition that Christ's 'stretched sinews taught all strings, what key/ Is best to celebrate this most high day' ('Easter', ll.11–12) is not a prettification of suffering; to understand the argument of these lines we have to supply the idea of Christ's guts performing the function of cat gut. We have to see the cost of our salvation, the suffering which is the bass to our music. Donne concludes his final sermon in a climax of affective piety:

> There now hangs that *sacred Body* upon the *Crosse, rebaptized* in his owne *teares* and *sweat*, and *embalmed* in his *owne blood alive*. There are those *bowells of compassion*, which are so conspicuous, so manifested, as that you may *see them through his wounds*.[17]

Donne insists that the metaphor which our embarrassment keeps dead—

'bowels of compassion'—is brought to life so that we see what compassion endures. The motivating of a dead metaphor is accomplished by attention to the Incarnation: the Incarnation realises the intelligible, extruding it into the sensible realm. Herbert's method in 'Easter' is quieter. The effect takes place off the page as we supply the shocking image of Christ's guts, without which the lines do not make sense.

The poem which presents the transformations of redemption most extensively is 'The Sacrifice'—a poem in which, in Empson's words, 'the contradictory impulses that are held in equilibrium by the doctrine of atonement may be seen in a luminous juxtaposition'.[18] The shock of zeugma which Herbert elsewhere recreates, or the indecorously naturalistic realision of intelligible typological 'symbols' (Tuve's word), are at the heart of the Incarnation:

> They buffet him, and box him as they list,
> Who grasps the earth and heaven with his fist,
> And never yet, whom he would punish, miss'd:
> > Was ever grief like mine?
> > (ll.129–32)

> *Now heal thy self, Physician; now come down.*
> Alas! I did so, when I left my crown
> And father's smile for you, to feel his frown:
> > Was ever grief like mine?
> > (ll.221–4)

'The Sacrifice', placed at the beginning of *The Temple*—immediately after 'The Altar'—creates the context for Herbert's subsequent wit. It demonstrates the contrarieties that Christ's sacrifice can resolve. To understand the weight of the resolution we must experience the clash and tug of contrariety. There is, in Herbert's poetry, a 'double motion' at work all the time. One is an anatomising impulse which represents by distinguishing. The other is an impulse to deny the ultimate existence of the boundaries which make a certain kind of representation through discrete particulars possible.

Helen Vendler remarks upon the variety of modes which Herbert employs and on the way in which he mixes them. She cites 'Love (iii)' as an example of verse allegory containing two 'stories': a secular story about a guest and a host, and a spiritual story about the arrival of a guilty soul at heaven:

A parabolic poet would have told the first story, and let us guess the application; an emblematic poet would have told the first story, and added the second by way of a gloss to his text. But Herbert, neither parabolic nor allegorical in any 'pure' way, has mixed text and gloss ...when we read the poem...we slide...from genre to genre, from love poem to allegory to homily to *débat*.[19]

She notices the way in which Herbert 'gives away his allegory' by the conjunction of 'dust' and 'sinne' which any systematic allegorist would keep on different planes. In Herbert's consciousness, however, 'they are simultaneous and coterminous'. A similar understanding lies behind Herbert's zeugmas (where dust and sin might well meet). The way in which he 'gives away' his allegories and mixes his modes derives from his belief that the distinctions which he reveals and through which he operates are known to be impermanent.

In Herbert's puns, the singleness of the graphic form or the acoustic unit is finally more significant than the semantic diversity which it contains. The single form is a token of reconciliation and atonement. But the different levels on which Herbert's language is operating and the different genres which he employs effectively isolate aspects of a meaning whose simultaneous fulness we cannot grasp.

'Providence' is Herbert's most sustained attempt to anatomise the fulness of the creation.[20] The creator's infinite presence can be intimated by itemising the wonderful provision evident within the finite sensible world:

> Thou art in small things great, not small in any:
> Thy even praise can neither rise, nor fall.
> Thou art in all things one, in each thing many:
> For thou art infinite in one and all.
>
> (ll.41–4)

This delighted catalogue of divine ingenuity seems at times like a series of answers to riddles:

> Light without winde is glasse: warm without weight
> Is wooll and furre: cool without closeness, shade:
> Speed without pains, a horse: tall without height,
> A servile hawk: low without losse, a spade.
>
> (ll.101–4)

For Herbert, riddles are like temporary accidents of our perception. They teach by illuminating a facet of congruence: the miraculous fittingness of the whole is dramatised and made apparent through the process of riddle and solution. 'Love-Joy' is a narrative involving the explication of a riddle by a persona who prides himself on his skill in such matters:

> As on a window late I cast mine eye,
> I saw a vine drop grapes with *J* and *C*
> Anneal'd on every bunch. One standing by
> Ask'd what it meant. I, who am never loth
> To spend my judgement, said, It seem'd to me
> To be the bodie and the letters both
> Of *Joy* and *Charitie*. Sir, you have not miss'd,
> The man reply'd; It figures *JESUS CHRIST*.

The persona is both right and wrong for the answer to this riddle is, ulti-mately, the answer to every riddle. The lineaments of the particular narra-tive, like the window it mentions, once seen, can be passed through.

Porfyrius' and Hrabanus' pages of letters which can be 'read in every direction' are like crossword puzzles with no blank squares. If such a puzzle should, completed, spell out a coherent message, though composed, horizontally and vertically, of discrete words, it would well represent the relation which Herbert conceives between the 'all' (which is God's Word) and the component parts with their own semantic integrity, through which we can discover the whole. The conceit of 'spelling' is central to Herbert's thought. Graphic and acoustic coincidences are tokens of a real congruity of meaning:

> How neatly doe we give one onely name
> To parents issue and the sunnes bright starre!
> ('The Sonne', ll.5−6)

> How well her name an *Army* doth present,
> In whom the *Lord of Hosts* did pitch his tent!
> ('Anagram of the Virgin Marie')

In the last example, the anagrammatic transformation of the word 'Mary' is presented as a revelation, not a destruction, of its meaning: it is re-membered thus. The couplet shows the two words to be isomorphic: the phonemes function as morphemes.[21]

The way in which the triplets of words in 'The Call' are shuffled through each stanza creates an effect of mutual information and mutual erasure:

> Come, my Way, my Truth, my Life:
> Such a Way, as gives us breath:
> Such a Truth, as ends all strife:
> Such a Life, as killeth death.

> Come, my Light, my Feast, my Strength:
> Such a Light, as shows a feast:
> Such a Feast, as mends in length:
> Such a Strength, as makes his guest.

> Come, my Joy, my Love, my Heart:
> Such a Joy, as none can move:
> Such a Love, as none can part:
> Such a Heart, as joyes in love.

The symmetries of this poem allow no word predominance. Each seems to be defined in terms of the others to a point which approaches transparency. By the end of the poem there is the impression that all the words mean the same thing: they are differentiated only in so far as their difference can illuminate the single meaning. Herbert comes closer in this poem than anywhere else to representing the way in which God's Word can flood and break down the distinctions between the individual words through which we work. This poem perfectly balances the distinguishing and the assimilating capacities of language.

'The Call' is an extraordinary poem in its achievement of level, brimming quietness. It presents a language on the brink of surrendering the partiality which gives it meaning. Elsewhere, Herbert creates poems which act as foils to the ensuing silence—poems which efface themselves by suberving that silence. But in 'The Call' the silence has been absorbed into the poem itself.

The tension between the poet's pride and the Christian's humility is constant and acute for Herbert. Often the resolution of the two in the suggestion that the poet's skill and wit is only a discovery of God's prior design is in some sense factitious. The final 'thine' of 'The Altar' does not settle the matter of authorship. We do not forget Herbert's skill and wit, nor should we if it is to be an image of divine care. The idea of placing his poetic gifts in the service of God can only resolve the conflict in a general way which glosses over the particular arrogances of poetic integrity. Whenever the statement is one of 'All this for you', the stress inclines as much to the first as to the last part. That Herbert was not ever entirely serene about the compatibility of his poetry and his faith is clear from his request that Nicholas Ferrar commit the manuscript of *The Temple* to the flames unless Ferrar thought that the poems might benefit others.[22]

'The Forerunners' presents a narrative of this preparedness to surrender wit:

> The harbingers are come. See, see their mark;
> White is their colour, and behold my head.
> But must they have my brain? must they dispark
> Those sparkling notions, which therein were bred?
>   Must dulnesse turn me to a clod?
> Yet have they left me, *Thou art still my God*.
>
> Good men ye be, to leave me my best room,
> Ev'n all my heart, and what is lodged there:
> I passe not, I, what of the rest become,
> So *Thou art still my God*, be out of fear.
>   He will be pleased with that dittie;
> And if I please him, I write fine and wittie.
>
> Farewell sweet phrases, lovely metaphors.
> But will ye leave me thus? when ye before
> Of stews and brothels onely knew the doores,
> Then did I wash you with my tears, and more,
>   Brought you to Church well drest and clad:
> My God must have my best, ev'n all I had.

Lovely enchanting language, sugar-cane,
Hony of roses, whither wilt thou flie?
Hath some fond lover tic'd thee to thy bane?
And wilt thou leave the Church, and love a stie?
    Fie, thou wilt soil thy broider'd coat,
And hurt thy self, and him that sings the note.

Let foolish lovers, if they will love dung,
With canvas, not with arras, clothe their shame:
Let follie speak in her own native tongue.
True beautie dwells on high: ours is a flame
    But borrow'd thence to light us thither.
Beautie and beauteous words should go together.

Yet if you go, I passe not; take your way:
For, *Thou art still my God*, is all that ye
Perhaps with more embellishment can say.
Go birds of spring: let winter have his fee;
    Let a bleak palenesse chalk the doore,
So all within be livelier then before.

Wit is surrendered with difficulty. It flares defiantly in 'dispark' as it contemplates its own darkening. Wit persists into the second stanza: 'Good men ye be, to leave me my best room,/ Ev'n all my heart, and what is lodged there.' But the room of the heart is different from that of a poetic stanza. An imaginative contraction is conveyed by these lines. The 'pretty rooms' of sonnets, even those rededicated to God, are, in their very expansiveness, of a different kind to the solemn and unindividualised chamber of the God-occupied heart. And, whereas elsewhere Herbert may seek to represent God's wit and care by some self-deprecating wit of his own, in 'The Forerunners' he acknowledges that divine and human wit may not be of the same kind and that he must be prepared to give up his own:

I passe not, I, what of the rest become,
So *Thou art still my God*, be out of fear.
    He will be pleased with that dittie;
And if I please him, I write fine and wittie.

For once Herbert represents his submission to God's will with a rhyme which is conspicuously flat,[23] acknowledging with pain that divine wit may comprehend, but not be comprehended by his own.

The next three stanzas ruefully relate a narrative of poetic service in a language which is expansively metaphorical and which sets off the constriction and reticence of the final stanza. In 'The Call' the very walls of Herbert's stanzas seem to dissolve. 'The Forerunners' is the work of a poet whose skill in showing, in juxtaposing and conjoining, has illuminated the way in which God's presence floods the world. This poem acknowledges that that flood may extinguish his own showing light.

Chapter 4

ANTONY AND CLEOPATRA

'We'll build in sonnets pretty roomes'

For George Herbert it is God, coextensive with this world but not coter-
minous, who makes the world visible, audible and knowable, before seal-
ing individual articulations in a silence of wholeness. Now I want to look
at the way in which erotic human love can be presented—and indeed
experienced—as the source of the world's illumination and coherence.

Most annotated editions of *Julius Caesar* include a note on the homo-
phony in Elizabethan pronunciation of 'Rome' and 'room'. Few can miss
the point of the pun that opposes the restrictions of Caesar's dictatorship
to the freedom of the desired republic:

> When could they say, till now, that talk'd of Rome,
> That her wide walks encompass'd but one man?
> Now is it Rome indeed and room enough,
> When there is in it but one only man.
>
> (I.ii.154−7)[1]

But no edition of *Antony and Cleopatra* that I know of, glosses this homo-
phone, though it is the source of a pivotal pun:

> Let Rome in Tiber melt, and the wide arch
> Of the rang'd empire fall! Here is my space
>
> (I.i.33−4)

These lines return to the concern of the play's first dialogue in which
questions of 'how much?' and 'how far?' were rebuked for their implica-
tions of limit. Philo, sensible Roman with a strong sense of decorum and
of when enough is enough, tells us at the start that 'this dotage of our
general's/ O'erflows the measure' (I.i.1−2). His speech, a variation on
the *quantum mutatus ab illo* theme, describes Antony's transformation
and invites our judgement:

> Look, where they come:
> Take but good note, and you shall see in him
> The triple pillar of the world transform'd
> Into a strumpet's fool: behold and see.
>
> (I.i.10−13)[2]

Our attention so alerted, we cannot fail to notice how the ensuing dialogue between Antony and Cleopatra refutes the validity of the frame of reference and judgement that Philo has set up:

> *Cleo.* If it be love indeed, tell me how much.
> *Ant.* There's beggary in the love that can be reckon'd.
> *Cleo.* I'll set a bourn how far to be belov'd.
> *Ant.* Then must thou needs find out new heaven, new earth.
>
> (I.i.14–17)

It is not that Antony and Cleopatra hold a different conception of 'measure' from Philo, or that they and Philo would disagree over the dimensions of the golden mean. It is that they reject as necessarily diminishing the very notion of such quantifying. Their dialogue replaces the world of dimensions and boundaries with an unrestricted world which corresponds to conceptual rather to actual capacity. The 'Rome' which Antony would let melt, is not just that place, capital of the Roman empire, but all place, every bounded location.

The numerous Renaissance poems on the theme of *exegi monumentum* opposed the immateriality of poetry to the vulnerable solidity of monuments of brass and stone even while, in the case of figured poems, imitating the contours of those material monuments. Shakespeare is offering a version of this theme in sonnet 55:

> When wasteful war shall statues overturn,
> And broils root out the work of masonry,
> Nor Mars his sword nor war's quick fire shall burn
> The living record of your memory.
> 'Gainst death and all oblivious enmity
> Shall you pace forth; your praise shall still find room,
> Ev'n in the eyes of all posterity
> That wear this world out to the ending doom.

The 'room' which is found for the boy's praise is that of the sonnet, only accidentally located on particular pages. Shakespeare may have intended the tacit bilingual pun with which Herbert is left in 'The Forerunners' ('Good men ye be, to leave me my best room') and upon which two lines of Donne's 'The Canonization' turn:

> And if no peece of Chronicle wee prove,
> We'll build in sonnets pretty roomes.
>
> (ll.31–2)

Certainly 'stanza' was a new and interesting import to English. 'Come, more, another stanzo: call you them stanzos?' asks the erudite Jacques (*As You Like It*, II.v.19). Puttenham writes of 'Staffe in our vulgare Poesie I know not why it should be so called... the Italian called it *Stanza*, as if we should say a resting place.'[3] The emphasis, at least as far as puns were concerned, shifted from the resting, propping connotations of *stanza* towards the place or room where such resting occurs. Marvell's Fleckno, 'though within one Cell so narrow pent/ [Had] *Stanzas* for a whole Appartment' ('Fleckno', ll.18–19).

In 'The Canonization' the solipsism of love combines with the elusiveness of poetic substance to offer an alternative to contingent space. The cities, rooms, or *stanze* of cartographers and builders are opposed in the indeterminate space of imaginative experience. This also happens in *Antony and Cleopatra*. And just as Donne's construction of pretty *stanze* exemplifies the powers of both love and poetry, so the contingency-defying love of Antony and Cleopatra is presented as much as a form of artistic and philosophic activity as an erotic one. Erotic love, in which the objective act bears so incongruous a relation to its subjective experience, shares some of the contradictions inherent in a poem (whatever its subject) in which a concise arrangement of words on paper both derives from, and initiates again in the reader, an unlocatable mental activity.

Erotic love and artistic production have traditionally been associated through the idea of procreation. The *locus classicus* for this is Diotima's speech in *The Symposium*:

> Those whose creative instinct is physical have recourse to women, and show their love in this way . . . but there are some whose creative desire is of the soul, and who long to beget spiritually, not physically, the progeny which it is the nature of the soul to create and bring to birth . . . of this all poets and such craftsmen as have found out some new thing may be said to be begetters.[4]

This association, which contains the idea that time can be cheated and a kind of immortality achieved with the creation of children or poems, both of which outlive their sources, provides the argument to the early sonnets in Shakespeare's 'sequence' as it was printed in 1609. Corporeal generation, initially presented as the only means of evading mortality, is first elided with, and then superseded by the immortality conferred by poetic fame.

But the relation between love and poetic creation is more intimate than the parallelism which a play on the notion of creativity suggests. Love of the boy is presented as impetus and food for the work of poetic creation while, reciprocally, poetry bestows on this love its own capacity to elude spatial and temporal limits. The relation between love and the mental powers involved in poetic creation is one of analogy and reciprocation. Poetry's time-cheating powers are extended to shelter the poet's love and its object; that love, in turn, extends its care to the particulars conceived by the imagination in the process of executing a poem. This is the source of that cherishing of particularity which allows images a distinct and autonomous beauty independent of their 'use' in analogy. The Sonnets do seem to 'consider every thing that grows'.

The coincidence of love and imagination in the Sonnets leads to the presentation of love as a way of seeing. This is most evident in a sonnet which laments in flat tones the failure of the imagination, the lack of responsive capacity, which derives from the absence of the boy, love's energising source:

> From you have I been absent in the spring,
> When proud-pied April, dressed in all his trim,
> Hath put a spirit of youth in everything,
> That heavy Saturn laughed and leapt with him.
> Yet nor the lays of birds, nor the sweet smell
> Of different flow'rs in odor and in hue,
> Could make me any summer's story tell,
> Or from their proud lap pluck them where they grew.
> Nor did I wonder at the lily's white,
> Nor praise the deep vermilion in the rose;
> They were but sweet, but figures of delight,
> Drawn after you, you pattern of all those.
> > Yet seemed it winter still, and, you away,
> > As with your shadow I with these did play.

> (98)

The monosyllables enact the nullity of the response—the dactyl of 'different' rising only to register the variegation that a fuller response would cherish and explore. It is the direct antecedent (via Wordsworth's 'Immortality Ode') of Coleridge's 'Dejection', one of the language's fullest accounts of imaginative failure. L.C. Knights describes this sonnet and 102 as 'direct developments of the Spenserian mode' in which 'no object is sharply forced upon the consciousness'.[5] When the boy is away the world cannot be seen.

To some extent all the sonnets which deal with the absence of the boy reveal love's ignorance and independence of the real world, but only 98 records a failure of imagination in this situation. The others involve more positive demonstrations of this independence—a flaunting of the imagination's transformative power. In 43 the antithesis between the unrewarding sight of the bodily eye by day and the wish-fulfilling visions of the mind's eye in dreams—a commonplace antithesis in the vocabulary of deprived love[6]—is sharpened into an account of the difference:

> When most I wink, then do my eyes best see,
> For all the day they view things unrespected,
> But when I sleep, in dreams they look on thee,
> And darkly bright, are bright in dark directed.

The real world, without the illuminating presence of the boy, is seen as meaningless and valueless, viewed at random. 'Unrespected' is both adverbial and adjectival, and this double function brings into prominence the word's origins in *respectus* and the extent to which value is bestowed by the look, the regard, which holds it. When we have been reminded of the word's etymology, the second line reads as an oxymoron: 'they view things that they do not (re)-view'. This prepares for the next line in which sightless eyes are described, not just as seeing, but 'directed'. The presence of the boy's image has the effect of providing a focus for vision, of directing the visual rays. The next quatrain suggests not only how brilliantly clear and defined the boy's form would appear to waking eyes, but that his form would endow his daylight environment with the clarity and definition which, without him, it lacks:

> Then thou, whose shadow shadows doth make bright—
> How would thy shadow's form form happy show
> To the clear day with thy much clearer light,
> When to unseeing eyes thy shade shines so!

This sonnet suggests that the presence of the loved boy is needed to make sense of the visible world. His light brings the tone of the visible world into a higher key so that forms, previously obscured in dullness, reveal themselves. The boy's 'form', through its distinction, illuminates and structures what would otherwise be a dull, undifferentiated world.

What the Sonnets and *Antony and Cleopatra* share is the way in which they explore romantic love, not as the source of tragedy or the proper end of comedy, but as a mode of thought, a way of seeing and organising experience. Love is not madness but elucidation. Cleopatra describes the effect of Antony's death as the collapse of experience into an undifferentiated continuum. In a world without Antony she 'views things unrespected':

> Hast thou no care of me, shall I abide
> In this dull world, which in thy absence is
> No better than a sty?...
> 　　　　　　　　　　　... young boys and girls
> Are level now with men: the odds is gone,
> And there is nothing left remarkable
> Beneath the visiting moon.
> 　　　　　　　　　　　(IV.xv.60–3; 65–8)

Even the distinction between antitheses has collapsed:

> ...All's but naught:
> Patience is sottish, and impatience does
> Become a dog that's mad:
> 　　　　　　　　　　　(IV.xv.78–80)

In sonnet 43 the boy's bright form showed up the contours of the otherwise 'dull world'. For Cleopatra, Antony was the differential, the form which anchored her gaze and in relation to which other forms could be distinguished. If the appropriate pictorial analogy for the effect which the

boy has on the world is a lightening of tone, Antony's function is compar-
able to that of the crucial figure in the foreground of a painting which is
needed to fix and give coherence to what would otherwise be seen as ran-
dom blobs of paint. In both *Antony and Cleopatra* and the Sonnets, lovers
are poets and the poet is a lover; in each, the poet-lovers see, shape and
speak a different world.

Of the eleven plays listed as 'tragedies' in the first folio of 1623, only
Antony and Cleopatra and *Julius Caesar* had stories with which an Eliza-
bethan audience would have been familiar.[7] While early audiences must
have watched *Macbeth* or *Othello* with as much interest in what would
happen as in how or why it would happen, the emphasis of interest with a
story as familiar as *Antony and Cleopatra* (Cleopatra, the first of Chaucer's
'good women') must have been much more upon the manner in which
the story was presented than in what happened next.

This familiarity with the outcome is something which affects not only
the audience's response but the quality of the play itself. This is accen-
tuated by the presence of the Soothsayer in the second scene. In response
to Charmian's 'Good sir, give me good fortune' he tells us 'I make not,
but foresee' (I.ii.14). His prophecies speak over the heads of the Egyptians
to an audience who recognise how illusory is the rich sense of possibility
which Charmian's playful misinterpretations reveal. The scope of once-
possible futures has contracted to the point of a restricted present. This
early in the play the Soothsayer has reminded us that the only flexibility
in the face of so rigid a destiny is that of interpretation.

In *Antony and Cleopatra* an accomplished destiny predates the play,
and scope of attitude replaces freedom of action. When Menas comes to
Pompey on the boat bearing the feasting triumvirs and suggests that he
cut the cable and slaughter Pompey's enemies, Pompey responds with a
consciousness of the relativity with which all action is valued in this play:

> Ah, this thou shouldst have done,
> And not have spoke on't! In me 'tis villainy,
> In thee, 't had been good service. Thou must know,
> 'Tis not my profit that does lead mine honour;
> Mine honour, it. Repent that e'er thy tongue
> Hath so betray'd thine act. Being done unknown,
> I should have found it afterwards well done,
> But must condemn it now.
>
> (II.vii.72–9)

The act remains the same but, according to who perceives it, the single
deed may be one of loyalty or treachery. To the more straightforward
Menas, Pompey's double-think seems pointlessly self-thwarting, but in
the next scene Antony's soldiers show a more sophisticated grasp of the
extent to which the act is constituted by its perceiver. Ventidius resists
Silius' exhortations to extend his martial triumphs through Media to

Mesopotamia, 'So thy grand captain Antony/ Shall set thee on triumphant chariots, and/ Put garlands on thy head'. (III.i.9–11) Ventidius knows better:

> O Silius, Silius,
> I have done enough. A lower place, note well,
> May make too great an act. For learn this, Silius;
> Better to leave undone, than by our deed
> Acquire too high a fame, when him we serve's away.
>
> .   .   .   .
>
> Who does i' the wars more than his captain can,
> Becomes his captain's captain: and ambition,
> The soldier's virtue, rather makes choice of loss,
> Than gain which darkens him.
> I could do more to do Antonius good,
> But 'twould offend him. And in his offence
> Should my performance perish.
>
> (ll. 11–15; 21–7)

This incompatibility between honour and loyalty is one example of a deadlock encountered frequently in this play. Action is paralysed by the mutually cancelling operation of two conflicting impulses.

The lack of opportunity with which the Soothsayer presents us in the second scene ('I make not, but foresee') suggests a restricted future. The claustrophobia is increased by a terminology which shrinks the globe— 'The little O, the earth' (V.ii.81)—to the dimensions of the stage. If Rome cannot be shared by Caesar and Antony it is because there is not 'room' for them, as Caesar perceives at Antony's death:

> I must perforce
> Have shown to thee such a declining day,
> Or look on thine: we could not stall together,
> In the whole world.
>
> (V.i.37–40)

The recalcitrance and mutual antipathy of the materials to be bound are presented as if physical laws. Caesar recognises this recalcitrance:

> Yet, if I knew
> What hoop should hold us staunch from edge to edge
> O' the world, I would pursue it.
>
> (II.ii.114–16)

A scene later, when a hoop has been improvised out of Octavia, the Soothsayer exhorts Antony to 'Make space enough between you' for Antony's 'lustre thickens,/ When he shines by' (II.iii.22; 26–7).

The ambition of Marlowe's Tamburlaine is to

> confute those blind geographers,
> That make a triple region in the world,
> Excluding regions which I mean to trace,
> And with this pen reduce them to a map.
> (Part 1, IV.iv.73−6)

But the world-shrinking capacities of martial and political might may involve a diminution of achievement. In *Antony and Cleopatra* the world is shrunk to the proportions of a general's map and the power that controls it thus seems less awesome than it might before the world was so harnessed. Pompey's 'quality, going on,/ The sides o' the world may danger' (I.ii.189−90). Yet phrases used to evoke the grandeur of the issues and the giant stature of the combatants, repeatedly have the contrary effect of diminishing the arena in which they operate. A few moments after Antony has spoken the words just quoted, Cleopatra, playing for Antony's attention, cries:

> Help me away, dear Charmian, I shall fall.
> It cannot be thus long, the sides of nature
> Will not sustain it.
> (I.iii.15−17)

Antony's words about the 'sides o' the world' are inevitably recalled and the effect is that of making Cleopatra's world at least commensurate with the real political one which Pompey's power threatened.

The claustrophobia which this play evokes with its bounded world and determined future affects the play's rhetorical structures. At the play's centre is the intransigence of the real world stubbornly refusing to yield in accordance with the dictates of the imagination. Antony's funny description of a crocodile to the drunken Lepidus employs a tautology which suggests the inflexibility of the object:

Lep. What manner o' thing is your crocodile?
Ant. It is shap'd, sir, like itself, and it is as broad as it hath breadth: it is just so high as it is, and moves with it own organs. It lives by that which nourisheth it, and the elements once out of it, it transmigrates.
Lep. What colour is it of?
Ant. Of it own colour too.
> (II.vii.40−6)

Such tautology parodies a mystical discourse of the exclusive and irreducible: 'And God answered Moses I AM THAT I AM' (Exodus iii.14). This inscrutable pronouncement is adopted by Shakespeare in sonnet 121 —a sonnet about opinion and about the distortions of projection inherent in all perception:

'Tis better to be vile than vile esteemed,
When not to be receives reproach of being,
And the just pleasure lost, which is so deemed,
Not by our feeling but by others' seeing.
For why should others' false adulterate eyes
Give salutation to my sportive blood?
Or on my frailties why are frailer spies,
Which in their wills count bad what I think good?
No, I am that I am, and they that level
At my abuses reckon up their own;

Sonnet 105 involves a more serious adaptation of religious discourse. The trinitarian miracle of unity in diversity and diversity in unity is discovered as a quality of the poet's love:

Kind is my love today, tomorrow kind,
Still constant in a wondrous excellence;
Therefore my verse to constancy confined,
One thing expressing, leaves out difference.
Fair, kind, and true, is all my argument,
Fair, kind, and true, varying to other words;
And in this change is my invention spent—
Three themes in one, which wondrous scope affords.

The confines of this sonnet's 'little room' ('Therefore my verse to constancy confined') yet allow for infinite variations. Difference is both excluded ('left out') by the constraints of formal and thematic unity, and generated as the variety which coexists with this unity becomes the source for the various 'leaves' of paper on which the many sonnets are inscribed.

Whilst tautology suggests limitation—of the object, in that it is irreducible, or of the speaker, in that he or she is ignorant, or of the hearer, in that he or she is, like Moses, uncomprehending—puns and paradoxes reveal a range in the thinking subject. The alternatives offered by the puns in the 'Dark Lady' sonnets reveal the ambiguity of the poet's response to the situation: a disgust and shame inspired by the business of sexual behaviour coinciding with the precarious sense of exaltation which such behaviour inspires. The pun in the penultimate line of sonnet 150, playing on the woman's capacity to stimulate erections and on the accompanying elevation of spirits, expresses, not the reconcilation of these two responses, but their baffling, antipathetic coexistence:

Whence hast thou this becoming of things ill,
That in the very refuse of thy deeds
There is such strength and warrantise of skill,
That, in my mind, thy worst all best exceeds?
Who taught thee how to make me love thee more,

> The more I hear and see just cause of hate?
> O, though I love what others do abhor,
> With others thou shouldst not abhor my state:
> If thy unworthiness raised love in me,
> More worthy I to be belov'd of thee.

In *Antony and Cleopatra* sexual love is similarly presented as something equivocal. Before the battle at Actium, Enobarbus tells Cleopatra, 'Your presence needs must puzzle Antony' (III.vii.10). The word 'puzzle' recalls the homophonous 'puzzel' or 'whore'.[8] Our understanding of Enobarbus' words is determined by our estimation of Cleopatra's relationship with Antony. It is widely assumed that Cleopatra is referring to a type of 'anamorphic' image when she says of Antony, 'Though he be painted one way like a Gorgon,/ The other way's a Mars' (II.v.117–18).[9] Whether or not her reference is so particular, anamorphic images, carefully calculated according to rules of perspective, to gather into recognisable forms only when viewed laterally (or from some other viewpoint not parallel with the picture plane) emphasise the subjectivity of perception and the extent to which the viewer constitutes the image seen. The type of two-sided anamorphosis which Cleopatra may be referring to is a kind of visual pun—two images in the space of one. This kind of picture provides a good analogy for the manner of this play in which all perceptions seem reversible or at least equivocal, and in which the rapid sequence of scenes shifting between Egypt and Rome communicate nothing so much as the instability of judgements.[10] Cleopatra is, depending on the view point, a 'strumpet' (I.i.13) and a 'gypsy' (I.i.10) or the 'day o' the world' (IV.viii.13) and the 'eastern star' (V.ii.307). The former appraisals are the loveless ones of the political world —the world of Rome and bounded 'room'. The latter—significantly images of luminosity—are the transformed perceptions of love. In this play, the lovers' cliché by which the loved one is the light of the lover's life, is realised so that love does indeed become a source of illumination, providing the visible world with distinction and significance.

As the uneasy pun of sonnet 150 testified, erotic love, with its dependence upon, often ludicrous, bodily expression, is particularly suggestive of the sort of two-sided perceptions which *Antony and Cleopatra* offers. In act V the clown enters with a basket filled with figs and snakes, visually suggestive of genitalia. Cleopatra's words, 'What poor an instrument/ May do a noble deed!' (V.ii.235–6) refer as much to the organs suggested by this basketful as to the basket's bearer:

> Things base and vile, holding no quantity,
> Love can transpose to form and dignity:
> (*A Midsummer Night's Dream*,
> I.i.232–3)[11]

In *A Midsummer Night's Dream* the play of *Pyramus and Thisbe* and the ludicrous problems of representation encountered and laboriously solved by Bottom and his fellow actors draw our attention to another kind of transformation: the kind which we, as auditors, perform as, in response to the language of the play, we fill out with our own imaginations the limited space, props and acting abilities in front of us. The mechanicals' play draws our attention to the mechanics of staging but also to the extent of our collaboration with the larger play of *A Midsummer Night's Dream* which works without the elaborate props that Bottom would require. Only when Bottom decides on the necessity of a character called 'Moonshine' do we realise that Shakespeare has flooded his own play with moonlight, and done so with language, not props.

In *Henry V* the Chorus repeatedly brings our attention back to the objective materiality of the stage, puncturing the illusion which it asks us to create. Speeches such as Grandprès' description of the English troops (IV.ii.39–52)—a piece of word-painting which compares in its fulness to Edgar's description of a precipice to the blind Gloucester—summon our 'imaginary forces' without alerting us, in the illusion-shattering way of the Chorus, to the need. The Chorus of *Henry V*, far from manifesting the 'imperfect dramatic faith' which Mark Van Doren finds in it,[12] is a mark of intense dramatic confidence on Shakespeare's part as he repeatedly shatters the illusion he has created, only to build it anew.

A similar act of confident self-reference occurs in *Antony and Cleopatra* when Cleopatra, who would have been played by a boy to the play's first audiences, recoils from the idea of giving in to Caesar and being made into a spectacle in Rome:

> Now, Iras, what think'st thou?
> Thou, an Egyptian puppet shall be shown
> In Rome as well as I: mechanic slaves
> With greasy aprons, rules, and hammers shall
> Uplift us to the view. In their thick breaths,
> Rank of gross diet, shall we be enclouded,
> And forc'd to drink their vapour...
>
>   .   .   .   .
>
> ...saucy lictors
> Will catch at us like strumpets, and scald rhymers
> Ballad us out o' tune. The quick comedians
> Extemporally will stage us, and present
> Our Alexandrian revels: Antony
> Shall be brought drunken forth, and I shall see
> Some squeaking Cleopatra boy my greatness
> I' the posture of a whore.
>
>   (V.ii.206–20)

Henry V encourages a doubleness in our vision and in our moral understanding of it. Shakespeare, playing on the contrast between the stage's material presence and the imaginary presence of the world suggested by the play's language, is offering us alternative evaluations. 'Can this cockpit hold/ The vasty fields of France?' (Chorus, I.ii.11 – 12) 'Cockpit' refers to the shabby stage surrounded by a restless audience, and also to the sordid and gratuitously violent world of cock-fights—a suggestion which might undermine our sense of the glory of Agincourt. In *Antony and Cleopatra* the daring passage of self-reference, which offers us a glimpse of the materials which furnish the stage whilst insisting that that is not what we see if we listen as we watch, makes us aware of the extent to which we have collaborated with the play and of the (at least) two-sidedness of our perceptions. In this play 'The little O, the earth' is no larger or more worthy than 'this wooden O' the stage. They both provide the bare materials which may or may not be transformed and enlarged by the loving imagination.

With events as fixed as they are in *Antony and Cleopatra*, interpretative range is the only range available. Yet antitheses, whilst offering conceptual scope, may work upon each other to produce a mutually-cancelling stasis:

> It hath been taught us from the primal state
> That he which is was wish'd, until he were;
> And the ebb'd man, ne'er lov'd till ne'er worth love,
> Comes dear'd, by being lack'd. This common body,
> Like to a vagabond flag upon the stream,
> Goes to, and back, lackeying the varying tide,
> To rot itself with motion.
>
> (I.iv.41 – 7)

The paralysis of will from which Octavia suffers also derives from the mutually-cancelling pulls of two contrary motions:

> Her tongue will not obey her heart, nor can
> Her heart inform her tongue—the swan's down feather,
> That stands upon the swell at the full of tide,
> And neither way inclines.
>
> (III.ii.46 – 50)

> Husband win, win brother,
> Prays, and destroys the prayer, no midway
> 'Twixt these extremes at all.
>
> (III.iv.18 – 20)

The ebb and flow of private opinion is as self-thwarting, as rotten through motion, as that of the 'common body' and works to give a sense of temporal, as well as spatial deadlock. Antony, on hearing of Fulvia's death, is the first to express this sense of paralysing reversibility:

> ... Thus did I desire it:
> What our contempts doth often hurl from us,
> We wish it ours again. The present pleasure,
> By revolution lowering, does become
> The opposite of itself; she's good, being gone,
> The hand could pluck her back that shov'd her on.
>> (I.ii.119–24)

Enobarbus calls upon the moon to bear witness to his repentance and death (IV.ix.7–10) and we are throughout made conscious of the mutability of the sublunary world and of the tidal ebb and flow which the moon controls. The one and a half line clusters into which blank verse often falls, may be expressively charged. In this play they frequently are: the first full line is expansive whilst the second half line shrinks back. Several of the lines which have this motion deal with the process of change, providing narratives of their own acoustic patterns:

> And is become the bellows and the fan
> To cool a gipsy's lust.
>> (I.i.9–10)

> Or thou, the greatest soldier of the world,
> Art turn'd the greatest liar.
>> (I.iii.38–9)

> O'er-picturing that Venus where we see
> The fancy outwork nature.
>> (II.ii.200–1)

> The loyalty well held to fools does make
> Our faith mere folly:
>> (III.xiii.42–3)

> And there is nothing left remarkable
> Beneath the visiting moon.
>> (IV.xv.67–8)

The moon, which seems itself to dissolve each month in the sky, is the initiator and representative of change. Only the occupants of the superlunary world are immutable and possessed of a stasis which is not compounded of deadlock. This is the achieved stasis which Cleopatra seeks as she makes of herself a vital artefact. Dead, she is that oxymoronic thing, a still life: 'now the fleeting moon/ No planet is of mine' (V.ii.239–40). The transformations which take place in the sublunary world are ones which mimic the fluidity of the moon's appearance and the ebb and flow of its effects.

> Let Rome in Tiber melt
>> (I.i.33)

> Melt Egypt into Nile!
> (II.v.77)

> Authority melts from me:
> (III.xii.90)

Ant. Cold-hearted toward me?
Cleo.   Ah, dear, if I be so,
From my cold heart let heaven engender hail,
And poison it in the source, and the first stone
Drop in my neck: as it determines, so
Dissolve my life; the next Caesarion smite
Till by degrees the memory of my womb,
Together with my brave Egyptians all,
By the discandying of this pelleted storm,
Lie graveless, till the flies and gnats of Nile
Have buried them for prey!

> (III.xiii.158−67)

> ... The hearts
> That spaniel'd me at heels, to whom I gave
> Their wishes, do discandy, melt their sweets
> On blossoming Caesar.

> (IV.xii.20−3)

> The crown o' the earth doth melt.

> (IV.xv.63)

> Dissolve, thick cloud, and rain...

> (V.ii.298)[13]

When the messenger is slow and ambiguous in delivering news of Antony, Cleopatra threatens to 'melt and pour' the gold she has just offered him down his 'ill-uttering throat' (II.v.34−5). The uses of coined or molten gold are too specific in this context for us to read this threat as yet another reference to the instability of forms, but the very idea of transforming a reward into a punishment is typical of the reversals of which this play is full.

Cleopatra's 'From my cold heart let heaven engender hail' would have punned more obviously to Elizabethan ears than to ours. The play on 'hail' ('hell') suggests that the poles of the moral universe stretching from heaven to hell may be found within her private drama—a secular psychomachia. I mentioned earlier the tendency of the play's grand terms to have the paradoxical effect of shrinking the world to the proportions of the stage rather than expanding the stage to those of the world, and of making the sides of individual nature at least equal in weight to the sides of the world; though without the fiendish equivocation of *Macbeth*, single phrases in *Antony and Cleopatra* seem double-sided. There can be no doubt as to the weight of intent which Scarus gives to his words after the battle of Actium: 'The greater cantle of the world is lost/ With very ignorance, we have kiss'd away/ Kingdoms, and provinces' (III.x.6–8). But it is hard not to hear the possibility of affirmation in such words with their echoes of Catullus' extravagant kisses and their anticipation of Cleopatra's retrospective celebration: 'realms and islands were/ As plates dropp'd from his pocket' (V.ii.91–2).

The traditional appropriation of martial terminology in erotic contexts may lead to conspicuous irony. Kyd achieves this in the second act of *The Spanish Tragedy* where the erotic banter between Horatio and Bel-Imperia receives a sinister commentary through the presence of Balthazar and Lorenzo who are hidden in readiness to murder Horatio (II.ii.25–40). The violence of the language used innocently by Horatio is realised by the murderers who revive the dead metaphors. This kind of literalistic irony (so characteristic of *Richard III* where words are proved to be 'only too true') involves only a one-way shift between intents. In *Antony and Cleopatra* the constant juxtaposition, in both metaphor and scene construction, of the erotic and the martial involves a relationship less static and more reciprocal:

> Mark Antony
> In Egypt sits at dinner, and will make
> No wars without doors.
>
> (II.i.11–13)

After Actium, Antony tells Cleopatra, 'You did know/ How much you were my conqueror' (III.xi.65–6). Nor does Shakespeare miss many chances to play on the word 'die'—'she hath such a celerity in dying' (I.ii.141–2). But such demonstration of martial language is a commonplace in Elizabethan writing. What is different in *Antony and Cleopatra* is the mutuality of the exchange of terms. Bodily death is eroticised:

> I will be
> A bridegroom in my death, and run into 't
> As to a lover's bed.
>
> (IV.xiv.99–101)

> If thou and nature can so gently part,
> The stroke of death is as a lover's pinch,
> Which hurts, and is desir'd.
>
> (V.ii.293–5)

As in Herbert's 'Shall thy strokes be my stroking?', 'stroke' is calmed from blow to caress. This reciprocal action between the two parts of the martial/erotic analogy is another example of the anamorphic instability of the play's perceptions. The last two quotations also demonstrate the extent to which perception constitutes its objects—a point made more emphatically in this play than elsewhere. The rigidity of the play's tragic end can be mollified only by another way of seeing that end: 'The eye altering alters all.' Enobarbus dead appears asleep (IV.ix.25–30). Antony's words to Eros, 'the long day's task is done,/ And we must sleep' (IV.xiv. 35–6), employ the common analogy between death and sleep in an uncommon way: not as the usual pious euphemism but to lend weight to the sense of weariness that attends fulfilment and to diminish the violence of the act when its violence is not the point. Cleopatra picks up the analogy: 'Dost thou not see my baby at my breast,/ That sucks the nurse asleep?' (V.ii.308–9). Dead, 'she looks like sleep,/ As she would catch another Antony/ In her strong toil of grace' (V.ii.344–6).

Act IV, scene xiv opens with an abrupt query from Antony: 'Eros, thou yet behold'st me?' That this is a genuine question and not just a tetchy demand for attention becomes evident as Antony proceeds:

> Sometime we see a cloud that's dragonish,
> A vapour sometime, like a bear, or lion,
> A tower'd citadel, a pendent rock,
> A forked mountain, or blue promontory
> With trees upon't, that nod unto the world,
> And mock our eyes with air. Thou hast seen these signs,
> They are black vesper's pageants.

Eros   Ay, my lord.
Ant.   That which is now a horse, even with a thought
> The rack dislimns, and makes it indistinct
> As water is in water.

Eros   It does, my lord.
Ant.   My good knave Eros, now thy captain is
> Even such a body: here I am Antony,
> Yet cannot hold this visible shape, my knave.

(IV.xiv.2–14)

M.R. Ridley, in the New Arden edition of the play, glosses 'even with a thought' as meaning 'as fast as thought'. Yet this passage seems to be referring to the projective imagination and the extent to which we interpret forms by the mental superimposition of those we already know. The rack dislimns 'even with a thought' because the maintenance of recognisable images in random configurations is dependent upon concentration. The lack of distinction in the world with which Cleopatra is left after Antony's death is comparable to the lapse into a continuum which Antony describes when the 'rack dislimns' and becomes 'indistinct/ As water is in water':

>   young boys and girls
> Are level now with men: the odds is gone,
> And there is nothing left remarkable
> Beneath the visiting moon.

(IV.xv.65–8)

Both Antony and Cleopatra use the idea of the loved other as a defining differential in their perception of the world. The idea of the other gives illumination and coherence to the world they see ('How would thy shadow's form form happy show/ To the clear day with thy much clearer light'). Othello uses his love for Desdemona as the key which fixes the universe in place—'when I love thee not,/ Chaos is come again (III.iii. 91–2). Similarly Antony and Cleopatra use the idea of their love, represented by the presence of the other, as the source of all significance. Antony's words to Eros indicate that even his perception of himself is informed and determined by the controlling idea of Cleopatra. Cleopatra's supposed betrayal of Antony leads him to feel that he has lost his hold over himself since that hold, surrendered to Cleopatra, has been dispersed to the enemy. Antony's sense of his own form is dependent upon the knowledge that it is acknowledged in Cleopatra's mirroring love. Without this he cannot 'think' that form which would compound his 'visible shape'.

In addition to the importance of the loved other to Antony and Cleopatra's conceptions of themselves, the sense in which this play is presented as a re-enactment of an already famous history affects the play's principals. Both Antony and Cleopatra seem aware of their mythic stature as something which has to be lived up to:[14]

> I am Antony yet.
> > (III.xiii.93)

> What's her name,
> Since she was Cleopatra?
> > (III.xiii.98–9)

> since my lord
> Is Antony again, I will be Cleopatra.
> > (III.xiii.186–7)

They are both the accomplished figures of myth and the perishing and inconsequential creatures that gave rise to that myth.

The Sonnets too seem to address two boys: one the archetypal figure who is seen as the source of all beauty and all poetry; the other, a fallible and perishable mortal loved for precisely those qualities and whom the poetry tries to exempt from mortality by capturing it in language. The paradox of 'eternal love in love's fresh case' (108, l.9) captures a dual sense of love as something both lived through and outside time. The two contrary motions—a rage against the mortality which will destroy the lovely boy, conflicting with the recognition that it is just that mortality, that sense of transience, which makes the beauty so precious and worth saving—combine in an urge toward the eternally mutable, beautifully imaged in the nearly oxymoronic notion of 'summer's distillation...A liquid pris'ner pent in walls of glass' (5, ll.9–10). This capture of the

transitory—a fly in amber effect—is achieved in Enobarbus' description of
Antony:

> I saw her once
> Hop forty paces through the public street,
> And having lost her breath, she spoke, and panted,
> That she did make defect perfection,
> And, breathless, power breathe forth.
>
> (II.ii.228—32)

Shakespeare stresses Cleopatra's volatility and childlikeness as much as
her grandeur.

This double sense of being both an achieved mythic figure and an erro-
neous mortal living that myth for the first time, is the source of many
reflexive constructions:

> Good madam, keep yourself within yourself,
> The man is innocent.
>
> (II.v.75—6)

> I will not hurt him.
> These hands do lack nobility, that they strike
> A meaner than myself; since I myself
> Have given myself the cause.
>
> (II.v.81—4)

> I have fled myself, and have instructed cowards
> To run, and show their shoulders.
>
> (III.xi.7—8)

> Nay, weep not, gentle Eros, there is left us
> Ourselves to end ourselves.
>
> (IV.xiv.21—2)

> Not Caesar's valour hath o'erthrown Antony,
> But Antony's hath triumph'd on itself.
>
> (IV.xv.15—16)

Loss of love coincides with a failure of imaginative energy. Antony's ina-
bility to sustain and hold his 'visible shape' is the inability of the tired
mortal to maintain an identity with his mythic image. To himself he is not
at home.

A few minutes later, when Antony has heard from Mardian of Cleo-
patra's supposed death, his sense of 'visible shape' is to come back with a
vengeance. This time it is not experienced as the vulnerable form which
needs to be sustained by thought, but as recalcitrant matter which may
refuse to yield in response to thought:

Heart, once be stronger than thy continent,
Crack thy frail case! . . .

.   .   .   .   .   .

All length is torture: since the torch is out,
Lie down and stray no farther. Now all labour
Mars what it does: yea, very force entangles
Itself with strength:
                    (IV.xiv.40−1; 46−9)

That aspect of Antony which is painted like a Mars is now self-thwarting. The linguistic density, the almost meaningless puns in this passage ('All length is torture: since the torch is out'; 'Now all labour/ Mars what it does') represent the resistance of Antony's unwilled strength and his desire to unify that self which he experiences as divided.

Antony dies of a sword wound rather than of thought, but the latter is possible in this play. The contrast between Rome and Egypt is not so much one between a world preoccupied with martial action and another with sexual action, as between a real world of action and an imaginative world of thought. The presence of Mardian the eunuch has an emblematic as well as an atmospheric function. The most obvious way to read this is as a signal of the emasculation which Antony, in Roman minds at any rate, undergoes in his relation to Cleopatra. At the moment he suspects Cleopatra of betrayal Antony himself seems to subscribe to this view, with Mardian's presence acting as a mnemonic. Mardian enters and Antony cries, 'O, thy vile lady!/ She has robb'd me of my sword' (IV.xiv.22−3).

In act I the burden of the banter between Cleopatra and Mardian is upon Mardian's difference from sexual beings:

Cleo. Thou, eunuch Mardian!
Mar.   What's your highness' pleasure?
Cleo. Not now to hear thee sing. I take no pleasure
         In aught an eunuch has: 'tis well for thee
         That, being unseminar'd, thy freer thoughts
         May not fly forth of Egypt. Hast thou affections?
Mar. Yes, gracious madam.
Cleo.   Indeed?
Mar. Not in deed, madam, for I can do nothing
         But what indeed is honest to be done:
         Yet have I fierce affections, and think
         What Venus did with Mars.
                              (I.v.8−18)

The rather heavy and predictable joke establishes that Mardian's eroticism does not lie 'in deed', but more important is the suggestion that the satisfactions of the imagination are adequate compensations. Venus and Mars inevitably suggest Cleopatra and Antony, and Mardian's words reinforce the impression that the love between the two is more an imaginative experience, a mental and linguistic event, than a physical one. Or perhaps it would be truer to say that thought, in this play, is presented as a form of action. Enobarbus dies of thought (IV.vi.31–6; IV.ix.15–18) and while Antony and Cleopatra depend upon external agents to instigate their deaths, the significance and experience of those deaths is transformed by the mental attitude with which they approach them. When Caesar comes to bargain with Cleopatra he chivvies her with 'be cheer'd,/ Make not your thoughts your prisons' (V.ii.183–4). The words are revealing of Caesar and singularly inappropriate to Cleopatra since, in the play's restricted world, the freedom of thought and attitude is the only kind she has.

Cleopatra's memory of her and Antony's dressing up in each other's clothes would be heard by Roman ears as further evidence of humiliation and emasculation. She 'drunk him to his bed;/ Then put [her] tires and mantles on him, whilst/ [She] wore his sword Philippan' (II.v.21–3). It is a moment of childlike make-believe which suggests the imaginative fulness of their world. These associations are picked up by Charmian as she makes the last adjustment to the dead Cleopatra: 'Your crown's awry,/ I'll mend it, and then play' (V.ii.317–18). The significance of the conventional elision between death and sleep is here tightened by the suggestion that what they share is the complete access into a world of imaginative experience—the world of child's play and dream.

The child's belief, which is also the poet's, in the efficacy of language, is vindicated more conspicuously than in most plays here where our perception of single events undergoes radical transformations depending upon the way in which those events are described. Amongst the characters in the play, Cleopatra seems most conscious of this creative capacity in language. Her retrospective evocation of Antony is described as a dream, not because it is illusory, but because its cosmic referents isolate the figure from local particulars and place him in the wholly significant realm of myth:

> I dreamt there was an Emperor Antony.
> O such another sleep, that I might see
> But such another man!
> .   .   .   .
> His face was as the heavens, and therein stuck
> A sun and moon, which kept their course, and lighted
> The little O, the earth.
> .   .   .   .
> His legs bestrid the ocean, his rear'd arm
> Crested the world: his voice was propertied
> As all the tuned spheres, and that to friends:
> But when he meant to quail, and shake the orb,
> He was as rattling thunder. For his bounty,

> There was no winter in 't: an autumn 'twas
> That grew the more by reaping: his delights
> Were dolphin-like, they show'd his back above
> The element they lived in: in his livery
> Walk'd crowns and crownets: realms and islands were
> As plates dropp'd from his pocket.
>
> (V.ii.76–92)

The Roman Dolabella retains a plain man's scepticism:

> *Cleo.* Think you there was, or might be such a man
>   As this I dreamt of?
> *Dol.*   Gentle madam, no.

Cleopatra's reply firmly asserts that the reality of this dream figure (whose abstraction from temporality is suggested by her uncertainty as to tense —'was, or might be') is not more flimsy, but rather more intense than the kind which Dolabella recognises:

> You lie up to the hearing of the gods.
> But if there be, or ever were one such,
> It's past the size of dreaming: nature wants stuff
> To vie strange forms with fancy, yet to imagine
> An Antony were nature's piece, 'gainst fancy,
> Condemning shadows quite.
>
> (V.ii.95–100)

The compounding creativity of the imagination usually multiplies and enlarges the given forms of nature. In this play the cramped real world has given way to the conceptual and imaginative freedom of the lovers—an internal freedom which ignores the constrictions of Rome/room. Antony, Colossus-like, straddles both of the play's worlds and operates in both kinds of room, material and internal. But Cleopatra's words, 'if there be, or ever were one such,/ It's past the size of dreaming', suggest a reversal of the usual proportions, to which the play has so far conformed, in which the world conceived by the imagination is always an extension and enlargement of the natural world. Here Cleopatra suggests that the presence of Antony signifies a largeness in the natural world capable of including and superseding the already expanded world of the imagination. The modes of existence which have been opposed throughout the play are here reconciled as, in contrast to the usual direction of the comparison, 'Nature's' creativity is seen as a form of imagination.

The image of Antony, dressed in woman's clothes is, most powerfully, one of creative androgyny. The two kinds of creativity of which Diotima speaks are elided in this play where erotic and imaginative experience are identified.

The lover's cliché by which the world seems to be a different place than it was before the access of love, is very precisely realised in *Antony and Cleopatra*. Antony and Cleopatra use each other, as Othello does Desdemona, as the object which holds the world together in significance. Chaos returns with loss of love for Othello. The worlds of Antony and Cleopatra collapse into incoherence when not illuminated by the idea of the other. Each makes of the other the light by which to see:

> His face was as the heavens, and therein stuck
> A sun and moon, which kept their course, and lighted
> The little O, the earth.
>
> (V.ii.78–81)

Cleopatra is the 'torch', the 'day o' the world'. Iras' words anticipate Cleopatra's death:

> Finish, good lady, the bright day is done,
> And we are for the dark.
>
> (V.ii.192–3)

Charmian, perfecting our final image of Cleopatra, seems as much to be shutting light away from the world as excluding the world's light from those eyes. The word 'windows' clinches this ambiguity.[15]

> Downy windows, close,
> And golden Phoebus, never be beheld
> Of eyes again so royal!
>
> (V.ii.315–17)

Othello also recognises the presence of two kinds of light: 'Put out the light, and then put out the light:' (V.ii.7). But chaos comes again when those lights are gone. And the return of that chaos is heralded by the loss of linguistic distinction.

Chapter 5

QUICK THOUGHT AND ITS VEHICLES

In *Antony and Cleopatra* and in Shakespeare's Sonnets it is love that illuminates and distinguishes the world. Love is presented as the source of mental stamina—the energy that Antony needs to sustain his 'visible shape'. Some kind of mental stamina is also needed to distinguish meaning at the most intimate verbal level:

> Then thou, whose shadow shadows doth make bright—
> How would thy shadow's form form happy show
> To the clear day with thy much clearer light,
> When to unseeing eyes thy shade shines so!
> (43, ll.5–8)

Love's candour enables the lover to distinguish not only the visible forms of the world but also its inaudible intentions. The formal, but not semantic repetition of 'form' in line 6 demands that we create and sustain a distinction between substantive and verb before the line can make sense. In the case of the second 'form' the distinction is reversible: the meaning of the last three words flickers between 'show a happy form' and 'form a happy show'. We are made to contemplate the extent to which our own mental clarity contributes to the formation of the meaning—and shows— we perceive.

In sonnet 43 Shakespeare makes use of the rhetorical figure of *antanaclasis* (repetition of the same word in a different or contrary sense). This same figure (which Puttenham named 'the Rebounde') is used self-illustratingly by Herbert in 'The Pulley'. This poem demands a restless seeking energy on our parts if we are to prize meaning from the apparent repetitions. This energy is the poem's subject:

> When God at first made man,
> Having a glasse of blessings standing by;
> Let us (said he) poure on him all we can:
> Let the worlds riches, which dispersed lie,
> Contract into a span.

> So strength first made a way;
> Then beautie flow'd, then wisdome, honour, pleasure:
> When almost all was out, God made a stay,
> Perceiving that alone of all his treasure
>   Rest in the bottome lay.
>
> For if I should (said he)
> Bestow this jewell also on my creature,
> He would adore my gifts in stead of me,
> And rest in Nature, not the God of Nature:
>   So both should losers be.
>
> Yet let him keep the rest,
> But keep them with repining restlesnesse:
> Let him be rich and wearie, that at least,
> If goodnesse leade him not, yet wearinesse
>   May tosse him to my breast.

There is a world of difference between such *antanaclasis* in which the perceiving mind holds meaning taut, and the slack repetition that signals the loss of grip:

> That which is now a horse, even with a thought
> The rack dislimns, and makes it indistinct
> As water is in water.

Othello's words as he smothers Desdemona—'Put out the light, and then put out the light'—seem to slide from vestigial *antanaclasis* into the inchoate repetition of a man now lost in this dull world.

John Donne also plays on the word 'light', but he does so in a context that makes the semantic distinctions clear:

> ...I will through the wave, and fome,
> And shall, in sad lone wayes a lively spright,
> Make my darke heavy Poem light, and light.
>   ('The Progresse of the Soule', ll.53–5)

In 'The Progresse of the Soule' a sharpened sense of the particularity of the world's objects extends to a sense of language as amongst those objects. The ability to make semantic distinctions between homophones is continuous with the ability to explore other physical quantities. 'The Progresse of the Soule', which traces the itinerary of a transmigrating soul, is a poem which brings together two traditions that might appear distinct. These are, firstly, the theological tradition which supposes an ubiquitous God and which attributes to the soul a freedom of movement which is the next best thing to ubiquity and, secondly, the poetic tradition by which small, unregarded objects—a glove, a gnat, a bead of sweat—are celebrated because of their free access to desired bodies. I propose to look at both traditions in terms of the opportunities that they provide for a poetry which explores the physical contours of the world.

AN UBIQUITOUS GOD AND THE MOCK ENCOMIUM

> ...the human mind participates in the Divine, which with the self-same Divinity dwells in the marshes and in the stars, and from the most sordid made the most divine of corporeal creatures.[1]

In these terms the Italian poetic theorist, Emanuele Tesauro, found divine endorsement for the indecorous conjunctions of poetic wit. To know at all is to know part of what God knows. I quoted in the third chapter Galileo's description of the way in which our intellect can begin to apprehend 'with time and gradual motion' that which the 'Divine Wisdom, like light, penetrates in an instant'. God, being a circle whose centre is everywhere and circumference nowhere, combines omniscience with ubiquity. In God knowledge and presence are identical. Divine knowledge cannot be said to derive from divine presence in the way that human knowledge can, since such derivation supposes a time lag.

The closest a temporally bound human can get to divine ubiquity is by moving very fast and very far. The divine part of man—his *mens* or *anima*—was traditionally endowed with a capacity for such motion. Galileo is using, and up-dating, the terms of the Church Fathers when he writes about the way in which alphabetic writing allows a man to 'communicate his most secret thoughts to any other person, though very far distant either in time or place, speaking with those who are in the Indies, speaking to those who are not yet born'.[2] So too is Hobbes when he writes of the way in which the fancy 'seemeth to fly from one Indies to the other, and from heaven to earth, and to penetrate into the hardest matter and obscurest places, into the future, and into herself, and all this in a point of time'.[3] This is the language in which the Church Fathers described the soul's capacity for flight. The 'point of time' in which Hobbesian fancy seems to accomplish its motion echoes Lactantius' 'temporis punctum':

> Can any fail to admire that that living and heavenly faculty which is called the mind or the soul, is of such volubility that it does not rest even when it is asleep; of such rapidity, that it surveys the whole heaven at one moment of time; and if it wills, flies over seas, traverses lands and cities,—in short, places in its own sight all things which it pleases, however far and widely they are removed?[4]

The Indies which Galileo and Hobbes both mention have their equivalents in the Persia and Africa that Ambrose mentions:

> Therefore the flesh cannot be after the image of God, but our soul which

is free and in widespread thoughts and deliberations roams hither and thither, which in considering looks at everything. Behold we are now in Italy and we think of those things which seem to look towards eastern or western parts and we seem to live with those who are placed in Persia and we see those who live in Africa if that land has received any who are known to us ... The soul therefore is after the image of God, being measured not by bodily but by mental activity, for it sees those who are absent, casts its gaze upon things across the sea, scans them with its glance, examines what is hidden, and hither and thither in a single moment makes its perceptions range throughout the limits of the world and the secrets of the universe.[5]

Augustine mentions Carthage and Alexandria as imaginable places: Aelfric, in a passage in the *Lives of the Saints* based very closely on Lactantius, mentions Rome and Jerusalem.[6]

While these patristic writers may have found in the notino of *anima*'s flight a good explanation for the phenomenon of imaginative range, most clearly experienced in dreaming but also observable in waking thought, the duty of these passages is towards the nature of the divinity thus imitated, rather than to any incidental bonuses derived from such imitation. It *is* wonderful that the mind can view Persia, Carthage, Alexandria and Rome, but this wonderfulness derives from and points back to God's amazing ubiquity. Any interest intrinsic to these places is secondary. Marlowe's Doctor Faustus, who experiences in the flesh this usually incorporeal mobility, is interested in what he is thus enabled to see: 'I swear/ That I do long to see the monuments/ And situation of bright-splendant Rome' (viii.49−51)[7]. But it is symptomatic of Faustus' self-damning mentality that he should long to be freed from the physical constraints of an earth-dweller only to cling more avidly to that earth.

Properly such flights are undertaken by flyers who are qualified for flight by their indifference to what they see. The wings which Philosophy bestows in *De Consolatione Philosophiae* are the means to a moral superiority to which the physical superiority is both analogy and means:

> Pennas etiam tuae menti quibus se in altum tollere possit adfigam, ut perturbatione depulsa sospes in patriam meo ductu, mea semita, meis etiam vehiculis revertaris.

> Sunt etenim pennae volucres mihi
>   Quae celsa conscendant poli
> Quas sibi cum velox mens induit
>   Terras perosa despicit
> Aeris immensi superat globum,
>   Nubesque postergum videt.
>   (IV.i)

(And I wyll fasten fethers of resones in thy mynde, whereby it may ryse up in heith, so that after thou hast cast awaye all trouble of worldly and temporall thynges, thou mayst reuert and turne into thy countrye safe and sounde, by my leding, by my path way and by my steppes.

Phylosophy

Certes I haue swyft fethers that is to say: vertue and wysedome that ascendeth unto the hygh heven. Whyche fethers when a swyfte mynde hath put on, it being disdainefull, dispiseth all earthly thynges and sur-mounteth the globe, that is to say: the grete body of the airy element, and seyth the cloudes behynde hys back...)[8]

Though Chaucer, in describing Troilus' ascent to the eighth sphere, betrays a lingering tenderness for this 'litel spot of erthe, that with the se/ Embraced is' (V.1815–16), the sea's embrace sheltering the earth from Troilus' philosophically proper scorn, heavenly flyers should find the world and its concerns in both senses 'beneath them'.

Nothing, however, is beneath an ubiquitous God, as attentive to the deaths of sparrows as of saints. Whilst the Church Fathers and medieval writers may have been concerned with the human mind's capacity to escape the trammels of the corporeal and the particular, the God whom this mind resembles confounds high and low by his presence in both. George Herbert, whose 'Providence' describes an intricate carefulness on God's part, writes elsewhere of Grace 'Op'ning the souls most subtile roomes' ('The H. Communion', l.22). Ben Jonson extends this intimate knowledge to the body and describes God as a delicate surgeon who:

> ...knowes the hearts of all, and can dissect
> The smallest Fibre of our flesh; he can
>   Find all out Atomes from a point t[o]'a span!
> Our closest Creekes, and Corners...
>   (*The Underwood*, lxxxiv.9. ll.150–3)

God's presence in the minute could, and in the seventeenth century often does, provide literary treatments of the otherwise trivial with theo-logical respectability. Nothing is beneath the attention of the God whom Herbert describes in 'Providence' and nothing is unworthy of being men-tioned by the poet.[9]

The literary genre of the mock *encomium* in which evidently unworthy objects are formally praised, depends for its comic effect on the reader's continued sense of the object's intrinsic unworth. The difficulty with which this tension was sustained (the *encomium* must not be too success-ful or its listeners will be unaware of the rhetorical skill that has contri-buted to its success) is exemplified in the fate of the originally mockingly encomiastic praises of Helen of Troy, that once unworthy object whose subsequent dignity owes much to her early encomiasts.[10]

Amongst the conspicuously valueless objects singled out for rhetorical exercises in praise are many whose triviality is mainly a matter of size.

Arthur Pease, writing about 'Things without honor', mentions praises of mice, ants, bees, flies, gnats and bedbugs. The technique of εὐφημια—the conversion of an unpleasant fact into a pleasant one—can discover in such tiny creatures the laudable, or at least enviable, ability to creep into small places unhindered or unobserved: to be flies on the walls.

METAMORPHOSIS AND THE SENSITIVE ENVIRONMENT

Ovid (whose mock *enconium* on Corinna's parrot (*Amores*, II.vi) was, along with Catullus' on Lesbia's sparrow (*Carmina* (ii)) one of the most imitated) makes the most of the small size and inoffensive inanimacy of a signet ring he gives Corinna (*Amores*, II.xv). What is paradoxical here is that the real monetary value of the ring is ignored and it is valued solely on account of the intimate proximity which it will be permitted with Corinna's flesh. Tolerated because inanimate, the ring is endowed with an androgynous life by the poet's participating imagination:

> tam bene convenias quam mecum convenit illi,
> et digitum iusto commodus orbe teras

> (Fit her so well, as she is fit for me,
> And of just compass for her knuckles be)[11]

As if his erotic imagination were stimulated by the analogy he plays with the idea of metamorphosis into a ring and with the intimate possibilities that this would offer:

> o utinam fieri subito mea munera possem
> artibus Aeaeae Carpathiive senis!

> tunc ego cum cupiam dominae tetigisse papillas
> et laevam tunicis inseruisse manum,

> elabar digito quamvis angustus et haerens
> inque sinum mira laxus ab arte cadam.

(O would that suddenly into my gift/ I could myself by secret magic shift!/ Then would I wish thee touch my mistress' pap,/ And hide thy left hand underneath her lap;/ I would get off though strait, and sticking fast,/ And in her bosom strangely fall at last.)

The idea of transformation which this elegy plays with is the unifying concept of Ovid's *Metamorphoses*. There the many transformations of human into vegetable and animal life create a cumulative sense of a world that is densely animated and responsive. We are given the intelligent human genealogies of plants and animals and the suggestion is that any plant may have a human ancestry comparable to that of the hyacinth or laurel, and that it may in some vital way contain its intelligent ancestor.

In such a world there is always the possibility of a reciprocal relation between man and his environment: the 'pathetic fallacy' may not be fallacious. It also becomes possible to describe human actions from alternative points of view: from the vantage points of the sensitive environment.

This habit of looking from the viewpoint of the environment is very much a feature of the Ovidian *epyllia* (small epics) popular in the late Renaissance. The *Metamorphoses* had been habitually moralised during the Christian middle ages by those who wanted their pleasure in Ovid to be consistent with moral rectitude. Raphael Regius' edition of 1492[12] was a breakthrough in that its commentary restricted itself to glossing philological and historical difficulties and offered no allegorical or moral reading of the text. The late Renaissance *epyllia*, whilst often retaining the moralising habit in the form of explanatory insertions, undo the tendency of medieval Ovidians to separate the presented world from its significance as if they existed in allegorical relation.[13] The environment presented by Marlowe (who had translated the *Amores*) in *Hero and Leander* is erotically animated, feelingly responsive to the human protagonists who inhabit and touch it:

> With that he stripped him to the ivory skin,
> And crying, 'Love, I come', leapt lively in.
> Whereat the sapphire-visaged god grew proud,
> And made his capering Triton sound aloud,
> Imagining that Ganymede, displeased,
> Had left the heavens; therefore on him he seized.
> Leander strived, the waves about him wound,
> And pulled him to the bottom, where the ground
> Was strewed with pearl, and in low coral groves
> Sweet singing mermaids sported with their loves
> On heaps of heavy gold, and took great pleasure
> To spurn in careless sort the shipwreck treasure.
> For here the stately azure palace stood
> Where kingly Neptune and his train abode.
> The lusty god embraced him, called him love,
> And swore he never should return to Jove.
> But when he knew it was not Ganymede,
> For under water he was almost dead,
> He heaved him up, and looking on his face,
> Beat down the bold waves with his triple mace,
> Which mounted up, intending to have kissed him,
> And fell in drops like tears because they missed him.
> Leander being up, began to swim,
> And, looking back, saw Neptune follow him;
> Wheareat aghast, the pour soul 'gan to cry,
> 'O let me visit Hero ere I die.'

> The god put Helle's bracelet on his arm,
> And swore the sea should never do him harm.
> He clapped his plump cheeks, with his tresses played,
> And smiling wantonly, his love bewrayed.
> He watched his arms, and as they opened wide
> At every stroke, betwixt them would he slide
> And steal a kiss, and then run out and dance,
> And as he turned, cast many a lustful glance,
> And threw him gaudy toys to please his eye,
> And dive into the water, and there pry
> Upon his breast, his thighs, and every limb,
> And up again, and close beside him swim,
> And talk of love.

(II.153–91)

Here Neptune has a double existence. On one level he is a personified abstraction—an old man with beard, crown, mace and submarine palace. As such he is separable from his significance: he 'stands for' the sea. But in Marlowe's poem Neptune also *is* the sea. As such his sentience gives definition to the body of Leander with which he comes into intimate contact. This is another example of the contrary pulls of language towards the particular and towards the universal, becoming a feature of narrative content. As in George Herbert's reworkings of traditional Christian images, the real, particular, sensible reference has the effect of remotivating, by animating, the wider intelligible reference.

In Shakespeare's *Venus and Adonis* we are presented with another dual nature. One is the nature in which the gods still dwell, participating in and coextensive with the environment which they control; the other is an alienated post-lapsarian nature in which the gods only walk in the form of personified abstractions. The poem occupies a time-scale that is correspondingly double: both before and after this divisive fall. It accounts for the fall in terms which become operative only when the events in the poem have taken place. Adonis rejects Venus with a haughty sense of distinction:

> "Call it not love, for love to heaven is fled,
> Since sweating lust on earth usurp'd his name;
> (ll.793–4)

Yet the separation of love and lust is one of the consequences of the poem's events—events which culminate in Venus' malediction on *future* lovers, and in her flight to heaven ('Thus weary of the world, away she hies', l.1189). Venus' dilemma—'She's love, she loves, and yet she is not lov'd' (l.610)—enacts the fall of love in the declension of the verb. Sidney's suggestion that grammatical distinctions of mood and tense are part of Babel's curse is borne out here, though the myth is pagan. In many ways Venus—Love—is coextensive with the environment in which this narrative unfolds. Stock Petrarchan metaphors like 'windy sighs' become unusually authentic in an environment which does sigh with love:

> "Fondling", she saith, "since I have hemm'd thee here
> Within the circuit of this ivory pale,
> I'll be a park, and thou shalt be my deer:
> Feed where thou wilt, on mountain or in dale;
>   Graze on my lips, and if those hills be dry,
>   Stray lower, where the pleasant fountains lie.

> "Within this limit is relief enough,
> Sweet bottom grass and high delightful plain,
> Round rising hillocks, brakes obscure and rough,
> To shelter thee from tempest and from rain:
>   Then be my deer, since I am such a park,
>   No dog shall rouse thee, though a thousand bark."
>   (ll.229–40)

If Venus here seems to be suggestively metaphorical about her body, other passages suggest that the erotic responsiveness of her particular body is shared by the landscape as a whole.[14] This landscape is one in which the influence of Love is pervasive and not confined to the *figure* of Venus:

> And as she runs, the bushes in the way,
> Some catch her by the neck, some kiss her face,
> Some twine about her thigh to make her stay;
> She wildly breaketh from their strict embrace,
>   (ll.871–4)

Here Love is loved, but caught in her own snare.

This way of describing the, often unwelcome, resistance of the natural world (Leander may think he's drowning but from Neptune's point of view Leander is being kissed; Venus may be flailing around in the hedgerow but the hedge craves and delights in this proximity) is a kind of sophistry. Venus consciously employs this sophistry when she tries to woo Adonis:

> "In night," quoth she, "desire sees best of all.

> "But if thou fall, O then imagine this:
> The earth in love with thee, thy footing trips,
> And all is but to rob thee of a kiss.
>   (ll.720–3)

Later, as she strives to accommodate the brutality of Adonis' death, she directs such sophistry at herself and converts the boar's act of murder into one of loving penetration:

'Tis true, 'tis true, thus was Adonis slain:
He ran upon the boar with his sharp spear,
Who did not whet his teeth at him again,
But by a kiss thought to persuade him there;
And nuzzling in his flank, the loving swine
Sheathed unaware the tusk in his soft groin.

"Had I been tooth'd like him, I must confess,
With kissing him I should have kill'd him first.
(ll.1111–18)

Elizabeth Donno has called this kind of explanation the 'aetiological conceit'.[15] Like all explanatory myths, the aetiological conceit works from how things are and is thus, however extravagant the given history of that present may be, rooted in a kind of realism. The whole of *Venus and Adonis* can be seen as an explanation of how love fell, initiating the separate concept of lust. But the local examples just quoted—the mini-myths which involve a teleological inversion of the usual way of looking at something and so convert an unpleasant fact into one which is benign in intent —do not extend their significance beyond their particular narrative moments. They do not explain how the world works, only how that particular bit of the world worked at that particular moment.

The inversion of our usual way of understanding an event shocks us into attention:

Apollo hunted *Daphne* so,
Only that She might Laurel grow.
And *Pan* did after *Syrinx* speed,
Not as a Nymph, but for a Reed.
(Marvell, 'The Garden',
ll.29–32)

A sharpened sense of physical delineation often accompanies such witty reversals. Our attention is concentrated on the boundaries on whose other side we now find ourselves:

'These Walls restrain the World Without,
'But hedge our Liberty about.
'These Bars inclose that wider Den
'Of those wild Creatures, called Men.
'The Cloyster outward shuts its Gates,
'And, from us, locks on them the Grates.
(Marvell, 'Upon Appleton House'
ll.99–104)

To grasp such a reversal it is necessary to imagine the boundary where the two opposed areas, the two possible directions from which to look,

meet. The loving environments of Leander and Adonis make us attentive
to the contours of the bodies with which they come into contact.

THE TREATMENT OF THE SENSITIVE ENVIRONMENT BY THE 'CAVALIER' POETS

The responsive sensitivity of natural phenomena—a sensitivity injected
into nature by the myths of Ovid's *Metamorphoses* and recovered in the
imaginations of those who de-moralised Ovid—becomes, in the hands of
some of the 'Cavalier' poets, a merely lecherous conceit: a way of invigor-
ating the device of the *blazon* which catalogues a woman's parts, with a
sense of resistant flesh. Thus Carew addresses the wind:

> Boldly light upon her lip,
> There suck odours, and thence skip
> To her bosome; lastly fall
> Downe, and wander over all:'
> ('A Prayer to the Wind',
> ll.9–12)

Lovelace, in 'Lucasta, taking the Waters at Tunbridge', recalls Marlowe's
description of the amorous sea, but lacks Marlowe's larger mythological
sense of a responsive and animated nature. In Lovelace's poem it is a
conceit which exists solely for the purpose of lecherous contemplation:

> I
> Yee happy floods! that now must passe
>   The sacred conduicts of her Wombe,
> Smooth, and transparent as your face,
>   When you are deafe, and windes are dumbe.
>
> .   .   .   .
>
> III
> And when her Rosie gates y'have trac'd,
>   Continue yet some Orient wet,
> 'Till turn'd into a Gemme, y'are plac'd
>   Like Diamonds with Rubies set.[16]

Herrick, in 'The Vine', employs the idea of metamorphosis to evoke a
fantasy of bondage in which he is the sentient bond:

> I dream'd this mortal part of mine
> Was Metamorphoz'd to a Vine;
> Which crawling one and every way,
> Enthrall'd my dainty *Lucia*.
> Me thought, her long small legs & thighs

I with my *Tendrils* did surprize;
Her Belly, Buttocks, and her Waste
By my soft *Nerv'lits* were embrac'd:
About her head I writhing hung,
And with rich clusters (hid among
The leaves) her temples I behung:
So that my *Lucia* seem'd to me
Young *Bacchus* ravisht by his tree.
My curles about her neck did craule,
And armes and hands they did enthrall:
So that she could not freely stir,
(All parts there made one prisoner.)
But when I crept with leaves to hide
Those parts, which maids keep unespy'd,
Such fleeting pleasures there I took,
That with the fancie I awook;
And found (Ah me!) this flesh of mine
More like a *Stock*, than like a *Vine*.

The resistance of Lucia's body is evoked principally through the contrast in textures, the vine's 'soft *Nerv'lits*' which crawl and hang contrast with Lucia's body and with the erection which this fantasy stimulates.[17]

Randolph writes 'Of a Snake which embrac'd Lycoris'.[18] He envies the licence of the non-human slitherer and uses its motions as a vehicle for his own roving eyes. At first he is alarmed by the danger with which the snake threatens the sleeping Lycoris:

But when I found he wore a guiltlesse sting,
And more of love did then of treason bring:
How quickly could my former feare depart,
And to a greater leave my iealous heart!
For the smooth Viper every member scands.
Africk he loaths now, and the barren sands
That nurst him, wondring at the glorious sight
Of thighs and belly, and her breasts more white
Then their own milke. *Ah! might I still* (quoth he)
Crawle in such fields, 'twixt two such mountaines be!

. . . .

Downe slips he, and about each limbe he hurles
His wanton body into numerous curles.

Lycoris wakes and, unafraid of the snake, plays suggestively with it:

And in her hand the tender worm she grasp'd,
While it sometimes about her finger clasp'd
A ring enamell'd, then her tender wast
In manner of a girdle round inbrac'd,

> And now upon her arme a braselet hung,
> Where, for the greater ornament, he flung
> His limber body into severall folds
> And twenty winding figures, where it holds
> Her amorous pulse, in many a various twist,
> And many a love-knot tyes upon her wrist.
> (ll.25–34; 53–4; 81–90)

The *Oxford English Dictionary* does not record the use of sense 6 of 'scan'—'To look at searchingly, examine with the eyes'—before 1798, but this is a fairly straightforward extension of sense 1—'To analyse (verse)'. The verb comes from the Latin *scandere* 'to climb', and Randolph's recollection of this origin is clear from his spelling of the word.[19] His use of the word accentuates the way in which sight and touch coincide for the snake and for the poet who uses the snake as an imaginative vehicle.

Lycoris's use of the snake as an ornament is characteristic of an almost fetishistic Cavalier focus on clothes and jewelry. Earl Miner has isolated a motif which he calls 'the embellishment of the woman',[20] and cites several poems devoted to moles, beauty patches, roses in enviable positions, and clothes. But what distinguishes many of these poems is not so much the act of looking *at* the woman so adorned as an attempt to *feel with* the adornment. Lovelace's 'sonnet,' 'Ellinda's Glove', displaces the interest in Ellinda's inaccessible contours onto a playfully solemn examination of the glove's turnings:

I

> Thou snowy Farme with thy five Tenements!
>   Tell thy white Mistris here was one
>   That call'd to pay his dayly Rents:
> But she a-gathering Flowr's and Hearts is gone,
> And thou left voyd to rude Possession.

II

> But grieve not, pretty *Ermin* Cabinet,
>   Thy Alabaster Lady will come home;
>   If not, what Tenant can there fit
> The slender turnings of thy narrow Roome,
> But must ejected be by his own dombe?

III

> Then give me leave to leave my Rent with thee;
>   Five kisses, one unto a place:
>   For though the *Lute*'s too high for me;
> Yet Servants knowing Minikin nor Base,
> Are still allow'd to fiddle with the Case.[21]

Of course the main point of the poem lies in the knowingly ludicrous exaltation of the trivial in the tradition of the mock *encomia*. But the trivial is exalted in a way which attends to structure and contour—the contours of Ellinda's absence and thus, indirectly, of Ellinda herself. It is as if Lovelace were imagining what it would be like to climb into her skin which might then fit him like a glove. In the first scene of *The Changeling*, Beatrice-Joanna, alight with a sensual awareness of De Flores which she as yet identifies as repulsion, refuses to touch again the glove that De Flores has picked up for her, preferring to throw down the other glove for him to keep: 'Take 'em and draw thine own skin off with 'em' (I.i.230). De Flores's ensuing comment— 'She had rather wear my pelt tann'd in a pair/ Of dancing pumps, than I should thrust my fingers/ Into her sockets here' (I.i.232–4)—violently brings out the eroticism latent in Lovelace's poem. The triviality which George Herbert scorns in 'Love (i)'—'onely a skarf or glove/ Doth warm our hands, and make them write of love'—is cultivated by some of the Cavalier poets into the occasion for focused imaginative experience.

SPARROWS AND FLEAS

Ovid's ring poem is evidence that the use of a trivial vehicle for imaginative experience was nothing new in the seventeenth century. The same kind of fantasy is present in the Harley lyric:

> Ich wolde ich were a þrestelcok,
> a bountyng oþer a lauerok,
>   swete bryd!
> Bituene hire curtel ant hire smok
>   y wolde ben hyd.[22]

I doubt whether this lyric shows evidence of Catullus' influence, but Catullus' two poems on Lesbia's sparrow (*Carmina* (ii) and (iii)) did generate many obvious imitations in the Renaissance.[23] Yet, though Lesbia's sparrow perches on her breast, nibbles her fingertips and hops about her lap, Catullus does not envy the bird this freedom. Rather he envies Lesbia her capacity for this kind of relaxation:

> Passer, deliciae meae puellae,
> quicum ludere, quem in sinu tenere,
> cui primum digitum dare appetenti
> et acris solet incitare morsus,
> cum desiderio meo nitenti
> carum nescio quid lubet iocari,
> et solaciolum sui doloris,
> credo, ut tum grauis acquiescat ardor:
> tecum ludere sicut ipsa possem
> et tristis animi leuare curas!

(Sparrow, my Lesbia's darling pet,/ Her playmate whom she loves to let/ Perch in her bosom and then tease/ With tantalising finger-tips,/ Provoking angry little nips/ (For my bright beauty seems to get/ A kind of pleasure from these games,/ Even relief, this being her way,/ I think, of damping down the flames/ Of passion), I wish I could play/ Silly games with you, too, to ease/ My worries and my miseries.[24])

It is only Catullus' later imitators who enviously imagine themselves in the position of the bird.

Skelton's 'Phyllyp Sparrowe' (which oddly omits Catullus from an impressive list of classical names) dwells a little more salaciously on the freedom of the bird:

> For it wold come and go,
> And fly so to and fro;
> And on me it wolde lepe
> Whan I was aslepe,
> And his fethers shake,
> Wherewith he wolde make
> Me often for to wake
> And for to take him in
> Vpon my naked skyn,
> God wot, we thought no syn:
> What though he crept so lowe?
> It was no hurt, I trowe;
> He dyd nothynge, perde
> But syt vpon my kne:
> Phyllyp, though he were nyse,
> In him it was no vyse;
> Phyllyp had leue to go
> To pyke my lyttell too;
> Phillip myght be bolde
> And do what he wolde;
> Phillip wolde seke and take
> All the flees blake
> That he coulde there espye
> With his wanton eye.
> (ll.159–82)[25]

Still, this poem is more in the tradition of the mock *encomium* than it is an imaginative exploration of contours. In *Astrophil and Stella* 83, Sidney seems to be remembering both Catullus and Skelton, though his Philip Sparrow (and the name suggests that the sparrow is an envied *alter ego*) is seen from the viewpoint of a rival:

I bare (with Envie) yet I bare your song,
    When in her necke you did *Love* ditties peepe;
    Nay, more foole I, oft suffered you to sleepe
In Lillies' neast, where *Love*'s selfe lies along.
    What, doth high place ambitious thoughts augment?
In sawcinesse reward of curtesie?
Cannot such grace your silly selfe content
But you must needs with those lips billing be?
    And through those lips drinke Nectar from that toong;
    Leave that sir *Phip*, least off your necke be wroong.
                        (ll.5−14)[26]

The 'black-silke cap' which a maid sets on another sparrow in one of Sidney's pastorals is another direct recollection of Skelton's sparrow who

    ...had a veluet cap,
    And wold syt vpon my lap,
    And seke after small wormes,
    And sometyme white bred crommes;
    And many tymes and ofte
    Betwene my brestes softe
    It wolde lye and rest;
    It was propre and prest.
                (ll.120−7)

But it's obviously a mistake to ascribe every expression of a theme—except of a very peculiar one—to the influence of a continuous tradition. When Keats wrote:

I scarcely remember counting upon any Happiness—I look not for it if it be not in the present hour—nothing startles me beyond the Moment. The setting sun will always set me to rights—or if a Sparrow come before my Window I take part in its existence and pick about the Gravel,[27]

subliminal literary memories may have prompted him to think of sparrows as particularly appropriate vessels for imaginative inhabitation, but it seems more likely that he simply saw a sparrow outside his window when he was writing his letter.

But Herrick's elegy 'Upon the death of his Sparrow' is clearly a very literary piece, recalling Skelton with '*Phill*, the late dead, the late dead Deare' and, behind Skelton, Catullus with 'Had *Lesbia* (too-too-kind) but known/ This Sparrow, she had scorn'd her own'. The last line of this elegy—'Not *Virgil*'s Gnat had such a Tomb'—clearly allies the poem with classical mock *encomia*. In another mock *encomium*, 'Upon a Flie', Herrick honours the fly as much by literary reference as with the ivory box which he speaks of. The verse container is the more enduring:

> Not *Virgils Gnat*, to whom the Spring
> All Flowers sent to 'is burying.
> Not *Marshals Bee*, which in a Bead
> Of *Amber* quick was buried.
> Nor that fine Worme that do's interre
> Her self i' th' *silken Sepulchre*.
> Nor my rare *Phil*, that lately was
> With Lillies Tomb'd up in a Glasse;
> More honour had, then this same *Flie*;
> Dead, and clos'd up in *Yvorie*.
>
> (ll.9−18)

The 'Gnat' or *Culex* which Herrick refers to, attributed to Virgil, is more an exercise in tone than in the perception of the miniature. It is the best known of several classical mockingly encomiastic or heroic pieces dealing with insects.[28] Less classical (though this was not recognised by those Renaissance readers who believed this poem to be by Ovid) is the medieval, neo-Latin 'Carmen de Pulice' ('Song of the Flea'), often printed in conjunction with a poem about a louse, 'De Pediculo'.[29] In the 'Carmen de Pulice' the poet envies the flea his freedom to go wherever he wants: 'nil tibi saeve latet' (Nothing is hidden from you, you brute.') The poet wonders what charm or drug might effect such a transformation on himself. If he could be so metamorphosed:

> Haererem in tunicae margine virgineae
> Inde means per crura meae sub veste puellae
> Ad loca quae vellem me cito surriperem

(I would fasten on to the edge of her maidenly tunic, and making my way from there between her legs, under my girl's shift, I would swiftly proceed to the parts of my desire.)

A great many 'I wish I were' poems take their cue from this. In France Ronsard, in his *Folastrie vi* (1553) writes 'Que pleust à Dieu que je pusse/ Pour une soir devenir puce' ('Would to God that I might/ Become a flea for one night').[30] And in 1582 a remarkable volume appeared in Paris commemorating the appearance of a flea in the cleavage of Catherine des Roches. This occurrence was remarked upon, and subsequently commemorated in verse, by the historian Estienne Pasquier. Mademoiselle des Roches replied, and the circulation of these two poems inspired a number of other contributions on the same topic—in French, Spanish, Latin and Greek. The volume is entitled, *La Puce ou Ieus Poetiques Francois & Latins Composez sur la Puce aux grands Iours de Poictiers l'an MDLXXIX dont Pasquier feut le premier motif*. Both Pasquier and Catherine des Roches dignify the flea by referring to Ovidian metamorphosis. Pasquier writes:

Je ne veux ni du Taureau,
Ni du Cyne blanc oyseau,
Ni d'Amphitrion la forme,
Ni qu'en pluie on me transforme:
Puis que Madame se paist
Sans plus de ce qu'il te plaist,
Pleust or à Dieu que je pusse
Seulement deuenir Puce:
Tantost ie prendrois mon vol
Tout au plus beau de ton col,
Ou d'une douce rapine
Ie succerois ta poitrine,
Ou lentement pas à pas
Ie me glisserois plus bas,
Et d'un muselin folastre
Je serois Puce idolatre,
Pinçottant ie ne scay quoy
Que i'ayme trop plus que moy.[31]

(I do not want the Bull's form, or that of the white bird, the Swan, nor of Amphitryon; nor do I wish to be turned into rain. Since madam is contented with so little of what pleases you, then would to God that I could just become a flea: then I would take flight to the loveliest part of your neck, or I would suck at your breast in an act of tender theft, or slowly, step by step, I would slither lower down, and be the flea adorer of a piece of playful muslin, pinching what I cannot tell, but which I love more than myself.)

Mademoiselle des Roches' reply is more subtle and inventive. In Ovidian fashion she gives the flea's history and tells of how Pan fell in love with the flea during its human girlhood:

Puce quand vous estiez pucelle,
Gentille, sage, douce & belle,
Vous mouuant d'un pied si leger,
A sauter & à voltiger,
Que vous eussiez peu d'Atalante
Deuancer la course trop lente.
Pan voyant vos perfections,
Sentit un feu d'affections,
Desirant vostre mariage:
Mais quoy? vostre vierge courage
Aima mieux vous faire changer
En puce, à fin de l'etranger
Et que perdant toute esperance
Il rompit sa perseuerance.

Diane sçeut vostre souhait
Vous le voulustes, il fut fait:
Elle voila vostre figures
Sous une noire couverture.[32]

(Flea, when you were a maid, gracious, good, sweet and lovely, so light-footed when you moved, skipping and fluttering around, that you could have overtaken Atalanta's too-slow pace. Pan, seeing your perfections and wanting to marry you, felt a fire of affection: but what? Your virgin heart would rather you were changed into a flea in order to distance him, so that, losing all hope, he'd relinquish his persistence. Diana knew what you wished. No sooner wished than it was done: she covered your face with a black veil.)

This fleaess makes a change with her resourceful chastity.

*   *   *

Sparrows and fleas bring with them evaluative associations which are connected, but not identical, with the small size that enables them to nip enviably around. The sparrow's traditional reputation for lechery[33] has little to do with its behaviour as a lady's pet (its lechery being directed more towards other sparrows than humans).[34] But, though the poems about pet sparrows often stress the innocence of the bird's behaviour in provocative environments, traditional associations are inevitably evoked when the birds nestle between human breasts. Emblematically these sparrows stand for the poet's lust, but imaginatively they gratify that lust. The pejorative associations of 'parasites' are clear in the metaphorical extension of the word; but even non-parasitic insects tend to be considered as at best insignificant and at worst repellent.

Whilst many fly/flea poems—perhaps with the 'Carmen de Pulice' as their model—involve an imaginative participation with the insect's life, using the unpleasant associations of the insect to suggest wittily that even so base a creature is more fortunate than the poet, there are many other poems which use their insect subjects as moral *exempla*. Lovelace, in 'A Fly Caught in a Cobweb' and 'A Fly about a Glasse of Burnt Claret', does not take up the opportunities which these flies offer for the sort of imaginative exploration he engages in elsewhere. Instead he uses these flies in a more Spenserian way—as miniature examples to point to a larger moral. The fly caught in a cobweb is a 'Small type of great ones, that do hum/ Within this whole World's narrow Room'. This is the method of Spenser's '*Muiopotmos*: or the Fate of the Butterflie' in which the mock heroic tone of the opening stanzas does not so much mock the heroic mode as suggest the heroic limits of the poem's moral implications.[35]

This method of *exemplum* and moral is closer to that of the *Ovid*

Moralisé than to that of Ovid himself or some of his Renaissance imitators who do not present a prior or ulterior moral which is separable from the body of the narrative. But what remains characteristically 'metaphysical' about these poems is the incongruous conjunction of weighty implication and apparently trivial vehicle.

Arthur Pease comments on the difficulty involved in drawing boundaries between the mock and the real *encomium*, and mentions the Greek interest in the natural sciences in which 'no least detail was too trivial for earnest consideration', as something capable of converting facetious into genuine praise.[36]

Bacon writes in the *New Organon*:

> And for things that are mean or even filthy,—things which (as Pliny says) must be introduced with an apology,—such things, no less than the most splendid and costly, must be admitted into natural history. Nor is natural history polluted thereby; for the sun enters the sewer no less than the palace, yet takes no pollution . . . For whatever deserves to exist deserves also to be known, for knowledge is the image of existence; and things mean and splendid exist alike. Moreover as from certain putrid substances—musk, for instance, and civet—the sweetest odors are sometimes generated, so too, from mean and sordid instances there sometimes emanates excellent light and information.[37]

However antique this idea may have been it seems to have needed fairly emphatic reaffirmation at the time when Bacon was writing—a time when written authority was being challenged, modified and extended by new observation of the actual. And the opportunities for this observation were greatly extended by the development of optical isntruments which Bacon describes as:

> those recently invented glasses which disclose the latent and invisible minutiae of bodies, and their hidden configurations and motions, by greatly increasing their apparent size; instruments by the aid of which the exact shape and outline of body in a flea, a fly, a worm, and also colours and motions before unseen, are not without astonishment discerned.[38]

The specific suggestiveness of one of the fine illustrations to Hooke's *Micrographia*, depicting a louse clinging to a hair is behind Marvell's lines in 'Last Instructions to a Painter':

> With *Hook* then through the *microscope*, take aim
> Where, like the new *Controller*, all men laugh
> To see a tall Lowse brandish the white Staff.
>
> (ll. 16–18)

But more important than such specific sources is the sense of worlds being made newly accessible to the corporeal eye by the means of telescope and microscope—an accessibility which surely stimulated and nourished with new detail the imaginative vision that had never been thwarted by the lack of optical instruments (Fig. 13).

What the development of optical instruments suggests in particular is the relativity of size. The small is no longer absolutely small and will, if correctly approached, reveal as complex and interesting a structure as the, relatively, large. The facility with which Marvell moves between marshes and stars in stanza LVIII of 'Upon Appleton House' derives from this perception of the relativity of scale:

> They seem within the polisht Grass
> A Landskip drawn in Looking-Glass.
> And shrunk in the huge Pasture show
> As Spots, so shap'd, on Faces do.
> Such Fleas, ere they approach the Eye,
> In Multiplying Glasses lye.
> They feed so wide, so slowly move,
> As *Constellations* do above.[40]

The mention of 'Multiplying Glasses' glosses the way in which Marvell's focus has been adjusting itself in this passage.

Looking at a flea is of course not the same as looking and feeling—'scanding'—with one. But the encouragement afforded by divine and scientific interest might vindicate writing about either act. Augustine writes:

> It is God who effects that miraculous combination of an immaterial with a material substance, with the former in command, the latter in subjection; God unites them to make a living creature. This is a work of such wonder and grandeur as to astound the mind that seriously considers it, and to evoke praise to the Creator; and this is true not only as that work is observed in man, a rational being and on that account of more excellence and greater worth than all other creatures, but even in the case of the tiniest fly.[41]

The concerns of God are not the same as the concerns of the naturalist—the former subsume the latter—but it is in their comparable extensiveness that Jonson's analogy between God and the surgeon-anatomist is rooted. Gerard Manley Hopkins, in 'The Blessed Virgin Compared to the Air we Breathe', was to image the ubiquity of grace with the air's infinitely delicate, but penetrating and pervasive contact:

> Wild air, world-mothering air,
> Nestling me everywhere,
> That each eyelash or hair
> Girdles, goes home betwixt
> The fleeciest, frailest-flixed
> Snowflake...

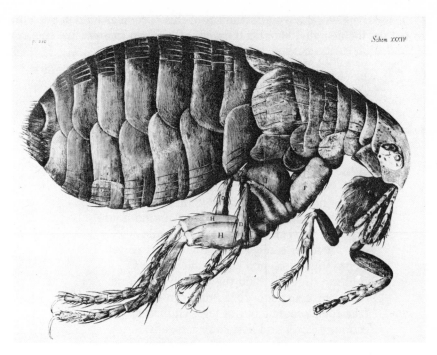

13. Flea, Robert Hooke, *Micrographia*, 1665, Schem. XXXIV.

> I say that we are wound
> With mercy round and round
> As if with air:
>
> (ll.1–6; 34–6)

The figure of Pride in *Doctor Faustus* compares itself to the enviable flea in the 'Carmen de Pulice':

> I am like to Ovid's flea; I can creep into every corner of a wench: some-
> times, like a periwig, I sit upon her brow; next, like a necklace, I hang
> about her neck; then, like a fan of feathers, I kiss her lips; and then,
> turning myself to a wrought smock, do what I list.
>
> (vi.115–20)

Whilst Lovelace and Herrick are both capable of an imaginative mobility which 'scands' and renders palpable the bodies they present, they only seem to do so in poems that are morally vacuous (such as 'Lucasta, taking the Waters at Tunbridge' or 'The Vine'). Both write poems of moral significance elsewhere but their method for these is different. What Marlowe does in Pride's speech is present a moral universe which is coextensive with the physical rather than in an allegorical relation to it.

Jonson gives to Mosca, the parasite in *Volpone*, a speech which plays with the mobility and freedom of access that parasites traditionally have, to image the energetic resourcefulness of this particular kind of evil (and to tell us, incidentally, about the nature of his own imaginative energy):

> ...I could skip
> Out of my skin, now, like a subtill snake,
> I am so limber. O! Your Parasite
> Is a most precious thing, dropped from aboue,
> Not bred 'mongst clods and clot-poules, here on earth.
> I muse, the mysterie was not made a science,
> It is so liberally profest, almost
> All the wise world is little else, in nature,
> But Parasites, or Sub-parasites. And, yet
> I meane not those, that haue your bare towne-arte,
> To know who's fit to feed 'hem; haue no house,
> No family, no care, and therefore mould
> Tales for mens eares, to bait that sense; or get
> Kitchin-inuention, and some stale receipts
> To please the belly, and the groine; nor those,
> With their court-dog-tricks, that can fawne, and fleere,
> Make their reuenue out of legs, and faces,
> Eccho my-Lord, and lick away a moath:
> But your fine, elegant rascall, that can rise,
> And stoope (almost together) like an arrow;
> Shoot through the aire, as nimbly as a starre;
> Turne short, as doth a swallow; and be here,
> And there, and here, and yonder, all at once;
> Present to any humour, all occasion;
> And change a visor, swifter, then a thought!
> This is the creature, had the art borne with him;
> Toiles not to learne it, but doth practise it
> Out of most excellent nature: and such sparkes,
> Are the true Parasites ...
>
> (III.i.5–33)

The ubiquitous Pride and Volpone's astonishingly capable parasite, Mosca, both possess a significance which is inseparable from their mobile capacity. Their terminology brings together the two apparently distinct areas in which such agility was discussed: solemn discussions of the *anima*'s God-imitative powers and playful, bordering on obscene, speculation about what fleas and other small things can get up to.

JOHN DONNE: 'THE FLEA' AND 'METEMPSYCHOSIS'

In John Donne's '*Metempsychosis*, The Progresse of the Soule', there is a perfect fusion between a moral relativism and the kind of imaginative elasticity demanded of a poet following a soul into such variously sized and structured dwellings. I will conclude this chapter with a study of that poem but shall look first at Donne's famous contribution to the genre of flea poem:

> Marke but this flea, and marke in this,
> How little that which thou deny'st me is;
> It suck'd me first, and now sucks thee,
> And in this flea, our two bloods mingled bee;
> Thou know'st that this cannot be said
> A sinne, nor shame, nor losse of maidenhead,
>   Yet this enjoyes before it wooe,
>   And pamper'd swells with one blood made of two,
>   And this, alas, is more then wee would doe.
>
> O stay, three lives in one flea spare,
> Where wee almost, yea more then maryed are.
> This flea is you and I, and this
> Our mariage bed, and mariage temple is;
> Though parents grudge, and you, w'are met,
> And cloysterd in these living walls of Jet.
>   Though use make you apt to kill mee,
>   Let not to that, selfe murder added bee,
>   And sacrilege, three sinnes in killing three.
>
> Cruell and sodaine, hast thou since
> Purpled thy naile, in blood of innocence?
> Wherein could this flea guilty bee,
> Except in that drop which it suckt from thee?
> Yet thou triumph'st, and saist that thou
> Find'st not thy selfe, nor mee the weaker now;
>   'Tis true, then learne how false, feares bee;
>   Just so much honor, when thou yeeld'st to mee,
>   Will wast, as this flea's death tooke life from thee.

The opening phrase, 'Marke but this flea', not only creates an intimacy of tone, but also introduces an immediate visual focus. We are asked to concentrate upon this low but familiar object. The second phrase, 'and marke in this', maintains the demand for visual (or imaginative) focus, but this demand is elided with another for conceptual abstraction. The flea must not simply be seen, but re-marked upon. The specious success of the poem's argumentation largely derives from Donne's insistence that we hold together these two kinds of 'marking' and by the sleight of hand with which he elides the two. The flea is not invoked as an analogue—a simile which might lose its persuasive force if developed autonomously beyond its point of contact with the objects to which it is compared—but as a *demonstration*. The words 'marke in this' do not mean only 'notice how in this case', but also, 'notice how in *this case*, these living walls of jet which encase our two bloods'. The casualness of 'Marke but this flea' is deceptive but useful. It gives the impression of an object being plucked from the environment at random and the implication is that other objects could demonstrate the following proposition equally well, as if all the objects in the world would point to the same incontrovertible conclusion. But, as the fourth line makes clear, the 'in this' of line 1 refers specifically to the interior of a particular insect body.

The poem's sophistical argument is carefully developed by capitalising on the visual focus which it has demanded and glossing over the shifts from the material object to the proposition it is supposed to demonstrate. The word 'this' is used six times in the first stanza and creates the illusion of scrupulous particularity (picked up in the 'just' of the penultimate line). The 'this'-es of lines 1 and 4 are directly referential. That of line 5 derives a reasonable supposition from already observed particulars; the 'this' of line 9 does not.

The suggestions of pregnancy in line 8, developing the accuracy of the fourth line, are uncomfortably counter-productive as if, in expanding his sophistical theme, the speaker has inadvertently leaked out one of the most reasonable grounds for resisting his plea—fear of pregnancy. Line 9 represents a rapid disavowal of such a notion and the cover-up is improved upon in the second stanza where the potentially explosive notion of two bloods mingled in one flea is converted into the analogy with the Trinity (and a return to demonstrative precision since there really are three bloods in that flea's case). The speaker's blasphemy is cleverly off-loaded onto the addressee of the poem with the hint that her move to squash the flea is not only suicidal but sacrilegious. A similar off-loading takes place at the start of the third stanza where the innocence of the unyielding woman is shifted onto the squashed flea. The woman, guilty of this, has lost her innocence as inconspicuously as she did in line 11. The immaculate conception suggested in lines 4 to 6 has been dropped in favour of the suggestion that innocence has already been mislaid and conception avoided.

It is hard to know the limits of the implications that a poem like this asks its readers to unravel. How far starwards is it permissible to ascend? It seems to me that the sacrilege—destruction of a temple and the murder of the Trinity—suggested at the end of the second stanza is elaborated at the beginning of the third: 'hast thou since/ Purpled thy naile, in blood of innocence?' The innocent blood is Christ's; the purpled nail, one of the nails of the cross. But the triumph over death has already been written into the poem. The 'living walls of Jet' suggest a sepulchre whose deathly nature Romeo and Juliet attempted and failed to defy. Only Christ converted a sepulchre into a source of life, making (in one of the period's favourite rhymes) the tomb a womb.

Were this triumph over death not already written into the poem, the guilt suggested in lines 19–20 might be too weighty for the poem to bear. But after a momentary shock at the facetiousness of such profound implications in a poem of apparently libertine levity, we should be more educatively shocked by the recognition that they are not inappropriate: that Christ is crucified at every moment, if not especially by flea-squashers, by all mankind engaged in the most mundane and trivial occupations. God is not limited by concepts of decorum. If we think fleas are trivial the limitation is ours, not God's.

God's interest in fleas (which Augustine had recorded) may permit the extent of the poem's covert implications—but that is a theological rather than an imaginative point. Donne does not, in this poem, use the small flea as a vehicle for imaginative exploration or show that interest in the minute which God and scientists share. The image of the flea provides a deliberately misleading focus which apparently anchors a spurious argument in a careful particularity which is not the poem's real concern. Apart from the useful fact that the flea sucks and contains blood, Donne is no more interested in its structure than is Lovelace in his 'Fly Caught in a Cobweb'. But by a sleight of hand Donne seems to be fusing rather than merely juxtaposing abstract argument and physical demonstration. Though the intelligible argument is not the consequence of the sensible demonstration it is significant that it gathers plausibility by seeming so. Donne appeals to the logic of matter ('the substance of matter is better than the beauty of words') though he does not use it. He constructs a fine-meshed sieve and passes it off for a watertight bowl.

However, in his strange and black long poem on metempsychosis, intellectual and imaginative stance coincide and corroborate one another. Jonson's parasite and Marlowe's Pride both imaged the nimble resourcefulness of evil—a resourcefulness which attempts to match the providential ubiquity of the good it combats. In his 'Progresse of the Soule' Donne conveys a sense of sin which is at once pervasive and minute. An eternal presence (or rather one that extends from the Fall to the Last Judgement) is traced in the course of a temporal sequence.

This sequence is a 'progresse' of two kinds. In that the poem gives us a genealogy of sin, tracing the soul of the apple eaten by Eve, the *malum malum*, in its ascent from vegetable to human accommodation (Queen Elizabeth), the progress described is one of dignity and self-consciousness —a progression from low to high. But the poem is also about a 'progresse' of the Elizabethan courtly type—a journey involving extended stays at various houses, each of which strives, more or less, to accommodate its guest.

The soul recommends itself as the subject of an epic by the range of its vision and by the variety of forms which it, and its follower, can perceive:

II

Thee, eye of heaven, this great Soule envies not,
By thy male force, is all wee have, begot.
In the first East, thou now beginst to shine,
Suck'st early balme, and Iland spices there,
And wilt anon in thy loose-rein'd careere
At Tagus, Po, Sene, Thames, and Danow dine,
And see at night thy Westerne land of Myne,
Yet hast thou not more nations seene then shee,
That before thee, one day beganne to bee,
    And thy fraile light being quench'd, shall long, long out live thee.

III

Nor, holy *Ianus*, in whose soveraigne boate
The Church, and all the Monarchies did floate;
That swimming Colledge, and free Hospitall
Of all mankinde, that cage and vivarie
Of fowles, and beasts, in whose wombe, Destinie
Us, and our latest nephewes did install
(From thence are all deriv'd, that fill this All,)
Did'st thou in that great stewardship embarke
So diverse shapes into that floating parke,
    As have beene moved, and inform'd by this heavenly sparke.

'This heavenly sparke' offers a closeness to the shapes which it informs
and a particularity of vision denied those poets who in an earlier epic style
had followed the career of Phoebus' steeds. The moral 'perspective'
obtained in these epic flights is replaced in Donne's poem by a precise and
exploratory scepticism:

As lightning, which one scarce dares say, he saw,
'Tis so soone gone, (and better proofe the law
Of sense, then faith requires) swiftly she flew
To a darke and foggie Plot; Her, her fates threw
    There through th' earth's pores, and in a Plant hous'd her anew.
                                                        (ll.126–30)

Too quick, too fine, for the sense to grasp, this soul is nevertheless con-
ceived in material terms. It is quantitatively, not qualitatively, different
from the objects of ordinary sense perception:

To an unfetterd soules quick nimble hast
Are falling stars, and hearts thoughts, but slow pac'd:
Thinner then burnt aire flies this soule.
                                                        (ll.171–3)

'Burnt aire', than which this not insubstantial soul is thin*er*, is air made
visible. By an effort of imaginative contraction and hypersensitivity Donne

presents us with an environment in which there are no *vacui*. The birds
move freely about the air because it is 'Plyant' (1.215) and yields to their
denser forms; it is not no thing. Even reverberated sound is seen for-
mally—as a material and conceivably visible quantity. When the whale
moves:

> At every stroake his brazen finnes do take,
> More circles in the broken sea they make
> Then cannons voices, when the aire they teare.
>
> (ll.311–13)

While the progress of the soul is supposedly controlled by 'Fate', the
account of this progress is in terms of strictly material causality. The soul
is not freed from the confines of one lodging until there is a space through
which it may escape:

> Just in that instant when the serpents gripe,
> Broke the slight veines, and tender conduit-pipe,
> Through which this soule from the trees root did draw
> Life, and growth to this apple, fled away
> This loose soule...
>
> (ll.121–5)

Inside the fish that the swan then swallowed:

> ...this Soule in double walls was shut,
> Till melted with the Swans digestive fire,
> She left her house the fish, and vapour'd forth;
>
> (ll.242–4)

Nor do the creatures which this soul inhabits move themselves unless
their environment yield them a place. The mandrake, whose form the
soul has entered by way of the earth's pores:

> ...to it selfe did force
> A place, where no place was; by natures course
> As aire from water, water fleets away
> From thicker bodies, by this root thronged so
> His spungie confines gave him place to grow:
> Just as in our streets, when the people stay
> To see the Prince, and have so fill'd the way
> That weesels scarce could passe, when she comes nere
> They throng and cleave up, and a passage cleare,
>   As if, for that time, their round bodies flatned were.
>
> (ll.131–40)

The *horror vacui* which determines this densely filled universe is
informed by an ubiquitous moral condition. The paradoxical ubiquity

and particularity of the Cross and its burden is shared by the evil fruit of the tree with which, in traditional typology, it is linked.

> This soule to whom *Luther*, and *Mahomet* were
> Prisons of flesh; this soule which oft did teare,
> And mend the wracks of th'Empire, and late Rome,
> And liv'd when every great change did come,
>   Had first in paradise, a low, but fatall roome.

> VII
> Yet no low roome, nor then the greatest, lesse,
> If (as devout and sharpe men fitly guesse)
> That Crosse, our joy, and griefe, where nailes did tye
> That All, which alwayes was all, every where;
> Which could not sinne, and yet all sinnes did beare;
> Stood in the selfe same roome in Calvarie,
> Where first grew the forbidden learned tree,
> For on that tree hung in security
>   This Soule, made by the Makers will from pulling free,
>   (ll.66–80)

Once the soul has animated the apple and been consumed by Adam and Eve, sin begins to rival redemption in its pervasiveness:

> Man all at once was there by woman slaine,
> And one by one we'are here slaine o'er againe
> By them. The mother poison'd the well-head;
> The daughters here corrupt us, Rivolets;
> No smalnesse scapes, no greatnesse breaks their nets.
>   (ll.91–5)

The pervasiveness which is the poem's subject is mirrored in the texture of the verse. One line runs into the next without cesura; the rhythms are impatient, restless, searching. The tight rhyme scheme, frequent internal rhymes, and curious use of homophones reinforce our sense of the density of this poem's world:

> ...I will through the wave, and fome,
> And shall, in sad lone wayes a lively spright,
> Make my darke heavy Poem light, and light.
>   (ll.53–5)

> ...Her, her fates threw
> There through th'earth's pores, and in a Plant hous'd her anew.
>   (ll.129–30)

Donne's adherence to laws of material causality and his sense of that matter, distinguishes his treatment of, sometimes traditional, *exempla* from that of Spenser in his 'Visions of the Worlds Vanitie', written only ten years before Donne's poem. Spenser describes the advent of these visions as the result of 'meditation deepe/ Of things exceeding reach of common reason' (ll.3−4). The 'visions' that follow are not the objects of that initial meditation but *illustrations* of it:

> Vnto my eyes strange showes presented were,
> Picturing that, which I in minde embraced
>
> (ll.10−11)

In each of Spenser's *exempla* the moral clearly pre-exists the anecdote which seems to yield it. Indeed the *exempla* are no more than a string of anecdotes which all illustrate the same point:

> So by the small the great is oft diseased.
>
> (l.28)

> Why then should greatest things the least disdaine,
> Sith that so small so mightie can constraine?
>
> (ll.41−2)

> O how great vainnesse is it then to scorne
> The weake, that hath the strong so oft forlorne.
>
> (ll.83−4)

Spenser's method here is inductive; his vivid descriptions serve only to impress his foregone conclusions upon us.

This is not the case with Donne. The moralisations which arise from various points in his poem read rather more as asides, wry comments on the preceding action, than as the conclusions to which the whole poem tends. The soul-harbouring fish, plucked from the water by the sea Pie,

> Exalted ... is, but to the exalters good,
> As are by great ones, men which lowly stood.
>   It's raised, to be the Raisers instrument and food.
>
> (ll.278−80)

The literal, physical act of 'exaltation' generates, rather than illustrates, this conclusion. Similarly the kneeless elephant who 'up-props' himself and 'on himselfe relies' (l.386) does so quite literally. The moral caution against negligent self-reliance is implicit in this particular description; the description does not read as one, of many possible, illustrations which could impress this caution upon us.

Spenser's treatment of a very similar elephant story is remarkably different. The description does not lack detail but that detail is only sufficient to impress the reader with a lively and memorable illustration of the final moral. The allegorical meaning of the anecdote is insistently pushed forward:

> Soone after this I saw an Elephant,
> Adorn'd with bells and bosses gorgeouslie,
> That on his backe did beare (as batteilant)
> A gilden towre, which shone exceedinglie;
>   That he himselfe through foolish vanitie,
> Both for his rich attire, and goodly forme,
> Was puffed vp with passing surquedrie,
> And shortly gan all other beasts to scorne,
>   Till that a little Ant, a silly worme,
> Into his nosthrils creeping, so him pained.
> .   That casting downe his towres, he did deforme
> Both borrowed pride, and natiue beautie stained,
>   Let therefore nought that great is, therein glorie,
>   Sith so small thing his happines may varie.
>   (ll. 99–112)

In Spenser the emphasis is upon the meaning which the 'visions' illustrate. The meaning is prior to the illustrations. The manner is that of moralised Ovid rather than of Ovid himself. But in Donne's poem the illustrations have ceased to be illustrations in the strict sense, for meaning is derived from them and is not prior or separable.

Spenser is a static observer: 'Vnto my eyes strange showes presented were'. Where these 'showes' came from and where they go to is not explained, for the rooted eye is unable to follow them once they have passed. Nor is the unmoving eye able to see beyond the surface. It cannot, as Donne's does, move 'Before, behind, between, above, below', thus gaining a sense of the structure and solidity of the thing perceived. Spenser's visions are pure appearance. They are like the figures which Faustus summons to pass across the stage, 'but shadows, not substantial'.

Donne on the other hand, 'a lively spright' (l. 53), uses his imagination as a mobile and exploratory instrument. In the soul with which he travels he finds the perfect vehicle with which to explore the forms of the world. The *anima*'s God-imitative capacity to range freely and delicately is shared by the soul, whose progress the poem traces, and by the 'spright' of Donne's imagination.[42] The terminology of swift and subtle mobility which derives from theological descriptions of God and the soul and which was only later extended to a human imagination not necessarily associated with the numinous, is here applicable to both. Donne writes about the soul and he exercises its powers in doing so, using it as a means to explore the material world with an imaginative eye freed from the limitations of corporeal vision.

The sceptical and inconclusive conclusion to the poem is:

> Of every quality comparison,
>   The onely measure is, and judge, opinion.
>   (ll. 519–20)

In the fallen world there is no absolute measure against which to judge and see. Yet one of the consolations of relativistic scepticism is the new areas of possible interest which are opened up when absolutes have fled. Donne displays such an interst as he uses the imagination's elastic capacity to expand or contract itself according to the nature of its objects. In the relativistic world of this poem quantity is only significant when juxtaposed with other quantities. Donne, in imaginatively tracking the soul, employs a soul's traditional flexibility to observe both the movement of land masses and the internal structure of plants. The microscopic detail which he observes in the forms of small creatures demonstrates that small is not less. The body of the larval fish in stanza XXIII is small only because it is smaller than other bodies which we are accustomed to seeing. Its smallness has no meaning, does not preclude the precise observation of its parchment-like scales, until it is foiled and contained by the greater volume of the swan when it 'swome a prison in a prison put' (l.241). The growth of the young sparrow is defined in terms of relative capacities:

> A mouth he opes, which would as much containe
> As his late house...
>
> (ll.186–7)

The bird is seen to have grown because he can now contain that which once contained him. Similarly the hugeness of the whale is a relative hugeness:

> Swimme in him swallow'd Dolphins, without feare,
> And feele no sides...
>
> (ll.316–7)

The largeness or smallness of these creatures consists in their ability to contain or be contained. They are displayed by their containers, revealed in relationship. Noah's ark is envisaged as a sort of display case for 'diverse shapes':

> That swimming Colledge, and free Hospitall
> Of all mankinde; that cage and vivarie
> Of fowles, and beasts...
>
> (ll.23–5)

As such it is inferior only to Donne's poem, which displays, and explores, the more diverse shapes which the 'deathlesse soule' has inhabited.

Boxes are put into boxes and prisons into prisons. The creatures which are contained by their materially perceived environment ('the free inhabitants of the Plyant aire' (l.215)) are themselves the containers and lodgings of souls. Donne takes up and imaginatively realises the Platonic notion of the flesh as the house of the soul (ll.70; 159; 177; 241; 244; 314; 391ff; 401, 490). Following the soul as it inhabits these dwelling places, Donne is able to survey their interiors. The mouse, in whose

'streight cloyster' the soul is lodged, comes across the 'sinewy Proboscis'
of the elephant:

> In which as in a gallery this mouse
> Walk'd, and surveid the roomes of this vast house,
> And to the braine, the soules bedchamber, went,
> And gnaw'd the life cords there;
>
> (ll.391–4)

Whilst Spenser had not been interested in his ant's eye view of the ele-
phant's insides, Donne travels with the mouse to envisage the long dark
tunnel of the trunk and the ascent to the domed chamber of its skull.[43]

Not only does Donne survey the interiors of the soul's dwellings. He
also achieves a new perspective on the world by looking out onto it from
within them. When the soul is confined inside 'a small blew shell, the
which a poore/ Warme bird orespread.../ Till her inclos'd child kickt, and
pick't it selfe a dore' (ll.178–80) the warmth of the bird is warmth felt from
within the egg, and the door which the fledgling picks is a door which opens
out onto the rest of the world. To the small fish, the mesh of a net forms
windows (l.254)—open ones through whose frames it may swim.

In Spenser's poem the 'point of view' was unvarying. The eye of the
imagination was no more versatile than that of the body; that poem's
energies were not engaged in looking. But in Donne's more sceptical
poem the directions in which and from which we are directed to look are
varied; our customary ways of seeing are revealed as not absolute, but
conditional. This mobility, which is very much part of the poem's relativ-
istic scepticism, allows for the wonderfully precise and delicate descrip-
tions whose tenderness points back to that providential attentiveness
which is the obverse of scepticism:

> Outcrept a sparrow, this soules moving Inne,
> On whose raw armes stiffe feathers now begin,
> As childrens teeth through gummes, to breake with paine,
> His flesh is jelly yet, and his bones threds,
> All a new downy mantle overspreads...
>
> (ll.181–5)

> ...A female fishes sandie Roe
> With the males jelly, newly lev'ned was,
> For they had intertouch'd as they did passe,
> And one of those small bodies, fitted so,
> This soule inform'd, and abled it to rowe
> It selfe with finnie oares, which she did fit:
> Her scales seem'd yet of parchment, and as yet
>   Perchance a fish, but by no name you could call it.
>
> (ll.223–30)

Chapter 6

A MIDSUMMER NIGHT'S DREAM

'Things base and vile'

I have stressed the difference between Spenser's inductive, analogising technique in which the sensible world illustrates, but does not generate, the intelligible, and Donne's technique in 'The Progresse of the Soule', in which the intelligible is found within the sensible world. Janel Mueller has suggested that Donne's poem has behind it an engagement with gnostic thought, according to which the soul can liberate itself from the body only by going through the body and completing its quota of earthly experience.[1] More loosely, the dualistic, gnostic association of evil with the material world may be behind such speeches as those of Marlowe's Pride and Jonson's Mosca. In both cases it is evil which presents itself in terms of such intimate and resourceful familiarity with the material world.

The association of evil with matter—dualist and anti-incarnationist—is traditional and persistent. Ben Jonson's 'realism'—his use of locally and temporally specific vocabulary—is restricted to his treatment of the morally, if not socially, 'low'. He observes the decorum of comedy. But a conception of divine Providence—more observantly resourceful than any evil in its attention to each detail of the creation, none of which can be 'beneath it'—allows the minute, the low and the particular to be referred to without denigration. It is in the workings of Providence that an ubiquitous God finds material expression and in which the sense-confounding paradox of Cusanus' description of God as a circle whose centre is everywhere and circumference nowhere is translated into a sensibly apprehensible *plenum*.

In the last chapter I looked at some of the ways in which poets explored the contours of the physical world, converting lexical into imaginative range and finding their occasions in narratives of creaturely mobility. In this chapter I want to look in some detail at *A Midsummer Night's Dream* and briefly at *The Tempest* to see how an extension of moral sympathy may both permit and suggest new areas of imaginative vision. The concept of a God whose loving attentiveness to detail is manifested in the workings out of Providence is important here.

A Midsummer Night's Dream is a play about sublunary lovers. The moon determines the play's fictional time and provides the upper limit of the imaginary space which the play's events occupy. The area 'between the cold moon and the earth' (II.i.156) through which Oberon can fly is also the extent of the play's reference. Theseus, speaking of the range of a poet's vision, describes the same bounded area:

> The poet's eye, in a fine frenzy rolling,
> Doth glance from heaven to earth, from earth to heaven;
>
>   (V.i.12–13)

The polarities of the 'cold moon and the earth' form the 'top' and the 'bottom' of the play's world. The moon is experienced as both confine and influence. So fixed is it in the Ptolemaic universe that Hermia uses the idea of its dislocation as a rhetorical impossibility:

> ...Would he have stol'n away
> From sleeping Hermia? I'll believe as soon
> This whole earth may be bor'd, and that the moon
> May through the centre creep, and so displease
> Her brother's noon-tide with th'Antipodes.
>
>   (III.ii.51–5)

The extremes of moon and earth are brought into a mutual relation by means of the moon's illumination of the earth and influence over it. As light, the moon picks out and makes visible the world above which she shines:

> Tomorrow night, when Phoebe doth behold
> Her silver visage in the wat'ry glass,
> Decking with liquid pearl the bladed grass
>
>   (I.i.209–11)

Later in the play Titania describes a reciprocation more intimate than that of the purely visual phenomenon that Lysander described:

> The moon, methinks, looks with a watery eye,
> And when she weeps, weeps every little flower,
> Lamenting some enforced chastity.
>
>   (III.i.191–3)

The moon cares about the details she illumines.

The lunar sphere, as well as marking the upper limit of the play's world, exists as a measure of speed:

> Over hill, over dale,
>   Thorough bush, thorough briar,
> Over park, over pale,
>   Thorough flood, thorough fire,
> I do wander everywhere,
> Swifter than the moon's sphere.
>
>   (II.i.2–7)

> We the globe can compass soon,
> Swifter than the wandering moon.
> (IV.i.96−7)[2]

This speed, the speed of thought, the speed of God-imitative souls and the speed of the imagination, is possessed by the fairies who, in a way which is comparable to the soul in Donne's 'Progresse', become vehicles for an imaginative exploration of the world which they inhabit. More importantly, they are causally connected with this world. Like the classical Lars and Penates they exert a very particular influence over the communities which they inhabit. Titania's attendant fairies are, as Bottom is quick to realise, closely associated with minor domestic satisfactions:

Bot.   ...I beseech your worship's name?

Cob.   Cobweb.

Bot.   I shall desire you of more acquaintance, good Master Cobweb: if I cut my finger, I shall make bold with you. Your name, honest gentleman?

Peas. Peaseblossom.

Bot.   I pray you, commend me to Mistress Squash, your mother, and to Master Peascod, your father. Good Master Peaseblossom, I shall desire you of more acquaintance too. Your name, I beseech you sir?

Mus.   Mustardseed.

Bot.   Good Master Mustardseed, I know your patience well. That same cowardly giant-like ox-beef hath devoured many a gentleman of your house: I promise you, your kindred hath made my eyes water ere now. I desire you of more acquaintance, good Master Mustardseed.

> (III.i.171−89)

Puck, no less connected with material particulars, is, as practical joker, the explanatory source of minor domestic upsets. It is he:

> That frights the maidens of the villagery,
> Skim[s] milk, and sometimes labour[s] in the quern,
> And bootles make[s] the breathless housewife churn,
> And sometime make[s] the drink to bear no barm,
> (II.i.35−8)

Later in this scene, the first scene in which fairies have been encountered, Titania and Oberon extend the realm of explanatory mythologising which the figure of Puck has introduced. The rift between the two is, Titania tells us, the source of aberrant behaviour in the natural world:

> ...never, since the middle summer's spring,
> Met we on hill, in dale, forest or mead,
> By paved fountain, or by rushy brook,

Or in the beached margent of the sea
To dance our ringlets to the whistling wind,
But with thy brawls thou has disturb'd our sport.
Therefore the winds, piping to us in vain,
As in revenge have suck'd up from the sea
Contagious fogs; which, falling in the land,
Hath every pelting river made so proud
That they have overborne their continents.
The ox hath therefore stretch'd his yoke in vain,
The ploughman lost his sweat, and the green corn
Hath rotted ere his youth attain'd a beard;
The fold stands empty in the drowned field,
And crows are fatted with the murrion flock;
The nine-men's-morris is fill'd up with mud,
And the quaint mazes in the wanton green
For lack of tread are undistinguishable.
The human mortals want their winter cheer:
No night is now with hymn or carol blest.
Therefore the moon, the governess of floods,
Pale in her anger, washes all the air,
That rheumatic diseases do abound.
And thorough this distemperature we see
The seasons alter: hoary-headed frosts
Fall in the fresh lap of the crimson rose;
And on old Hiems' thin and icy crown,
An odorous chaplet of sweet summer buds
Is, as in mockery, set; the spring, the summer,
The childing autumn, angry winter, change
Their wonted liveries; and the mazed world,
By their increase, now knows not which is which.
And this same progeny of evils comes
From our debate, from our dissension;
We are their parents and original.

                                    (II.i.82–117)

This poetry, in the Ovidian tradition, presents a densely responsive universe. The plenitude of reference in the last passage imaginatively fills the gap between the play's polarities of earth's surface and lunar sphere. The air is made palpable as wind, visible as moonshine and, in Titania's subsequent account of the Indian mother, fragrant with spice:

... in the spiced Indian air, by night,
Full often hath she gossip'd by my side;
And sat with me on Neptune's yellow sands,
Marking th'embarked traders on the flood:
When we have laugh'd to see the sails conceive

And grow big-bellied with the wanton wind;
Which she, with pretty and with swimming gait
Following (her womb then rich with my young squire),
Would imitate, and sail upon the land
To fetch me trifles, ...

(II.i.124–33)

The pungent, billowing air, sympathetically wanton, is presented with an imaginative hypersensitivity which responds to the almost imperceptible. The fairy world provides the imagination with vehicles with which to see and feel more minutely; it also, in revealing the extent of its control and concern, reinjects the natural world with intentionality.

There is a decorum involved in the difference in the poetry spoken by the fairy king and queen and that which is spoken by their servants. Whilst both rulers and subjects identify themselves with the natural world, the poetry of Titania and Oberon is wider in scope and more general in reference than that of the subject-fairies who identify themselves with a world of minute particulars. Whilst Titania refers to the consequences of her rift with Oberon in the large terms of seasonal disruption and crop failure, the fairies respond to this rift by a retreat into the minute:

And now they never meet in grove or green,
By fountain clear, or spangled starlight sheen,
But they do square; that all the elves for fear
Creep into acorn-cups, and hide them there.

(II.i.28–31)

The subject-fairies look after the details of the natural world. They decorate it:

And I serve the Fairy Queen,
To dew her orbs upon the green.
The cowslips tall her pensioners be,
In their gold coats spots you see;
Those be rubies, fairy favours,
In those freckles live their savours.
I must go seek some dew-drops here,
And hang a pearl in every cowslip's ear.

(II.i.8–15)

Other small occupants of the natural world they oppose:

You spotted snakes with double tongue,
Thorny hedgehogs, be not seen;
Newts and blind-worms, do no wrong,
Come not near our fairy queen.

> *Weaving spiders, come not here;*
> *Hence, you long-legg'd spinners, hence!*
> *Beetles black, approach not near;*
> *Worm nor snail, do no offence.*
>   (II.ii.9–12; 19–22)

While the fairies clearly regard the minute and the physically low as worthy of attention, they distinguish between small things which are benign and those which are not. When Oberon arrives immediately after the departure of the lullabying fairies, the spell he casts, though decorously referring to larger creatures than those mentioned in the lullaby, clearly undoes any charm that the lullaby has effected. The creatures mentioned in the lullaby are tacitly added to his own catalogue of what is 'vile':

> What thou seest when thou dost wake,
> Do it for thy true love take;
> Love and languish for his sake.
> Be it ounce, or cat, or bear,
> Pard, or boar with bristled hair,
> In thy eye that shall appear
> When thou wak'st, it is thy dear.
> Wake when some vile thing is near.
>   (II.ii.26–33)

The 'vile thing' that is near when Titania awakes is Bottom the weaver with the head of an ass.

Just as the play's imaginative topography, stretching between 'the cold moon and the earth', is one with a definite top and a definite bottom, so is the society of the Athenians clearly structured on a vertical scale with Theseus and Hippolyta at the top, Bottom and the other mechanicals at the bottom. The first act of the play introduces us to the Athenians in descending order of rank. And with the descent in social status comes a corresponding increase in the particularity of linguistic reference. The mechanicals, as their names as well as their occupations proclaim, belong to and work with the material world. Their attachment to matter is the source of comedy when it comes to the staging of *Pyramus and Thisbe*, for they demand a material representation of everything to which that play refers. Though the moon's maddening light has saturated the larger play and been felt as a continuous presence through the suggestions of language rather than stage props, the mechanicals see the need to cast Starveling in the part of Moonshine, *'with lantern, dog, and bush of thorn'* (V.i. 134). But while the mechanicals' attachment to material things is the source of comedy at their expense, it is also the source of their strength. What they have between them, as carpenter, weaver, bellows-mender, tinker, joiner and tailor, is a basic knowledge of how things work, how they fit together.

This knowledge, which the more elevated mortals lack, is what links the mechanicals, socially at the bottom of the hierarchy, with the fairies, and in particular with the servant-fairies who inhabit the ground and know about what goes on there. The names—Peaseblossom, Cobweb, Moth and Mustardseed—identify the fairies as much with real things—albeit natural and delicate ones—as do the names of the mechanicals. Both mechanicals and fairies work with and through things and it is this shared knowledge of how the world works and is put together that is the source of Bottom's serene accommodation of his marvellous encounter.

Of course the whole point of this encounter, in terms of plot and stage spectacle, lies in the contrast between Bottom's 'mortal grossness' (III.i. 153) and the delicacy of the fairies. It is on the basis of this contrast that Bottom is used as an instrument in the humiliation of Titania. Bottom's own transformation emphasises rather than contrasts with his original nature. Puck does not give Bottom the ass's head out of an entirely arbitrary malice, for the head in some sense reveals or underlines Bottom's nature. In disenchanting Bottom, Puck admits to an element of tautology in the initial enchantment: 'when thou waks't, with thine own fool's eyes peep' (IV.i.83). Bottom is both the most and the least changed of all the play's enchanted creatures. While Titania and the Athenian lovers have had their sight and their understanding changed by the juice of Love-in-Idleness, Bottom, the only one to undergo an ostensible (to everyone else) transformation, retains his own eyes and his own mind.

In a play so preoccupied with love, its rationality and its craziness, the transformation of one of the characters into the form of a beast would suggest that we are being shown love's bestial, carnal face. This is how Jan Kott understands it:

> The slender, tender and lyrical Titania longs for animal love. Puck and Oberon call the transformed Bottom a monster. The frail and sweet Titania drags the monster to bed, almost by force. This is the lover she wanted and dreamed of.[3]

On waking, her repudiation of her love—'O how mine eyes do loathe his visage now!' (IV.i.78)—has all the energy of Freudian *Verneinung*. Oberon, who has caused Titania to 'dote' upon the ass-headed Bottom out of spite, releases her from her delusion out of 'pity'. To Oberon, as to Titania, such love is a humiliation, a degradation. The mystery which Titania asks Oberon to unravel as she takes to the air again, is of how she came to be so debased, both in location and activity:

> Come my lord, and in our flight
> Tell me how it came this night
> That I sleeping here was found
> With these mortals on the ground.
> (IV.i.98–101)

Helena's words—'Things base and vile, holding no quantity,/ Love can transpose to form and dignity' (I.i.232–3)—could be heard as describing love's glory or its degradation. Whichever it is, Titania in her brief love for Bottom (whom Oberon's spell has identified as 'some vile thing') has exemplified Helena's sentence.

Bottom is clearly right when he says that 'reason and love keep little company together nowadays' (III.i.138–9). One of the most important questions which this play asks is whether the irrationality of love is above reason or below it. I think we are also made to consider whether the terms 'above' and 'below' have any absolute value.

Titania and the Athenian lovers repudiate, rather than learn from, their period of irrational dotage. The Athenians, who have been degraded into cruelty, are led to dismiss their period of enchantment and to think of it as *mere* dream:

> When they next wake, all this derision
> Shall seem a dream and fruitless vision;
> (III.ii.370–1)

Full of wonder, but also of relief, the awakened Athenians recount their 'dreams' to Theseus and Hippolyta. There is a lot of flesh-pinching to ensure that they are now awake, and awe at the strangeness of their recent experience, but, by the beginning of act V, their dreaming has served its function of sorting out rightful from wrongful lovers and can be relegated to what is safely past. Titania's dream is similarly both aberrant and functional. The function is to distract her attention and affections so that Oberon may prise away her Indian boy, and also—a related function—to chastise her through ridicule. Bottom's 'dream' (which was in fact no dream; he lay broad waking, unblinded by Love-in-Idleness) has a function as a component in Titania's chastisement, but, unlike the 'dreams' of Titania and the Athenian lovers, has no obvious function in relation to Bottom. He does not have to be moved from one position to another by the experience; there is no problem which only the licensed confusion of a dream could unravel for him.

Oberon seems to wish upon Bottom a dismissiveness about his night's experience like that expressed by Titania and the other Athenians:

> . . . gentle Puck, take this transformed scalp
> From off the head of this Athenian swain,
> That he awaking when the other do,
> May all to Athens back again repair,
> And think no more of this night's accidents
> But as the fierce vexation of a dream.
> (IV.i.63–8)

So it is all the more remarkable that Bottom's response to his 'dream' is the fullest, most wondering and most appreciative of all the responses recorded in the sequence of awakenings in act IV, scene i. It is true that, unlike the four lovers who have been degraded into cruelty, and unlike Titania who has loved what she would normally loathe, Bottom has no cause to regret any part of his behaviour whilst under the influence of Puck's spell. For all his 'mortal grossness', Bottom transformed has behaved with both dignity and courtesy.

Bottom's words on 'awaking' clearly bear some relation to *1 Corinthians* ii, 9–13:

> But as it is written, The things which the eye hathe not sene, nether eare hathe heard, nether came into mans heart, are, which God hathe prepared for them that loue him./ But God hath reueiled *them* vnto vs by his Spirit: for the Spirit searcheth all things, yea the deepe things of God./ . . . / Now we haue receiued not the Spirit of the worlde, but the Spirit, which is of God, that we might knowe the things that are giuen to vs of God./ Which things also we speake, not in the wordes which mans wisdome teacheth, but which the holie Gost teacheth, comparing spiritual things with spiritual things.

Frank Kermode calls Bottom's words a 'parody' of this Biblical passage.[4] But 'parody' assumes a less dignified relationship with the source than is suggested by Bottom's modest wonder:

> I have had a most rare vision. I have had a dream, past the wit of man to say what dream it was. Man is but an ass if he go about to expound this dream. Methought I was—there is no man can tell what. Methought I was—and methought I had—but man is but a patched fool if he will offer to say what methought I had. The eye of man hath not heard, the ear of man hath not seen, man's hand is not able to taste, his tongue to conceive, nor his heart to report, what my dream was. I will get Peter Quince to write a ballad of this dream: it shall be called 'Bottom's Dream', because it hath no bottom.
>
> (IV.i.203–215)

In many ways Bottom, with his 'misassignment of sense-experience',[5] out-Pauls Paul and improves upon his original by demonstrating, and not just telling us about, the sense-confounding nature of divine revelation.

The source of Bottom's wonder is that he has been loved. He has been utterly and irrationally cherished and has been given attendants—Peaseblossom, Cobweb and Mustardseed—inhabitants of the natural world whom Providence has stored for the service of man. George Herbert in his 'Providence', catalogues some of the innumerable particulars which, far from being beneath, manifest the attention of an ubiquitous God. Providence is:

> . . . in small things great, not small in any:
> Thy even praise can neither rise, nor fall,
> Thou art in all things one, in each thing many:
> For thou art infinite in one and all.

. . . .
How harsh are thorns to pears! and yet they make
A better hedge, and need lesse reparation.
How smooth are silks compared with a stake,
Or with a stone! Yet make no good foundation.

Sometimes thou dost divide thy gifts to man,
Sometimes unite. The Indian nut alone
Is clothing, meat and trencher, drink and can,
Boat, cable, sail and needle, all in one.
                    (ll.41–44; 121–128)

That last stanza evokes the new world of the 'Bermuda pamphlets' and *The Tempest*—texts that refer to the workings of Providence as such. I will come back to *The Tempest*. It is a play which develops and manifests many of the ideas which are latent in *A Midsummer Night's Dream* and which, for related reasons, includes the same kind of particularising natural poetry as the earlier play.

I don't want to overfreight these plays with biblical allusions; *A Midsummer Night's Dream* does not invite us to think about Providence in the way that *The Tempest* certainly does. But the relation between Bottom's speech and 1 Corinthians ii.9 is secure and, having been pointed in this direction, one finds more in this epistle to bring to the play. Helena's words—'Things base and vile, holding no quantity,/ Love can transpose to form and dignity'—seem almost as close to 1 Corinthians as Bottom's speech:

For the foolishnes of God is wiser then men, and the weakenes of God is stronger then men./ For brethren, you se your calling, how that not manie wise men after the flesh, not manie mightie, not manie noble *are called*./ But God hathe chosen the foolish things of the worlde, to confounde the wise, and God hathe chosen the weake things of the worlde, to confounde the mightie things./ And vile things of the world & things which are despised, hathe God chosen, & things which are not, to bring to noght things that are.

(1 Corinthians i.25–28)

What allies the 'foolishnes of God' as Paul describes it, with God's providential concern is the way in which the one values and the other works through the 'vile things of the world, & things which are despised'. Herbert's poem makes the point that even the unpleasant and the unlovely have their uses: thorns, stakes and stones are as good and necessary as pears and silk. Providence works through the vile and the 'foolishnes of God' led to the incarnation of God's son, not as the child of a prince but of a carpenter. This is the divinity who, to quote Tesauro again, 'dwells in the marshes and in the stars, and from the most sordid made the most divine of corporeal creatures.' While the image of Bottom with the ass's head makes Jan Kott think of the dark bestiality of Goya's *Caprichos*,[6] it might be more appropriate, and less anachronistic, to think of the ox and ass of the nativity tableaux in the mystery cycles.

Tesauro, writing about fifty years after the composition of *A Midsummer Night's Dream*, discovers in the Divinity's transforming attention to the sordid a vindication of a poetic method which ignores hierarchical decorum in its ability to range between mutually illuminating antitheses. In *A Midsummer Night's Dream* an imaginative range is both matched and permitted by a theologically derived moral perspective which values what is, in other systems considered 'base and vile'. The word 'base' implies both moral stature and physical location. The same is true of Bottom's name. In this play Bottom, socially, constitutionally, and by virtue of his name, the lowest and heaviest creature on the stage, is given the greatest and most gracious revelation. Since his 'dream' has no function in relation to himself—it is only a component in the manoeuvring of Titania—its reverberations are not circumscribed. While the other dreamers carry the effects of their dreaming into the notional future beyond the play, it is only Bottom who carries the incorporated experience of his dream into the future. While the other objects of enchantment—Titania and the Athenian lovers—are perplexed by the oddity of their dream experiences, it is only Bottom who responds with a sense of joyful wonder. Given the evocation of 1 Corinthians in Bottom's waking words and in Helena's earlier sentence, it would seem that what Bottom is responding to, with due and delighted humility, is a revelation of divine love. Titania may be the agent (and one who, on waking, doesn't much value the role), but the absolute and careful love which Bottom experiences, at a time when he is looking more than usually ludicrous in the eyes of mortals who believe in the dignity of their own form, is a version and token of divine love: 'And vile things of the world & things which are despised, hathe God chosen'.

This accordance of dignity to the low and solid is obliquely connected with the licence to imaginative range which the figures of the fairies provide. The fairies, in their capacity to fly with the speed of thought, are elementally constituted as air and fire—the ascending elements which Cleopatra retains, discarding the other two, on her entry into a wholly imaginative realm. Cicero's discussion of the nature and durability of the soul in the *Tusculan Disputations*, involves a description of the elements and their motions:

> ...we do not doubt that the nature of the four elements from which all things are begotten is such that, as though their laws of motion were mutually apportioned and divided, the earthy and the moist are carried perpendicularly into land and sea by their own tendency and weight, while the two remaining parts, one fiery, the other airy, precisely as the two first-mentioned are carried into the centre of the universe by

heaviness and weight, so the last two on the contrary fly vertically upward into the heavenly region, whether this be due to an upward tendency inherent in their nature, or because bodies naturally lighter are driven away from heavier bodies. And since these facts are established it ought to be clear that souls, on quitting the body, whether they are airy, that is to say, of the nature of breath, or fiery, are carried aloft . . . such a soul necessarily strives to reach higher regions; for the two lighter classes have no downward tendency and always seek the heights. Consequently if souls are dispersed in space, this takes place at a distance from the earth; if they survive and preserve their quality, all the more reason for their being carried to heaven and breaking their way through and parting asunder our dense and compact air which is nearest to earth; for the soul is hotter or, preferably, more glowing than our air which I just now described as dense and compact; and this may be known from the fact that our bodies, which are fashioned from the earthy class of elements, are heated by the glow of the soul.[7]

Titania, in promising to 'purge [Bottom's] mortal grossness so,/ That [he shall] like an airy spirit go' (III.i.153–4), is promising to convert his predominantly earthy constitution into one of fire and air. If *A Midsummer Night's Dream* were an allegorical play then one might read the striking tableau of Titania embracing Bottom as signifying the harmonious balance of the four elements.

There are two, connected, kinds of 'low'-ness in this play. There is social lowness, the bottom of the social scale where Bottom and his companions belong; and there is physical lowness—the height at which cowslips seem 'tall', the ground level which the fairies inhabit. Although so unlike in size and elemental constitution, it is appropriate that these two kinds of low life should come into contact with each other. It is appropriate not by means of a pun on lowness, but because they are the two parties in the play most implicated in the material world.

It is through the particulars of the material world that divine Providence works and, while the agility of the fairies, like that of the fleas, souls and sparrows discussed in the previous chapter, becomes a vehicle for the imagination of the poet that follows them, the concepts of divine Providence and of the holy foolishness that exalts the low, enrich the newly visible objects with significance. Bottom's dream, the suggestion that he is cherished, is therefore closely connected with the remarkable, and remarked-upon, delicacy of natural description which is to be found in this play. Hazlitt, having quoted Bottom's words to Cobweb—'good mounsieur, get you your weapons in your hand, and kill me a red-hipped humble-bee on the top of a thistle; and good mounsieur, bring me the honey-bag'—exclaims, 'What an exact knowledge is here shown of natural history!'.[8] This may be so—though I think it would be a mistake to make too much of 'Shakespeare the naturalist'—but the fact that this play should give an impression of such an 'exact knowledge' at a time when most poets would have turned to a pastoral vocabulary, is more surprising than Hazlitt's exclamation registers. In the course of their dialogue of mutual accusation, Titania reminds Oberon of the times:

> When thou hast stol'n away from fairy land,
> And in the shape of Corin, sat all day
> Playing on pipes of corn, and versing love
> To amorous Phillida.
>
> (II.i.65–8)

Titania reminds us of the pastoral idiom which Shakespeare might have used, and which he does use elsewhere. But it is not the idiom of fairy land which is, necessarily, an idiom of particularity.

The concepts of divine Providence and holy foolishness extend beyond evaluation of the creatures through whom and for whose sake they work. Both mortals and fairies have a clear sense that some things are 'vile'. For the fairies those creatures warded off in the lullaby to Titania are 'vile'; so are the larger creatures whom Oberon mentions: 'Be it ounce, or cat, or bear,/ Pard, or boar with bristled hair' (II.ii.29–30). Lysander, blinded by Love-in-Idleness into a love of Helena and a repudiation of his love for Hermia, tells Hermia to

> Hang off, thou cat, thou burr! Vile thing, let loose,
> Or I will shake thee from me like a serpent.
>
> (III.ii.260–1)

Later he adds insult to insult by comparing her to the physically base, though not particularly vile:

> Get you gone, you dwarf;
> You minimus, of hindering knot-grass made;
> You bead, you acorn.
>
> (III.ii.328–30)

Hermia feels she is being taunted about her stature—''"Little" again? Nothing but "low" and "little"?' (III.ii.326). The (confused) references to the different heights of Rosalind and Celia in *As You Like It* make it clear that two of the boy/female leads in the King's Men were of markedly different build. In making so much of this difference in *A Midsummer Night's Dream* Shakespeare accommodates it into a conceptual framework as yet another example of the apparent opposition between high and low. Lysander's taunts exemplify the identification of the low with the 'vile' but, when he has been disenchanted and his love for Hermia is restored, that identification no longer holds. Hermia remains low but is no longer held to be a 'vile thing'. Lysander's renewed love for Hermia brings with it some kind of recognition that the low is as good as the high.

This is a play in which antitheses are reconciled. The 'tedious-brief'

tragedy of Pyramus and Thisbe is the source of comedy. The reversals—
from love to hate, from hate to love—which Love-in-Idleness so frighten-
ingly induces testify to the close bond that unites antitheses, so that
extreme opposites have more in common with each other than interven-
ing states: black and white are more closely associated with each other
than with grey. The descent into darkness and madness when the lovers
are 'wood' and 'wooed' within the wood involves an encounter with this
fact—a recognition of the close bond between love and hate. The 'gentle
concord' (IV.i.142) which is achieved is one which has assimilated and
passed through discord. The 'musical...discord' (IV.i.117) of the Spar-
tan hounds recalled by Hippolyta is a harmony in which threat is con-
tained. Actaeon's fate—the price of revelation—is never mentioned in
this play but, with Diana so much in evidence, it cannot be forgotten.

Antitheses are reconciled, not destroyed; that reconciliation demands
an accommodation and an acceptance of what might otherwise be consid-
ered the 'bad' side of a pair of opposites. To quote Herbert's 'Providence'
again:

> Ev'n poysons praise thee. Should a thing be lost?
> Should creatures want for want of heed their due?
> Since where are poysons, antidotes are most:
> The help stands close, and keeps the fear in view.
>
>   (ll.85–8)

The belief that some things are, morally as well as physically, 'base and
vile', is one held by many of the characters in *A Midsummer Night's
Dream*. But the play as a whole, its structure and its poetry, suggest a
different way of seeing and understanding. Creatures which had custom-
arily wanted 'for want of heed their due' in poetry, are here dignified with
a particularising, and not conventionally pastoral, reference. The atten-
tion bestowed upon the socially and constitutionally low and earthy char-
acter of Bottom is very intimately connected with the quality of the poetry
associated with the fairies—with the 'exact knowledge of natural history'
which is considered worth showing. Bottom's 'bottomless' dream also
suggests that revelation isn't always the privilege of the 'high'. The
play's topographical polarities of moon and earth are seen as possibly
reversible, since the restrictions which govern the sublunary world are
passed as easily through descent as through ascent. Bottom has had some
intuition of the divine, not through ascent but, as it were, through the
bottom of the world.

The providential attention to detail which is imaged in Bottom's
encounter with the fairies emerges more conspicuously as a governing
concept in *The Tempest*. Prospero tells Miranda that they landed safely
on the island 'By Providence divine' (I.ii.159).[9] Ferdinand attributes his
encounter with and betrothal to Miranda to 'immortal Providence' (V.i.
189). Providential texts are recalled: in particular the account of the

'tempest' in Acts xxvii which occurred during Paul's crossing of the Mediterranean.[10] Despite the apparent danger, Paul recognises an ulti-mately benign control. He encourages the others on the boat to break their fast: 'for this is for your sauegarde: for there shal not an heere fall from the head of anie of you' (xxvii.34). Prospero, as he wrecks and saves the voyagers, mimics the work of divine Providence:

> The direful spectacle of the wrack...
>
> .   .   .   .
>
> I have with such provision in mine Art
> So safely ordered, that there is no soul—
> No, not so much perdition as an hair
> Betid to any creature in the vessel
> Which thou heard'st cry, which thou saw'st sink.
>
> (I.ii.26–32)

Later in the scene Ariel confirms that the shipwrecked voyagers are safe: 'Not a hair perish'd' (I.ii.217). Providence's attention to details as appar-ently insignificant as hairs is confirmed in Matthew x:

> Are not two sparrowes solde for a farthing, and one of them shal not fall on the ground without your Father?/ Yea, and all the heeres on your heade are nombrd.
>
> (ll.29–30)

The Bermuda pamphlets which lie behind many of the details of *The Tempest* laid considerable emphasis upon the role of divine Providence in the preservation of the voyagers.[11] This Providence manifests itself chiefly through timely provision. What it provides and what it attends to may be minute particulars.

Jan Kott, writing about the mythical structures that are present in *The Tempest*, says that in all voyage literature

> we always find this fundamental opposition between the new language of experience, which has a demystifying function, and the rhetoric of Scripture and of classical authors, which finally compose the providen-tial theology of the voyages to the west.[12]

What he does not take into account here is the way in which the theolog-ical concept of Providence provided a conventional and orthodox framework which was able to accommodate the particulars of the new discoveries. Because of its notorious attention to detail, the concept of divine Provi-dence could offer at least a temporary shelter to 'the new language of experience.'

In *A Midsummer Night's Dream* it was principally the mobile fairies who acted as imaginative vehicles for the sight and particularising of a world usually unregarded. The four elements that are emblematically united in Titania's embrace of Bottom are clearly portioned between the protagonists of *The Tempest*. Caliban, addressed by Prospero as 'Thou earth' (i.ii.316), is associated with the heavy, descending elements. In contrast, Ariel ('a spirit too delicate/ To act [the] earthy and abhorr'd commands' of Caliban's mother Sycorax (I.ii.272–3)), though capable of moving through all the elements, is predominantly associated with the ascending elements of air and fire.[13] He recalls Puck in his ability to shift shapes, and in his swift, delicate agility.[14] His song, '*Where the bee sucks, there suck I*' (V.i.88–94), recalls the poetry associated with the fairies in *A Midsummer Night's Dream*: the natural world is shown on a different scale. But the poetry most remarkable for its particularity in *The Tempest* is not that of Ariel, whose agility enables such exploration, but Caliban's, Ariel's earthy antithesis. Caliban asserts a prior claim to the island in a language which reveals his intimacy with it. The language was the gift of Prospero but the knowledge is Caliban's own:

> This island's mine, by Sycorax my mother,
> Which thou tak'st from me. When thou cam'st first,
> Thou strok'st me and made much of me; wouldst give me
> Water with berries in 't; and teach me how
> To name the bigger light, and how the less,
> That burn by day and night: and then I lov'd thee,
> And show'd thee all the qualities o' th' isle,
> The fresh springs, brine-pits, barren place and fertile:
> Curs'd be I that did so!
>
> > (I.ii.333–41)

The information which Caliban gives Prospero, showing him 'all the qualities o' th' isle', is of the kind which the Bermuda pamphleteers would have attributed to Providence. It is Caliban's generosity to show and, in his capacity to do this he reveals that in one sense the island is more his own than it will ever be his coloniser Prospero's. To Trinculo he says:

> I'll show thee the best springs; I'll pluck thee berries;
> I'll fish for thee, and get thee wood enough.
>
> .   .   .   .
>
> I prithee, let me bring thee where crabs grow;
> And I with my long nails will dig thee pig-nuts;
> Show thee a jay's nest, and instruct thee how
> To snare the nimble marmoset; I'll bring thee
> To clustering filberts, and sometimes I'll get thee
> Young scamels from the rock.
>
> > (II.ii.160–1; 167–72)

Caliban's long nails, like the stakes and thorns that Herbert mentions in his 'Providence', have their good uses. This is 'the new language of experience' which delights in the resources of the natural world.

Prospero continues to mimic the workings of divine Providence when he imposes a period of suffering on Ferdinand; and he shows that he has learned from Caliban to distinguish the good and bad amongst the island's natural resources. He prescribes only the bad for Ferdinand:

> Sea-water shalt thou drink; thy food shall be
> The fresh-brook mussels, wither'd roots, and husks
> Wherein the acorn cradled.
>
> (I.ii.465−7)

The poetry and structure of *A Midsummer Night's Dream* should, I think, qualify any preconceptions about what are, physically and morally, base and vile. So too in *The Tempest*; Ferdinand has the right attitude towards his suffering:

> There be some sports are painful, and their labour
> Delight in them sets off: some kinds of baseness
> Are nobly undergone; and most poor matters
> Point to rich ends.
>
> (III.i.1−4)

Caliban, though hated, is as necessary to Prospero as his other, loved, servant:

> We cannot miss him: he does make our fire,
> Fetch in our wood, and serves in offices
> That profit us.
>
> (I.ii.313−15)

But while Prospero manifests a grudging acceptance of the lower nature represented by Caliban—'this thing of darkness I/ Acknowledge mine'[15] —(V.i.275−6) the intricate detail of Caliban's reference, the exploratory energy of his speeches, show a more generous accommodation of Caliban's earthy nature on Shakespeare's part. The imaginative energy with which Bottom, in his encounter with the fairies, was juxtaposed, is assimilated by Caliban as his own. Ariel may be the more mobile but Caliban is the more observant.

Behind *A Midsummer Night's Dream* and *The Tempest*—plays whose spritely participants allow a new mobility and range to the imaginative eye that travels with them—lie biblical passages which support the cherishing of particularity which is so remarkable a feature of these plays' poetry. It is a new kind of poetry, attentive to the minutiae of natural life at earth and sea level. The representation of the imagination's powers of speed and lightness in the form of swift sprites has produced a poetry which explores and at the same time values creatures whose elemental constitutions would seem most antithetical to the fiery and airy imagination: Bottom and Caliban for example.

Chapter 7

ANDREW MARVELL

The Language of Restoration

In *A Midsummer Night's Dream* and *The Tempest* an extension of imaginative range, as evinced by a more particularising poetry, coincides with an extension of moral sympathy. Several of the works already looked at suggest an increasing identification of right understanding with clear observation of the material world. Language is the point at which meaning and matter intersect and Andrew Marvell seems to have been particularly conscious of this fact. The characteristic direction of his wit is of bringing together and seeming to reconcile a material with an interpretative dimension. This creates the impression of a world in which matter is invested with significance as well as with bulk and, correspondingly, of a language which has a natural, as opposed to an arbitrary connection with the world to which it refers. Such a language—a language which would communicate the nature of the things it named—was believed to have been spoken by Adam in Eden and it was the endeavour of several late Renaissance philologists to discover this original language.[1] Marvell's own use of language, in conjunction with his many pastoral settings, wittily suggests a status that is natural rather than arbitrary. Two poems which I shall look at in detail—'Bermudas' and 'The Garden'—present paradisal worlds and it is, I shall be arguing, a large part of Marvell's art to present his poems as acts of restoration.

But first I should like to look at 'Fleckno, *an English Priest at Rome*' (the play on 'room' still operating). This poem works by means of a witty obtuseness which denies the existence of any dimension other than the material. That matter is mere stuff—unredeemed by meaning—and is as such the fearful antithesis of the world which Marvell's poetry more often seeks to restore—a world whose matter sings its meaning.

Jokes about the materiality of literature—about its status as so much ink and paper—were not new. Martial and Catullus had made them. But they became conspicuously frequent in late seventeenth- and early eighteenth-century England.[2] The main force of these jokes is, like that of the figured poems, to foil the relative immateriality of language and its effects. But, with literature a low-priced commodity on Grub Street, there is an edge of fear to these later playings which distinguished them from earlier flauntings of imaginative incorporeality.

The material hardship suffered by the producers of literary works draws attention to the material, quantitative nature of the product. Jonson, resentfully and painfully dependent upon patronage, recognises that his imagination's independence of material restrictions—something he delightedly celebrates—is in fact dependent upon a degree of material prosperity which can release the mind from corporeal preoccupations. This he acknowledges in his 'Epistle Mendicant' to the Lord High Treasurer:

MY LORD:

Poore wretched states, prest by extremities,
Are faine to seeke for succours, and supplies
Of *Princes* aides, or *good mens* Charities.

Disease, the Enemie, and his Ingineeres,
Want, with the rest of his conceal'd compeeres,
Have cast a trench about mee, now, five yeares;

And made those strong approaches, by *False braies*,
Reduicts, *Halfe-moones*, *Horne-workes*, and such close wayes,
The Muse not peepes out, one of hundred dayes;

But lyes block'd up, and straightned, narrow'd in,
Fix'd to the bed, and boords, unlike to win
Health, or scarce breath, as she had never bin,

Unlesse some saving-*Honour* of the *Crowne*,
Dare think it, to relieve, no less renowne,
A *Bed-rid* Wit, then a *beseiged* Towne.

In *Timber* Jonson laments the poor taste of his age:

when wee shall heare those things commended, and cry'd up for the best writings, which a man would scarce vouchsafe, to wrap any wholesome drug in; hee would never light his *Tobacco* with them.[3]

But penury, and the marketing of literature as a commodity (which patronage only thinly disguises), has the effect of metamorphosing all literature into material quantities such as those for which it is exchanged.

In 'Fleckno, *an English Priest at Rome*', Marvell, whose poetry had never been his livelihood, combines a Puritan's attack on Catholic materialism with a gentleman's scorn for the commodity turned out by the literary hack. In the world of this peom, material is absolute. While quick shifts from corporeal to conceptual perception are demanded of the reader, the whole poem testifies to the intransigence of matter. For Donne, in 'The good-morrow', the magnanimity of love can make 'one little roome, an every where', but the only hope that Fleckno has of expanding his exiguous lodgings lies in exploiting a pun:

> And though within one Cell so narrow pent,
> He'd *Stanza's* for a whole Appartement.
>
> (ll.17–18)

And while Donne's comparable pun in 'The Canonization'—'We'll build in sonnets pretty roomes'—emphasises poetry's release from spatial restriction, this pun pulls us back to the confining materiality of Fleckno's leaden stanzas.

Within the material world there can be no coexistence—the rigidity of matter delimits possibility:

> Nature that hateth emptiness,
> Allows of penetration less:
> ('An Horatian Ode',
> ll.40–1)

The antithesis between Fleckno's 'suttle Body' (l.67) and his very solid poems has a geometric logic and inevitability. While it may be true that the real turgidity of his poetry is the cause of his poverty and undernourishment, it also seems right that when the poetry becomes too bulky, the poet's own body should be whittled away. Something has to make room.

The solidity of Fleckno's poetry is matched by the unyielding contours of his lodgings. In the sustained misunderstanding of the following passage, metaphor is confounded with substantial fact:

> I meet one on the Stairs who made me stand,
> Stopping the passage, and did him demand:
> I answer'd he is here *Sir*; but you see
> You cannot pass to him but thorow me.
> He thought himself affronted; and reply'd,
> I whom the Pallace never has deny'd
> Will make the way here; I said *Sir* you'l do
> Me a great favour, for I seek to go.
> He gathring fury still made sign to draw;
> But himself there clos'd in a Scabbard saw
> As narrow as his Sword's; and I, that was
> Delightful, said there can no Body pass
> Except by penetration hither, where
> Two make a crowd, nor can three Persons here
> Consist but in one substance.
>
> (ll.87–101)

Language is motivated perforce by this contact with reality:

> ...I said, the place doth us invite
> By its own narrowness, Sir, to unite.
> He ask'd me pardon;...
>
> .   .   .   .

> ...the propitiatory Priest had straight
> Oblig'd us, when below, to celebrate
> Together our attonement:...
> (ll.103–5; 107–9)

'Unite' and 'attonement' have acquired a literal force.

In this poem the gentleman poet who can afford to keep his work 'poetic' combines his ridicule of the hack's productions with a jibe at the Catholic priest's dependence upon externals. Marvell invites the hungry Fleckno to eat and break his pre-Mass fast:

> I ask'd if he eat flesh. And he, that was
> So hungry that though ready to say *Mass*
> Would break his fast before, said he was Sick,
> And th' *Ordinance* was only Politick.
> Nor was I longer to invite him Scant:
> Happy at once to make him Protestant,
> And Silent. Nothing now Dinner stay'd
> But till he had himself a Body made.
> I mean till he were drest: for else so thin
> He stands, as if he only fed had been
> With consecrated Wafers: and the *Host*
> Hath sure more flesh and blood then he can boast.
> (ll.51–62)

This literal understanding of Transubstantiation (with the hint of cannibalism in line 51) is complemented by Marvell's own version of the Trinity as three men stuck in a stairway.

The tyranny of the corporeal in this poem is that of a nightmare world emptied of spirit. It is a poem that anticipates the fearful comedy of *The Dunciad*. The spiritual and the material cannot be identified in the world of 'Fleckno' and the reconciliations that Marvell's puns effect in this poem proclaim themselves to be fallacious.

The puns in 'Fleckno', in their deliberate heavy-handedness, do not have what Empson has called the 'tact' of Marvell's puns.[4] Elsewhere in his work Marvell produces puns which do not strain into conflicting areas so much as unobtrusively affirm a reconciliation. In stanza LXXIII of 'Upon Appleton House', the phrase 'light *Mosaick*' precisely captures the dappling shadows of leaves under sunlight. And it is this precision which defuses and quietens a potentially outrageous allusion to the Pentateuch:

> Out of these scatter'd *Sibyls* Leaves
> Strange *Prophecies* my Phancy weaves:
> And in one History consumes,
> Like *Mexique Paintings*, all the *Plumes*.
> What *Rome*, *Greece*, *Palestine*, ere said

I in this light *Mosaick* read.
Thrice happy he who, not mistook,
Hath read in *Natures mystick Book*.

(ll.577–84)

The wit of this pun consists in an apparent restoration of meaning. Classical and Old Testament prophecy are conflated, and history is gathered back into a pastoral timelessness as the leaves on the trees, both Sybilline and Mosaic, are found to contain all knowledge.

The visual precision of 'light Mosaick' is a vital part of Marvell's pun. His language seems to be moving towards a reidentification of the conceptual with the material: right vision is inextricable from right understanding. In 'On a Drop of Dew' the 'naturalistic' precision and clarity of the image is essential for the understanding derived from it:

See how the Orient Dew,
Shed from the Bosom of the Morn
    Into the blowing Roses,
Yet careless of its Mansion new;
For the clear Region where 'twas born
    Round in its self incloses:
    And in its little Globes Extent,
Frames as it can its native Element.

(ll.1–8)

The drop of dew, whose mirror-like upper hemisphere literally reflects the light of the Eastern sun, 'framing' the image of its native element, is also, in its spherical perfection, its retentive self-sufficiency, and its merely notional point of contact with its 'Mansion new', a metaphor for the heavenly sphere from which it derives. This metaphorical level on which it is an 'image' is endorsed by the dew-drop's literal capacity to re-present the heavens on its mirrored surface. This endorsement of the metaphorical by the literal permits the analogical extension which follows between the drop of dew and the human soul which bears an ideal impression of its heavenly source:

So the Soul, that Drop, that Ray
Of the clear Fountain of Eternal Day,
Could it within the humane flow'r be seen,
    Remembring still its former height,
    Shuns the sweat leaves and blossoms green;
    And, recollecting its own Light,
Does, in its pure and circling thoughts, express
The greater Heaven in an Heaven less.

(ll.19–26)

Memory is here a localised accumulation of the past in the present.

'Recollecting' and 'remembring' are used in their most fully motivated senses. The soul gathers in and reconstitutes its heavenly source in the same way that the natural drop of dew gathers in, to re-present in miniature form, the light of the sun. The word 'express'—both pressing out and excluding, and representing and therefore including—anticipates the poem's final annihilation of the boundaries it has played with, when the image is assimilated into what it has imaged.

The next ten lines, by an ambiguity of pointing, suggest a possible extension of the recollective affinity of the soul with its heavenly source, to the sphere of the Copernican world whose rotation can be seen as an urge towards illumination by the sun:

> In how coy a Figure wound,
> Every way it turns away:
> So the World excluding round,
> Yet receiving in the Day.
> Dark beneath, but bright above:
> Here disdaining, there in Love.
> How loose and easie hence to go:
> How girt and ready to ascend.
> Moving but on a point below,
> It all about does upwards bend.
> (ll. 27–36)

'So the World excluding round' continues the description of the soul which, in its spherical perfection, shuns the world it inhabits. But it also initiates a redemptive extension of the analogy to the world itself which, in its roundness and in its light-seeking movement, demonstrates an affinity with the heavens.

'On a Drop of Dew' is Marvell's most explicitly religious poem. The relations it reveals, endorsed by the reflective qualities of the natural dew-drop, are relations which must culminate in a dissolution of distinctions as heaven re-collects its own. The dissolution is first enacted by the natural drop of dew which evaporates in the warmth of the westward-moving sun:

> Restless it roules and unsecure,
> Trembling lest it grow impure:
> Till the warm Sun pitty it's Pain,
> And to the Skies exhale it back again.
> (ll. 15–18)

The use of 'exhale' rather than the more predictable 'inhale' initiates the blurring of distinctions. The sun reabsorbs the drop of dew, not by suction but by emission. This dissolution of difference as the image is recollected into its source is described in full in the final lines of the poem:

How loose and easie hence to go:
How girt and ready to ascend.
Moving but on a point below,
It all about does upwards bend.
Such did the Manna's sacred Dew destil;
White, and intire, though congeal'd and chill.
Congeal'd on Earth: but does, dissolving, run
Into the Glories of th'Almighty Sun.

(ll.34—40)

In 'On a Drop of Dew' the annihilation of difference is described in the language of fluidity: the subject demands a liquefying dissolution. Almost always elsewhere, however, Marvell presents virtue as firm and compact. The stubborn materiality of Fleckno's world—a world in which matter resists and conquers spirit—has its antithesis in the other world which several of Marvell's poems create. In this world spirit is coextensive with matter; matter is radiantly significant. The way in which a metaphorical meaning is endorsed by one of literal, physical precision in so many of Marvell's poems, is part of a tendency of his language to reidentify the conceptual with the material. In his imaginative universe the density and compactness deriving from the assimilation of meaning into matter is self-evidently good.

'A Dialogue Between the Resolved Soul, and Created Pleasure' is couched in terms of softness versus firmness. The 'resolution' of the soul is the antithesis of dissolution, and its greater firmness is represented in the couplets which it characteristically employs in contrast to Pleasure's more diffuse quatrains. Pleasure offers softness to the soul:

On these downy Pillows lye,
Whose soft Plumes will thither fly:
On these Roses strow'd so plain
Lest one Leaf thy side should strain.

(ll.19—22)

In contrast to this contrived, artificial softness, the soul responds with an image of proper gentleness:

My gentler Rest is on a Thought.
Conscious of doing what I ought.

(ll.23—4)

Pleasure, having been outdone in its own terms of softness, begins to parody the firmness of the resolved soul:

Heark how Musick then prepares
For thy Stay these charming Aires:
Which the posting Winds recall,
And suspend the Rivers Fall.

(ll.36—40)

This temptation is sufficiently great to induce the soul to unclench and expand into a quatrain:

> Had I but any time to lose,
> On this I would it all dispose,
> Cease Tempter. None can chain a mind
> Whom this sweet Chordage cannot bind.
>   (ll.41–44)

But the Medusa-like capacity of Pleasure's music to charm, recall, and suspend is not the restorative power which Marvell's own art emulates. Pleasure merely mimics this true art. The Fall is suspended, not undone.

The kind of music which Marvell approves, and which he emulates in his poetry, is one that does not so much suspend and freeze time as ante-date it. In 'The First Anniversary of the Government under O.C.' Cromwell is compared to Amphion:

> Learning a Musique in the Region clear,
> To tune this lower to that higher Sphere.
>   (ll.47–8)

Proper music, like proper language, will duplicate rather than deviate from a heavenly music which will then reassimilate it, in the way that heaven reabsorbs the drop of dew which reflected it. The firmness and density which Marvell almost always presents as good, derives from such a duplicatory reaffirmation. This is the source of Amphion's constructive firmness:

> So when *Amphion* did the Lute command,
> Which the God gave him, with his gentle hand,
> The rougher Stones, unto his Measures hew'd,
> Dans'd up in order from the Quarreys rude;
> This took a Lower, that an Higher place,
> As he the Treble alter'd, or the Base:
> No Note he struck, but a new Story lay'd,
> And the great Work ascended while he play'd.
>   The listning Structures he with Wonder ey'd,
> And still new Stopps to various Time apply'd:
> Now through the strings a Martial rage he throws,
> And joyning streight the *Theban* Tow'r arose;
> Then as he strokes them with a Touch more sweet,
> The flocking Marbles in a Palace meet;
> But, for he most the graver Notes did try,
> Therefore the Temples rear'd their Columns high:
> Thus, ere he ceas'd, his sacred Lute creates
> Th'harmonious City of the seven Gates.
>   (ll.49–66)

Amphion's musical reconstruction of the walls of Thebes is the positive mythical counterpart of the linguistic and architectural chaos initiated at Babel. As well as providing the terms for this compliment to Cromwell, Amphion's wall-building myth is suggestive of the restorative firmness which Marvell's use of language elsewhere attempts.

*   *   *

All simile affirms a state of division. Empson makes this point very delicately in his essay on Marvell's 'The Garden':

> Any statement of identity between terms already defined ('God is love') is a contradiction because you already know they are not identical ... A vague sense that 'is' has other uses than the expression of identity makes us ready to find meanings in such sentences.[5]

This way in which all simile, any affirmation of similarity and comparability will simultaneously be an affirmation of difference, is something which the peculiar nature, the 'tact' of Marvell's characteristic puns manages in part to conceal. This 'tact' derives, I think, from the way in which they seem not to be reaching out in the direction of difference and diversity so much as gathering that difference in, re-collecting divergent meanings into an original compactness. Often his puns seem to realise conventional meanings by playing upon a meaning that has precise material and local implications: 'upbraid': to reprove by gathering up as in a plait ('The Garden', 1.6); 'imbark': to climb into a tree as if into a boat ('Upon Appleton House', 1.483); 'recollecting': gathering up again ('On a Drop of Dew', 1.24); the 'sweet Chordage' of the music that temptingly threatens to bind the soul ('Dialogue between the Resolved Soul, and Created Pleasure', 1.44); the unvoiced pun on 'reformation' that governs the narrative of the creation of Appleton House from a dissolved convent's ruins. These puns seem to bring us closer to a natural language which has a more than conventional relation to the things it denotes. They do this partly by means of etymological justification and partly by their precise, local and material reference.

At least twice Marvell reminds us of the way in which 'indurance' is connected with hardening and with matter. In 'A Dialogue Between the Soul and Body', spirit is affected by and beginning to take on the attributes of matter. The soul is 'Constrain'd not only to indure/ Diseases, but, whats worse, the Cure' (ll.27–8). In 'Upon Appleton House' he describes the opposite process at work as Fairfax's spirituality mollifies his firm house:

> Yet thus the laden House does sweat,
> And scarce indures the *Master* great:
> But where he comes the swelling Hall
> Stirs, and the *Square* grows *Spherical*;
> More by his *Magnitude* distrest,
> Then he is by its straitness prest:
> And too officiously it slights
> That in it self which him delights
>
> (ll.49–56)

The second part of this complimentary stanza points us back in the direc-
tion in which 'induring', hardening, may after all be good.

The world of mere matter—matter emptied of spirit—is what the poet
Marvell encounters and 'indure[s]' ('Fleckno', l.30) during his visit to
Fleckno; it is what threatens the soul when the body attempts to
take over. But to this reduced mere matter, Marvell's language opposes
significant matter. The kind of hardening of which he approves is towards
an original density in which spirit was coextensive with, not yet divided
from, matter. The 'Reformation' that he desires in 'The Picture of
Little T.C. in a Prospect of Flowers' involves a correcting and straighten-
ing of 'errour' (l.27) by returning Spring to a perfection in which
endurance derives from the assimilation of spiritual perfection into
material form:

> Mean time, whilst every verdant thing
> It self does at thy Beauty charm,
> Reform the errours of the Spring;
> Make that the Tulips may have share
> Of sweetness, seeing they are fair;
> And Roses of their thorns disarm:
>   But most procure
> That Violets may a longer Age endure.
>
> (ll.25–32)

The unfallen world and its natural language were both compact and
firm. Maria Fairfax, so the compliment goes, has a corrective effect upon
nature comparable to that of little T.C.:

> ...by her *Flames*, in *Heaven* try'd,
> *Nature* is wholly *vitrifi'd*.
>
> LXXXVII
> 'Tis *She* that to these Gardens gave
> That wondrous Beauty which they have;
> She streightness on the Woods bestows;
>
> ('Upon Appleton House', ll.687–91)

In 'Upon Appleton House', England's peaceful insularity is recalled as something lost. The Civil War painfully over, the first Dutch War had begun in 1652, the year of the poem:

> O Thou, that dear and happy Isle
> The Garden of the World ere while,
> Thou *Paradise* of four Seas,
> Which *Heaven* planted us to please,
> But, to exclude the World, did guard
> With watry if not flaming Sword;
> What luckless Apple did we tast,
> To make us Mortal, and The Wast?
>   (ll.321–8)

Without devaluing Fairfax's military achievements, Marvell regrets the necessity that provoked them. Into the garden of Fairfax's estate Marvell reads the garden of Eden, where belligerence is deprived of its sting—a benign metaphor which lacks a correlative:

> Unhappy! shall we never more
> That sweet *Militia* restore,
> When Gardens only had their Towrs,
> And all the Garrisons were Flowrs,
> When Roses only Arms might bear,
> And Men did rosie Garlands wear?
> Tulips, in several Colours barr'd,
> Were then the *Switzers* of our *Guard*.
>
>   XLIII
> The *Gardiner* had the *Souldiers* place,
> And his more gentle Forts did trace.
> The Nursery of all things green
> Was then the only *Magazeen*.
> The *Winter Quarters* were the Stoves,
> Where he the tender Plants removes.
> But War all this doth overgrow:
> We Ord'nance Plant and Powder sow.
>   (ll.329–44)

The military terminology which Marvell projects onto this garden-paradise is the product of fallen language.[6] The differences and divisions by which metaphors live are, by means of this particular narrative, shown to be the products of loss. The status of these military metaphors is comparable to that of the rosary with which the infant Christ plays in Hugo Van der Goes' *Virgin and Child* in the National Gallery, London (Fig.14). In Christ's hands the rosary is a plaything, an ordinary necklace. The intercession inscribed on the outer leaves of the painting reminds us that only God has no need of intercession, only Christ can play with rosaries: the rest must pray.

14. Hugo Van der Goes, *Virgin and Child* (London, National Gallery).

In 'The Picture of Little T.C. in a Prospect of Flowers', 'Upon Apple-
ton House' and 'The Garden' (about which I shall say more later), Mar-
vell describes cultivated gardens which have been brought back to a
benign near-identity with the first garden. This kind of restoration is the
business of art—the gardener's and the poet's. But the cultivated garden
in 'The Mower against Gardens' is presented by the mower as a corrupt
and fallen version of the original:

> Luxurious Man, to bring his Vice in use,
>   Did after him the World seduce:
> And from the fields the Flow'rs and Plants allure,
>   Where Nature was most plain and pure.
> He first enclos'd within the Gardens square
>   A dead and standing pool of Air:
> And a more luscious Earth for them did knead,
>   Which stupifi'd them while it fed.
> The Pink grew then as double as his Mind;
>   The nutriment did change the kind.
>
> (ll. 1–10)

Here the corrupt art of the fallen world is associated with softness and
malleability: 'And a more luscious Earth for them did knead'.[7] The argu-
ment, the same as Perdita's in act IV of *The Winter's Tale*, is that the art

which seeks to improve nature by enriching the already adequate soil and creating hybrids by grafting, is a corrupt and alienated art, symptomatic of the division and doubleness initiated at the Fall. Right art, the implication is, consists in a return to and a restoration of the source, rather than in a divisive departure from it. The poem ends with an image of mistaken art —an art of divided analogising:

> ...*Fauns* and *Faryes* do the Meadows till,
> More by their presence then their skill.
> Their Statues polish't by some ancient hand,
> May to adorn the Gardens stand:
> But howso'ere the Figures do excel,
> The *Gods* themselves with us do dwell.
>
> (ll.35–40)

True art reveals the living presence of the gods; false art creates inert replicas.

This notion of art as reaffirming rather than elaborating, restoring rather than duplicating, endorses the reflexiveness, the self-referentiality, of many of Marvell's phrases: 'Like its own Tear' ('On a Drop of Dew', l.13); 'the Mower mown' ('Damon the Mower', l.80); 'The River in it self is drown'd' ('Upon Appleton House', l.471). As in his restorative, almost tautologous puns, Marvell's language seems to double back on itself to re-produce and affirm an original, natural language.

Marvell's compacting puns and reflexive constructions suggest an attempt to restore an original language. But, to recall Empson's point about statements of identity between terms already defined, we are reminded of difference and division at the moment when they are being denied. In Marvell's poetry we are reminded of the act of compression as much as of its achievement. The perception of difference is the basis of all language and, though pre-linguistic fantasies may be entertained (as in stanza LXII of 'Upon Appleton House') poetic energies must depend upon differentiation. His poetry is witty because it presents us simultaneously with both a differentiated range and a unifying compression of it.

*   *   *

Thomas Sprat, in his *History of the Royal Society*, describes the Society's attempt 'to return back to the primitive purity, and shortness, when men deliver'd so many *things*, almost in an equal number of *words*.'[8] The absurdity latent in such an enterprise was picked up by Swift in Book III of *Gullivers Travels* where he describes a visit to the School of Language at the Grand Academy of Laputa:

The first Project was to shorten Discourse by cutting Polysyllables into one, and leaving out Verbs and Participles, because in reality all things imaginable are but Nouns.

The other Project was a Scheme for entirely abolishing all Words whatsoever...An Expedient was therefore offered, that since Words are only Names for *Things*, it would be more convenient for all Men to carry about them, such *Things* as were necessary to express the particular Business they are to discourse on...many of the most Learned and Wise adhere to the New Scheme of expressing themselves by *Things*, which hath only this Inconvenience attending it, that if a Man's Business be very great, and of various kinds, he must be obliged in Proportion to carry a greater Bundle of *Things* upon his Back, unless he can afford one or two strong Servants to attend him.[9]

Bacon's belief that 'the substance of matter is better than the beauty of words' may seem to have been taken to crude extremes by men like Sprat who hoped to make language work only in reference to material quantities. But their aim was to make language a more adequate medium through which to transmit the results of experimental science. Their obligations were towards 'the substance of matter'.

Apart from in 'Fleckno'—a poem about a poet whose work is worth no more (and whose worth is not of a different kind) than the paper it is written on—the sort of matter which Marvell's language emulates is unlike any in the natural world. The first distinction that language registers is that between speaker and everything else. But in the world before man and language fell the distinctions deriving from separation and division did not operate. In 'The Mower's Song' the speaker recalls a state in which difference and division had no place and in which perceiver matched perceived:

> My Mind was once the true survey
> Of all these Medows fresh and gay;
> And in the greenness of the Grass
> Did see its Hopes as in a Glass;
>
> (ll.1–4)

Cut down by the scornful Juliana, this innocent and happy unity is lost. The mind no longer re-presents its 'native Element' in the way that the drop of dew can. The fifth stanza of 'The Mower's Song' introduces a more artificial mode of representation than the simply reflective one of the first:

> And thus, ye Meadows, which have been
> Companions of my thoughts more green,
> Shall now the Heraldry become
> With which I shall adorn my Tomb;
> For *Juliana* comes, and She
> What I do to the Grass, does to my Thoughts and Me.
>
> (ll.25–30)

In 'The Mower against Gardens' a conventional statuary stands for—and apart from—the living gods who inhabit the landscape. In 'The Mower's Song' a conventional code of signification—heraldry—replaces a natural one. All post-lapsarian language is heraldic in this sense rather than naturally reflective or transparent.[10]

In 'Damon the Mower', the mower recognises his allegorical status—a status only acquired after the Fall which brought in death and division.[11] Marvell's mower both recognises and stands apart from the Great Reaper:

> While thus he threw his Elbow round,
> Depopulating all the Ground,
> And, with his whistling Sythe, does cut
> Each stroke between the Earth and Root,
> The edged Stele by careless chance
> Did into his own Ankle glance;
> And there among the Grass fell down,
> By his own Sythe, the Mower mown.
>
> Alas! said He, these hurts are slight
> To those that dye by Loves despight.
> With Shepherds-purse, and Clowns-all-heal,
> The Blood I stanch, and Wound I seal.
> Only for him no Cure is found,
> Whom *Julianas* Eyes do wound.
> 'Tis death alone that this must do:
> For Death thou art a Mower too.
>
> (ll.72–88)

The allegorical representation of *death* derives from the Fall of man more obviously than any other conceivable example. But beyond this there is a suggestion that all allegorical or heraldic signification is both fallen and deathly: fallen from the original fullness of identity when minds matched meadows. In the unfallen world a mower could represent nothing but the world of which he was part.

*   *   *

The urge to return to, to re-collect, an original integrity—an integrity which is epistemological, physical and ethical all at once—is suggested by Marvell's particular kind of poetic density. This density operates on a number of different levels. It is present, not just in the fact of his puns but in the particular nature of those puns: the way in which they seem to be pulling divergent meanings back to an earlier unity and the extra sense of solidity they gain from their precise local reference: 'imbark'. It is present in his fondness for reflexive constructions, constructions which double back on themselves: 'the Mower mown'. It is present in the way in which physical states of firmness and compactness are repeatedly associated with moral rectitude: 'by her *Flames*, in *Heaven* try'd,/ *Nature* is wholly *vitri-fi'd*'. And most of all it is present in the flawless tightness of his verse—his very 'good band' as Puttenham would have called it.

The law of *horror vacui* which is so relentlessly at work in the cramped world of 'Fleckno', has an ethical counterpart in the dense plenitude of providential attention. In 'Bermudas'—another response to the voyage accounts which placed so much emphasis upon the role of Providence—the flawlessly regular rhymed tetrameters mirror Providence's close weave. The proliferating prepositions of the poem's first four lines ('where', 'in', 'from', and an implicit 'to') convey the movement of a gaze from the ariel span of the first two lines, to the 'small Boat' of the third:

> Where the remote *Bermudas* ride
> In th'Oceans bosome unespy'd,
> From a small Boat, that row'd along,
> The listning Winds receiv'd this Song.
> (ll.1−4)

Our gaze is focused and contracted yet we have the impression that the points at which our looking began and ended delimit a random section of a continuum, as densely filled elsewhere as here.

There is no 'when' to the poem. The winds 'receiv'd' the song (l.4) which was 'sung' from the boat: that much is past. But the steady couplets which mimic the falling oars seem capable of perpetual renewal. The poem does not complete itself so much as stop, and again we have the impression of moving in at one of many possible moments, to hear the song of those who row, seemingly directionlessly, 'along'. They do not sing to maintain their energy in rowing: rather they row to make time for their singing:

> And all the way, to guide their Chime,
> With falling Oars they kept the time.
> (ll.39−40)

The song, which is the object of their rowing and which constitutes the body of the poem, is curiously undifferentiated, by metre or rhyme scheme, from the first and last four lines which bring us into and take us out of hearing range of the song. This lack of differentiation makes the poem appear to be part of a larger, continuous whole. Marvell manages to combine great formal tightness with a teasing reticence which suggests that there is more. Something like the poetic 'fragment' which the Romantics emulated is achieved in this poem and in the more obviously elusive 'Nymph complaining for the death of her Faun'.

The poem is without an 'I'. The plural singers are unidentified—hence the curiously neutral, egoless quality of the poem. Yet the world which it presents is an intended, designed world in which relationships are tight and revealing. The couplets, which mimic the metronome of the oars, convey also the taut reciprocity of this environment in which the winds are responsive to the notes they receive ('The listning Winds'). The weaving syntax and the enormous number of dependent clauses give the impression of tight, interdependent causality:

> What should we do but sing his Praise
> *That* led us through the watry Maze,
> Unto an Isle so long unknown,
> And yet far kinder than our own?
> *Where* he the huge Sea-Monsters wracks,
> *That* lift the Deep upon their Backs.
>
> (ll.5–10; my italics)

The closely dependent relationships in this world reflect a careful, providential structuring.

But the metre remains unchangingly simple and the clauses do not overrun their lines. The relationships, though multiple, are explicable and the impression we have is one of complexity being unravelled and simplified. The manner is like that of the nursery rhyme, 'The House that Jack Built'. But here the dominant genre is the hymn and this *encomium* shares with hymns the mnemonic simplification and enumeration of the marvellously complex. The word 'maze' (1.6) is used here, as it is in *The Tempest*,[12] to suggest the providential ordering of apparent chaos. In every maze there is a right path and it is this knowledge which enables Providence to discover the 'Isle so long unknown' (1.7) and 'In th'Oceans bosome unespy'd' (1.2). and, though a real place, this island seems a fictional dream-island which is floating rather than local (1.1), immune to time rather than temporal (1.13). Like the goals of fairy tales, this island will declare itself to those who are morally on the right path rather than to the best navigators. The island is both everywhere and nowhere.

But wherever, whenever, and if ever this island is, it is sufficient to itself. It is an artificial Eden, densely stacked with phenomena with which to delight the senses: sight (ll.13–14; 17–18); smell (1.28); taste (ll.19–22); hearing (ll.27; 32). Of the five senses only touch is not clearly suggested. So immediate is the gratification in this densely filled world that there is no distance between toucher and touched:

> He makes the Figs our mouths to meet;
> And throws the Melons at our feet.
>
> (ll.21–2)

The intent and care with which this island has been arranged is evident everywhere:

He gave us this eternal Spring,
Which here enamells every thing;
And sends the Fowl's to us in care,
On daily Visits through the Air.
He hangs in shades the Orange bright,
Like golden Lamps in a green Night.
And does in the Pomgranates close,
Jewels more rich than *Ormus* show's.
He makes the Figs our mouths to meet;
And throws the Melons at our feet.
But Apples plants of such a price,
No Tree could ever bear them twice.
With Cedars, chosen by his hand,
From *Lebanon*, he stores the Land.
And makes the hollow Seas, that roar,
Proclaime the Ambergris on shoar.
He cast (of which we rather boast)
The Gospels Pearl upon our Coast.
And in these Rocks for us did frame
A Temple, where to sound his Name.

(ll. 13–32)

Everything is static and enamelled for presentation. Only the daily packages of fowl move and these are presented as passive, inanimate missiles—unlike the comparable 'fat aged carp' of Jonson's Penshurst. The oranges do not appear organic. They have been carefully hung against a leafy background calculated to display their beauty. The pomegranates are no more organic than the oranges. Their ruby seeds are transformed into the jewels they resemble and wrapped in rinds. The apples and imported Lebanon cedars that grow on this island-*Wunderkammer* are valued as rare curios rather than for their utility. Indeed utility is redundant as a separable notion here where gratification is so immediate that want cannot be experienced. This is an unusual extension of the ways in which divine Providence can be celebrated. Divine provision is usually praised for its resourceful practicality, but Marvell has imagined a world in which needs are so thoroughly catered for that want is never felt. It is this which permits an aesthetic appreciation of the objects of gratification. This is not the decadent art for art's sake which both neglects and feeds on need. This art antedates need.

The reference to 'The Gospels Pearl' (l.30) elides the celebration of Christian Providence which the song purports to be, with the terms in which that Providence has been perceived: the provision of the rare, the beautiful and the precious. In this poem Marvell has done something comparable to what Shakespeare does with Hermione's 'statue' in *The Winter's Tale*. Our initial perception of Hermione as a statue, a work of art, leads to our reinvesting the familiar human form with a sense of its wonderfulness. To perceive God as an artist involves us in a new appreciation of the beauty and structure of the natural world.

*   *   *

In 'Bermudas' the natural is perceived as the carefully artificial, and Marvell provides us with an image of the sort of art to which his own writing aspires: an art which duplicates, restores and affirms an original nature rather than one which decorates and elaborates on it. The beautiful provisions of the island manifest the art *of* nature rather than any artful deviation from it.

In 'The Garden' Marvell presents a pastoral world which, in its compact sufficiency, acts as a corrective to artful or sexual elaborations away from the 'happy Garden-state' (l.57). He antedates the Fall of man to the moment of division and separation when Eve was taken from Adam's side:

> Such was that happy Garden-state,
> While Man there walk'd without a Mate:
> After a Place so pure, and sweet,
> What other Help could yet be meet!
> But 'twas beyond a Mortal's share
> To wander solitary there:
> Two Paradises 'twere in one
> To live in Paradise alone.
>
> (ll.57–64)

The 'Mortal's share' is to share and be divided. Moral and artistic rectitude, Marvell suggests, consist in an attempt to re-achieve the original, undivided compactness. (The mower against gardens inveighed against the false art of elaboration, multiplication and division.)

Diffusion is presented as both morally and aesthetically wrong-headed. The men of the first stanza are lost, through their own vanity and 'in vain' in a labyrinth of their own making. The maze they have created confounds ('amazes') them with its seeming potential and yet, like all mazes, it offers only one way out. The 'single Herb or Tree' (l.4) which is their symbolic and, if only they knew it, real reward, upbraids their vainglorious efforts and provides an exemplary corrective in its 'short and narrow verged Shade' (l.5). The compactness and reticence of this shade reproves the men, while it unifies and reconciles ('braids up') the snares ('Toyles') they have spun for themselves.

I wrote before about the way in which Marvell's wit often consists in combining a conceptual meaning with one of precise, local, physical reference. In this way his language moves towards assimilating the conceptual back into the physical to create a world of significant matter. The conventional,

'heraldic' mode of signification in which the natural world and its signifi-
cance are separable, is being replaced by an 'earlier' mode in which they
are identical. As far as the men of action in the first stanza are concerned,
the various crowns of palm, oak and bay that they seek as their rewards,
are only significant in a heraldic, conventional way. Marvell shows us
otherwise.

Tenses other than the present are rare in this poem which works to
establish a permanence. The only truly lost and finished past in the poem
is the time well lost described in lines 11–12 ('Mistaken long, I sought
you then/ In busie Companies of Men'). Elsewhere the perfect tense des-
cribes actions through which a permanent present is established and tran-
sience conquered (ll.9; 28–32; 65).

The divisive eroticism represented (heraldically!) by the 'white' and the
'red' contrasts with the consolidated satisfactions of the really green vege-
table world:

> No white nor red was ever seen
> So am'rous as this lovely green.
> (ll.17–18)

'Am'rous' and 'lovely' could be read as synonyms; if so this tautology
moves in the right direction of duplication as opposed to elaboration.
Whereas the 'Fond Lovers' of human loves 'Cut in these Trees their
Mistress name' (l.20), the poet inscribes only the names of the trees
themselves:

> Fair Trees! where s'eer your barkes I wound,
> No Name shall but your own be found.
> (ll.23–4)

Marvell, seeking a bond between words and the things they signify, chases a
chain of representation. The names both stand for and act as receptacles
for the trees' significance, just as the trees themselves are the incarnate
receptacles of the sacred and ideal plants of quiet and innocence:

> Fair quiet, have I found thee here,
> And Innocence thy Sister dear!
>
> .   .   .   .   .   .
> Your sacred Plants, if here below,
> Only among the Plants will grow.
> (ll.9–10; 13–14)

By cutting the names into the barks the poet has made them seem less
arbitrary—as if the difference between the word 'oak', an individual oak,
and an ideal oak was one of degree rather than of kind.

The real significance of names is further substantiated in stanza IV
where we learn that Daphne and Syrinx have been incorporated into the
plants that have traditionally stood for them. Our assumption that Daphne

and Syrinx sprouted leaves in order to save themselves from fates worse than immortality is up-ended in a teleological reading in which they are pursued only for the sakes of their metamorphosed selves:

> The *Gods* that mortal Beauty chase,
> Still in a Tree did end their race.
> *Apollo* hunted *Daphne* so,
> Only that She might Laurel grow.
> And *Pan* did after *Syrinx* speed,
> Not as a Nymph, but for a Reed.
>
> (ll.27–32)

Transient mortality is caught up in the still life of plant form.

The Fall, re-enacted in stanza V, is deprived of its terrors and of its consequence. It is an innocent fall, an act of participation with the vegetable world which stanzas II and IV have reinvested with significance. This fall is not a fall *from* anything but a fall onto and into a state of near-identity with the natural world—as if the poet hopes to be assimilated back into this world in the way that Daphne and Syrinx were. The real achievement of the creative mind (whose creativity we are reminded of in lines 43–6) is an act of annihilation which makes of itself a transparency, representing the ideal world which it inhabits. With the annihilation of 'all that's made/ To a green Thought in a green Shade' (ll.47–8) the divisive distinction between perceiver and perceived is lost.

The ecstasy described in stanza VII is necessarily incomplete (unlike the one at the end of 'On a Drop of Dew'). The soul must be corporeal if it is to confirm a leisured and permanent present in a world of significant matter. The seventeenth-century garden to which we return in the final stanza is modelled on the first Eden garden. The 'skilful Gardner' of this stanza has assumed the powers of a god. In planting a dial of flowers he has transformed fleeting time into a present, local and lovely substance from which bees may gather nectar. The hours are 'wholsome' because unified as a spatial entity; they are also, after the bee has made honey from them, 'wholesomely' nourishing. A delicious *sol étude* is discovered within the 'delicious solitude' of the garden.

Both the language and the narrative of 'The Garden' work in the direction of ravelling up ('up-braiding') the divisions inherent in the fallen world and reproducing a more compact world which is coextensive with its significance. This paradise works on an aesthetic of compactness. The 'streight' (l.44) and the 'narrow' (l.5) are good and beautiful.

A biblical reference which supports Marvell's conversion of this aesthetic good into an ethical one is Matthew vii. 13–14:

> Enter in at the streicte gate: for it is the wide gate, and the broad waye that leadeth to destruction: and manie there be which go in thereat,/ Because the gate is streicte, and the way narowe that leadeth vnto life, and fewe there be that finde it.

In 'Upon Appleton House' Marvell congratulates Fairfax on the closely fitting, unsuperfluous dimensions of his home:

> The low roof'd Tortoises do dwell
> In cases fit of Tortoise-shell:
> No Creature loves an empty space;
> Their Bodies measure out their Place.
> (ll.13−16)

He contrasts such right proportions—the proportions which existed before the Fall of man and before the fall and dispersal of language at Babel —with the vainglorious improportion of:

> ...he, superfluosly spread, [who]
> Demands more room alive then dead.
> And in his hollow Palace goes
> Where Winds as he themselves may lose.
> What need of all this Marble Crust
> T'impark the wanton Mote of Dust,
> That thinks by Breadth the World t'unite
> Though the first Builders fail'd in Height?
>
> IV
> But all things are composed here
> Like Nature, orderly and near:
> In which we the Dimensions find
> Of that more sober Age and Mind,
> When larger sized Men did stoop
> To enter at a narrow loop;
> As practising, in doors so strait,
> To strain themselves through *Heavens Gate*.
> (ll.17−32)

* * *

Both stylistically and topically Marvell is a poet of retreat. The compressed and the self-contained are, in his work, presented as both ethical and stylistic goods. The stance his poetry most consistently takes is that of a Christian stoicism. He was one of several English Renaissance poets to translate the Chorus from Seneca's *Thyestes* which advocates a retreat into self-sufficiency. The best, or at least most powerful, of these translations is Wyatt's, but Marvell's smooth and closely rhymed version mimes the discreet retreat that it advocates instead of underlining—as Wyatt's does—the horror of its converse:

Climb at *Court* for me that will
Tottering favors Pinacle;
All I seek is to lye still.
Settled in some secret Nest
In calm Leisure let me rest;
And far of the publick Stage
Pass away my silent Age.
Thus when without noise, unknown,
I have liv'd out all my span,
I shall dye, without a groan,
An old honest Country man.
Who expos'd to others Ey's,
Into his own Heart ne'r pry's,
Death to him's a Strange surprise.

The smoothness of Marvell's poetry—and his 'tactful' puns are part of this—enacts the retreat it advocates to an extent which is often riddlingly impermeable: oil-skinned compactness. This poetry seldom conveys the solemn recognition of any other than the self which should be sufficient. There is a rare moment of naked personal address to another in his 'Poem on the Death of O.C.' when he describes the sight of Cromwell dead:

I saw him dead, a leaden slumber lyes,
And mortal sleep over those wakefull eyes:
Those gentle rays under the lids were fled,
Which through his looks that piercing sweetnesse shed;
That port which so majestique was and strong,
Loose and depriv'd of vigour, stretch'd along:
All wither'd, all discolour'd, pale and wan,
How much another thing, no more that man?

(ll.247–54)

The energy of much of Marvell's poetry derives from the way in which his language seems to reidentify the conceptual with the material. He invests language with a semblance of density which recalls a state in which spirit was coextensive with matter. But he always retains a sense of the difference between the conceptual and the material and he is unusually sensitive to language's capacity to move between these states. While the urge of his poetry is towards a matter which is luminous with meaning, it shuns what is mere matter and just 'another thing'. The strength of his lines comes from an 'up-braiding' which brings *vir*tue to masculine force.

Notes and References

NOTE ON TEXTS AND TRANSLATIONS

I am responsible for what may appear an inconsistency in my choice of texts in that some retain the original spellings whilst others are modernized. My policy has been to use the best widely available texts and these tend to favour a modernized spelling. Where no modern edition has been the obvious choice I have gone back to earlier editions whose spelling I have retained.

A comparable unevenness will be evident in the translations. I have looked for serviceable translations which are roughly contemporaneous with the English material I am discussing. But these are not available in every instance so I have used good modern translations as well. In a few cases I have provided my own.

ABBREVIATIONS

Bib. d'Hum. et Ren.	*Bibliothèque d'Humanisme et Renaissance*
ELH	*English Literary History*
FQ	*The Faerie Queene*
JAAC	*Journal of Aesthetics and Art Criticism*
JHI	*Journal of the History of Ideas*
JWCI	*Journal of the Warburg and Courtauld Institutes*
JWI	*Journal of the Warburg Institute*
MLN	*Modern Language Notes*
OED	*The Oxford English Dictionary*
PL	Migne, *Patrologia Latina*
PMLA	*Publications of the Modern Language Association*
SEL	*Studies in English Literature*
SP	*Studies in Philology*

Unless otherwise stated, references to Shakespeare's plays are to *The Riverside Shakespeare*, ed. Gwynne Blakemore Evans, Boston, 1974. Bible quotations are from the 1560 edition of the Geneva Bible

INTRODUCTION

1. Svetlana Alpers, *The Art of Describing*, London, 1983, p.xxiv.
2. *The Works of Francis Bacon*, ed. James Spedding, 14 vols, London, 1857–1874, vol. iii, p.285. The passage is from *The Advancement of Learning*.
3. *Rhetoric* 1411b; see also Paul Ricoeur, *The Rule of Metaphor*, London, 1978, study 1.
4. '[God's] hidden power, penetrating all things by its presence, yet free from contamination, gives existence to whatever in any way exists, in so far as it exists at all. For the absence of God's creative activity would not merely mean that a thing would be different in some particular way; it simply could not exist.' Augustine, *City of God*, transl. Henry Bettenson, ed. David Knowles, Harmondsworth, 1972, p.506 (Lib.xii. cap. 26)

CHAPTER 1

1. The editions I shall be using throughout are *Ben Jonson*, ed. P. and E. Simpson, 11 vols, Oxford, 1970 and *The Poems and Letters of Andrew Marvell*, ed. H.M. Margoliouth, 2 vols, Oxford, 1971.
2. *The Works of Francis Bacon*, ed. cit., vol. iii, p.398.
3. Henry Reynolds, *Mythomystes* in *Critical Essays of the Seventeenth Century*, ed. J.E. Spingarn, Oxford, 1908, vol. i, p.157.
4. *Advice to a Son*, Oxford, 1656, p.9, quoted by George Williamson in 'Strong Lines', in *Seventeenth Century Contexts*, London, 1960, pp.120–31; see also Morris Croll, 'Muret and the History of "Attic Prose"' in the Seventeenth Century', *SP*, xviii, 1921, pp.79–128.
5. The edition I am using is *Antony and Cleopatra*, ed. M.R. Ridley, London, 1977.
6. *Ben Jonson*, vol. viii, p.623.
7. ibid. vol. viii, p.624.
8. *The English Works Of Thomas Hobbes* (hereafter *EW*), ed. Sir William Molesworth, 11 vols, London, 1839–1845, vol. iv, pp.453–4.
9. *EW*, vol. viii, p.xxiii.
10. ibid., vol. viii, pp.xxix–xxx. Gerard Manley Hopkins writes, in a letter to Robert Bridges dated 6 November 1881: 'Plainly if it is possible to express a subtle and recondite thought on a subtle and recondite subject in a subtle and recondite way and with great felicity and perfection, in the end, something must be sacrificed, with so trying a task, in the process, and this may be the being at once, nay perhaps even the being without explanation at all, intelligible.'

(*The Letters of Gerard Manley Hopkins to Robert Bridges*, ed. Claude C. Abbott, London, 1935, pp.265–6.)
11. The edition I am using is *The Poems of Sir Philip Sidney*, ed. W.A. Ringler, Oxford, 1965.
12. George Puttenham, *The Arte of English Poesie* (hereafter *Arte*), ed. Gladys Doidge Willcock and Alice Walker, Cambridge, 1936, p.183.
13. *Ben Jonson*, vol. viii, p.621.
14. *EW*, vol. vi, p.489.
15. *The Elements of Law Natural and Politic* ed. F. Tönnies, London, 1969, p.2; see also *EW*, vol. i, pp.91–2.
16. *EW*, vol. i, p.92.
17. *Peacham's Compleat Gentleman 1634*, with an Introduction by G.S. Gordon, Oxford, 1906, p.56.
18. *EW*, vol. iv, p.449. Hobbes lifted this passage, which occurs in the 'Answer to Davenant', from his earlier scientific work; see Appendix 2 to the *Critique du De Mundo de Thomas White*, ed. Jean Jacquot and Harold Whitmore Jones, Paris, 1973, p.449.
19. *Dialogue on the Great World Systems, in the Salusbury Translation*, ed. Giorgio de Santillana, Chicago, 1953, pp.116–17.
20. *Leviathan*, I. viii, *EW*, vol. iii, pp.56–7.
21. Translated by C.T. Wood, T.S.K. Scott-Craig, and B. Gert, in *Man and Citizen, Thomas Hobbes's De Homine and De Cive*, ed. B. Gert, New York, 1972, pp.63–4.
22. *EW*, vol. i, p.206; see also F. Brandt, *Thomas Hobbes's Mechanical Conception of Nature*, Copenhagen, 1928, pp.293 ff., and M.M. Goldsmith, *Hobbes's Science of Politics*, New York, 1966, pp.32–4.
23. *Leviathan*, I. vi, *EW*, vol. iii, p.39.
24. *EW*, vol. iv. p.449.
25. *Leviathan*, I. iii, *EW*, vol. iii, pp.12–13.
26. *Leviathan*, I. iii, *EW*, vol. iii, p.11; see also L. Tatarkiewicz, 'L'esthétique associationniste au XVIIe siècle, *Revue d'esthétique*, xii, 1960, pp.287–92.
27. *The Elements of Law*, ed. cit., p.13.
28. *Leviathan*, I. iii, *EW*, vol. iii, pp.12–13; Raman Selden notes the 'tone of celebration' in this passage, 'Hobbes and Late Metaphysical Poetry', *JHI*, xxxv, 1974, pp.197–210.
29. *Leviathan*, I. iv, *EW*, vol. iii, pp.23–4.
30. *Leviathan*, I. v, *EW*, vol. iii, pp.36–7.
31. *Leviathan*, I. iv, *EW*, vol. iii, p.28.
32. *The Whole Works of Jeremy Taylor*, ed. R. Heber, London, 1851, vol. ix, p.421.
33. ibid., vol. ix, p.423.
34. ibid., vol. ix, pp.422–3.

35. Rosemond Tuve, *Elizabethan and Meta-physical Imagery*, Chicago, 1972, p.409.

36. The edition I am using is *The Poems of John Donne*, ed. H.J.C. Grierson, 2 vols, Oxford, 1912.

37. I am using the Arden Shakespeare edition of *The Poems*, ed. F.T. Prince, London, 1960.

38. I am using *Shakespeare's Sonnets*, ed. Stephen Booth, New Haven, 1977.

39. I am using Edmund Spenser, *Poetical Works*, ed. J.C. Smith and E. de Selincourt, Oxford, 1912.

40. *Leviathan*, I. iv, *EW*, vol. iii, p.25.

41. *Leviathan*, I. iv, *EW*, vol. iii, p.21

CHAPTER 2

1. *The Spectator*, no. 58, 7 May 1711.

2. *EW*, vol. iv, pp.446–7.

3. Quoted by David Sylvester, *Catalogue of an Exhibition of Paintings by René Magritte, 1898–1967*, London, 1969, p.28.

4. Galileo Galilei, *The Assayer* (1623), transl. S. Drake in *Discoveries and Opinions of Galileo*, New York, 1957, p.238.

5. See for instance *The garden of Cyrus or the Quincunx* (1658) in vol. i of *The Works of Sir Thomas Browne*, ed. Geoffrey Keynes, London, 1928.

6. *Ovid's Metamorphosis Englished, Mythologiz'd and Represented in Figures by G[eorge] S[andys]*, London, 1632, p.342.

7. Readers of the *Purgatorio* may also discover an acrostic of VOM in canto xii, ll.24–58.

8. Juan Eusebio Nieremberg, *Oculta Filosofia de la Sympatia y Antipatia de las cosas, artificio de la naturaleza, noticia natural del mundo, y segunda parte de la Curiosa Filosofia*, Barcelona, 1645, cap. xi; quoted by Mario Praz in *Studies in Seventeenth Century Imagery*, London, 1939, vol. i, p.16.
   For a study of specifically labyrinthine figured poems see Ana Hatherly, 'Labirintos Portugueses dos seculos XVII & XVIII', in *Colóquio Artes*, xlv, 1980, pp.20–9.

9. *Publilii Optatiani Porfyrii Carmina*, Corpus Scriptorum Latinorum Paravianum, Turin, 1973; see also N.W. Helm, 'The Carmen Figuratum as shown in the work of Publilius Optatianus Porfyrius', *Transactions and Proceedings of the American Philological Association*, xxxiii, 1902, pp.43–9.

10. An account of the MS in the Nationalbibliothek in Vienna (MS 652 olim theol. 39) is given by Julius von Schlosser, 'Eine Fulder Miniaturhandschrift der KK. Hofbibliothek', *Jahrbuch der Kunsthistorischen Sammlungen des Allerhöchsten Kaiserhauses*, xiii, 1892, pp.1–36; my references will be to Migne, *PL*, vol. cvii, cols. 133–294.

11. An example of this can be found in the gloss to fig. xii, *PL*, cols 195–8: 'De nomine Adam protoplasti, quomodo secundum Adam significet, et ejus passionem demonstret.' The figure consists of the Greek letters of Adam's name arranged in cruciform. The gloss reveals that the numerological equivalents to these letters (alpha: 1; delta: 4; mu: 40) add up to 46 which was the number of years it took to build the temple in Jerusalem which Christ, referring to the temple of his body, promises to rebuild in three days.

12. Emanuele Tesauro, *Il Cannocchiale Aristotelico*, facsimile of 1670 Turin edition, ed. August Buck, Hamburg, 1968, p.59.

13. *M. Rabani Mauri De Laudibus Sanctae Crucis*, ed. Jakob Wimpheling, Pforzheim, 1503; this quotation is on the verso of the title page in this and in the 1605 edition.

14. J.E. Spingarn, *Critical Essays of the Seventeenth Century*, i, *1605–1650*, Oxford, 1908, p.159.

15. Edward Benlowes, *Theophila*, London, 1652, p.269.

16. Ernst Vogt, 'Das Acrostichon in der greichischen Literatur', *Antike und Abendland*, xiii, 1967, pp.88–95.

17. *Georgics*, i.424–37; ii.315–42; see Edwin Brown, *Numeri Vergiliani: Studies in 'Eclogues' and 'Georgics'*, (Collection Latomus lxiii), Brussels, 1963.

18. Here the tendency is not to bury the acrostic as if it were a secret code, but to draw attention to it by a visible separation of the component letters, and often by a formulaic phrase such as *is cuius per capita versorum nomen declaretur*.

19. F. Saxl, 'The Classical Inscription in Renaissance Art and Politics', *JWI*, iv, 1940–41, pp.19–46.

20. For an account of the development of this mode see John Sparrow, *Visible Words, a Study of Inscriptions in and as Works of Art*, Cambridge, 1969.

21. Petrus Apianus and Bartolomaeus Amantius, *Inscriptiones Sacrosanctae Vetustatis*, Ingolstadt, 1534.

22. Geoffrey Hartman, in his chapter 'Words and Wounds' (*Saving the Text*, Baltimore, 1981, pp.118–57) writes cautiously and well about the vulnerability of the ear.

23. 'Hearing a poem, as opposed to reading it on the page, means you miss so much—the shape, the punctuation, the italics, even knowing how far you are from the end.' (Philip Larkin, 'An Interview with *Paris Review*', in *Required Writing*, London, 1983, p.61.)

24. *Il Cannocchiale Aristotelico*, ed. cit., p.595:

'La Romana antiquità . . . componeua le sue Inscrittioni con una schietta grauità; ma senza viuezza ne acume niuno. S'aggiunse dapoi maggior' eleganza dello stile, con qualche tenerezza di affetto: ma ne l'occhio, ne l'orrecchio hauria distinta la Periodo Lapidaria.'

25. Epigraphs containing acrostics demand careful lineation to preserve their visible sense. The pride in straightness of line and margin taken by the stone-cutters who carved the acrostic epigraphs included in *Carmina Latina Epigraphica* must have been akin to that of the early printers to whom straight lineation and homogeneity of the page were hard ideals. See *Carmina Latina Epigraphica*, ed. F. Buecheler, Leipzig, 1895–1926.

26. W.J. Ong, 'System, Space and Intellect in Renaissance Symbolism', *Bib. d'Hum. et Ren.*, xviii, 1956, pp.222–39.

27. *Arte*, p.81.

28. ibid., p.85.

29. R. Wittkower, *Architectural Principles in the Age of Humanism*, London, 1974 (3rd edition), p.119.

30. *Arte*, p.87.

31. Simmias describes his 'Egg', which is read weaving inwards—from the first line to the last, from the second to the penultimate etc. —as a 'weave' (ατϱιον) (*The Greek Bucolic Poets*, transl. J.M. Edmonds, London, 1912, pp.496–7). Wimpheling, in his preface to *De Laudibus Sanctae Crucis*, uses the word *innectens* to describe Hrabanus' method of developing and involving the symbolism of the Cross. Abraham Fraunce, writing of 'conceited verses' says that '*Theocritus hath expressed the forme of an egge, and an alter in verse, so hath Willy* represented the figure of a swoard, and an old Abbot [Hrabanus?] the image of a crosse in verie laboured and intangled verses.' (*The Arcadian Rhetorike* (1588), ed. Ethel Seaton, Oxford, 1960, p.53.) Ezra Pound writes: 'Dante's rhyme is but a stiffer thread in the texture, to keep the whole from sprawling and pulling out of trim shape (c.f. weave of any high grade trouser material).' (*Literary Essays of Ezra Pound*, ed. T.S. Eliot, London, 1954 (repr. 1974), p.210.)

32. *Arte*, pp.91–2.

33. J.C. Scaliger, *Poetices libri VII*, Heidelberg, 1581, cap. xxv, p.175.

34. See Margaret Church, 'The First English Pattern Poems', *PMLA*, lxi, 1946, pp. 636–50, who attributes the figured poems of the Greek Anthology to Oriental influence at the School of Alexandria; see also A.L. Korne, 'Puttenham and the oriental Pattern Poem', *Comparative Literature*, vi, 1954, pp.289–303, who doubts any direct influence from the Orient.

35. *Arte*, pp.91–2.

36. Orazio Lombardelli praises Tasso's great work in these terms: 'that he should have succeeded so well in knotting and tying all the parts of this poem of his . . . to have promised to sing the glorious reconquest, and then to have delayed it so much, to have put so many things in its way, to have interrupted it, and to have brought it almost to the point of desperation . . . and with so much verisimilitude and interweaving, and correspondence of one part with another, that there are never any doubts of importance remaining and that the memory is never so disturbed that it would fail to attach quickly one thing to another; until at the end all obstacles give way' (quoted and translated in B. Weinberg, *A History of Literary Criticism in the Italian Renaissance*, Chicago, 1961, vol. ii, p.1028).

37. Jean Crispin, *Poetae graecae vetustissimi*, Geneva, 1600 (1st edition 1589) p.214.

38. The 'egg' which Pierius Valerianus inscribed to Daniele Barbaro is printed in a collection of poems appended to *Pro Sacerdotum Barbis*, Rome, 1531.

39. See note 33 above.

40. Richard Wills, *Poematum Liber*, London, 1573, no. 6. Wills, whilst conscious of his classical precedents, makes a point of Christianising his own versions. His altar, in contrast to the pagan originals of Besantinus and Dosiadas, is a Christian altar; his sword, an invention of his own and an addition to the repertoire of often-repeated forms, is the sword of the Spirit, 'quod est verbum Dei'.

41. Richard Wills, *De Re Poetica*, transl. and ed. from the 1573 edition A.D.S. Fowler, Oxford, 1958.

42. Quoted in *Elizabethan Critical Essays*, ed. G. Smith, Oxford, 1904, vol. i, p.126.

43. See Frances A. Yates, 'The Emblematic Conceit in Giordano Bruno's *De Gli Eroici Furori* and in the Elizabethan Sonnet Sequences', *JWI*, vi, 1943, pp.101–21. Bruno's work is particularly interesting in that the 'emblems' consist of verbal descriptions only; see also Hessel Miedema, 'The Term *Emblema* in Alciati', *JWCI*, xxxi, 1968, pp.234–50, where it is shown that Alciati used the term *Emblema* to refer to epigrams independent of visual representation.

The allegorical mode differs from the emblematic in that, as Frances Yates points out, 'its very strangeness and unnaturalness will not allow the mind to rest in it without seeking a further explanation' (art. cit above); see also W. J. Ong. 'From Allegory to Diagram in the Renaissance Mind', *JAAC*, xvii, 1959, pp.423–40, and Margery Corbett and R.W. Lightbown, *The Comely Frontispiece: the Emblematic Title Page in England 1550–1660*, London, 1979.

44. Thomas Fuller, *The History of the Worthies of England*, London, 1662, ed. J. Nichols, 2 vols, London, 1811, vol. i, p.355.

45. See Harold Jenkins, *Edward Benlowes, 1602–1676*, London, 1952, pp.78–9; Francis Quarles, *Emblemes*, London, 1635 (this volume is dedicated to Edward Benlowes); Francis Quarles, *Hieroglyphikes of the Life of Man*, London, 1638; Hermann Hugo, *Pia Desideria*, Antwerp, 1624; Collegium Societatis Jesu, *Typus Mundi*, Antwerp, 1627.

46. *The Works of Francis Bacon*, ed. cit., vol. iii, p.399.

47. ibid., vol. iii, p.285.

48. Joshua Sylvester, *Lachrimae Lachryma[rum], or the Spirit of Teares distilled for the vn-tymely Death of the incomparable Prince Panaretus*, London, 1613 (3rd edition).

49. *Du Bartas, his Divine weekes and workes translated and written by the famous Philomusus Joshua Sylvester Gent*, London, 1621, p.1176.

50. This is the translation of C.E. Bennett in *Horace, The Odes and Epodes*, London, 1927.

51. La Fontaine, *Oeuvres Complètes*, ed. Jean Marmier, Paris, 1965, pp.394–5.

52. William Gager, *Exequiae Illustrissimi Equitis D. Philippi Sidnaei, Gratissimae Memoriae ac Nomini Impensae*, Oxford, 1582, sigs B4v–D1v, printed in J.W. Binns, 'William Gager on the Death of Sir Philip Sidney', in *Humanistica Lovaniensia*, xxi, 1972, pp.221–38.

53. The edition I am using is *The Poetical Works of Robert Herrick*, ed. L.C. Martin, Oxford, 1956.

54. Herrick's attentiveness to the shaping of his work is shown in the order in which he published his two volumes. *Hesperides*, the secular volume, is printed first and is dated 1648; it is followed by *Noble Numbers* or *His Pious Pieces*, dated 1647. This arrangement, which reverses the order of composition, expresses a stepping out of the secular world of time into eternity. See A.B. Chambers, 'Herrick and the Trans-shifting of Time', *SP*, lxii, 1975, pp.85–114.

55. Leon Battista Alberti, *De Re Aedificatoria*, vi. cap. 2. This definition is translated by R. Wittkower in *Architectural Principles in the Age of Humanism*, ed. cit., p.33.

'ut sit pulchritudo quidem certa cum ratione concinnitas universarum partium in eo cuius sint: ita ut addi, aut diminui, aut immutari possit nihil, quam improbabilius reddat'.

56. *Ben Jonson*, vol. viii, p.583.

57. ibid., vol. viii, p.623.

58. See Stanley Fish, *The Living Temple, George Herbert and Catechising*, Los Angeles, 1978, pp.139–40; George Watson, 'The Fabric of Herbert's *Temple*', *JWCI*, xxvi, pp.354–8. Throughout I am using *The Works of George Herbert*, ed. F.E. Hutchinson, Oxford, 1945.

59. *Arte*, p.96.

60. Stanley Fish's analysis of this poem in his *Self-Consuming Artefacts*, Los Angeles, 1972, pp.207–15, has formed the basis of my reading.

61. 'The Church-Floore' may be another; Coburn Freer, in *Music for a King: George Herbert's Style and the Metrical Psalms*, Baltimore, 1972, p.121, argues that four stanzas are needed in this poem, each stanza constituting a triangle in a tiled floor.

62. Paschasius a Sancto Joanne, *Poesis artificiosa cum sibi praefixa perfacili manuductione ad Parnassum, tam veterum, quam recentiorum Poetarum authoritate Studiosae elaborata in usum studiosae Iuventutis proposita*, Würzburg, 1668. The work is dedicated to Count Roger of Staremberg whose chaplain Paschasius was for a while. There is little information to be found about Paschasius but he should not be confused (as he is in Zedler's *Universal Lexicon*) with a sixteenth-century Paschasius, also a Carmelite, working in Malines.

CHAPTER 3

1. *Complete Prose Works of John Milton*, vol. ii, *1643–1648*, New Haven, 1959, p.513. The passage is from *Areopagitica*.

2. Galileo Galilei, *Dialogue on the Great World Systems*, ed. cit., pp.114–15.

3. Psalm 94.ix: 'He that planted the eare, shal he not heare.?'

4. 'For the usual image of the Holy Ghost in the form of a dove the pretence is great . . . ; no less than the words of the scripture . . . To this I answer, that the Holy Ghost did not appear in the shape of a dove at all; but the dove mentioned in the story relates only to the manner of His descending, and hovering over Christ.' *The Whole Works of Jeremy Taylor*, ed. cit., vol. ix, p.424.

5. Rosemond Tuve, *A Reading of George Herbert*, Chicago, 1952, p.88.

6. ibid., p.128.

7. Compare Wilfred Owen's 'Greater Love': 'Red lips are not so red/ As the stained stones kissed by the English dead'.

8. Girolamo Maripiero, *Il Petrarcha Spirituale*, Venice, 1536, fol. 2^v.

9. G.K. Hunter writes of Marlowe's deliberately blasphemous appropriation of a traditional theme for Christ *in utero Virinis* in his 'infinite riches in a little room' ('The Theology of Marlowe's *The Jew of Malta*', *JWCI*, xxvii, 1964, pp.211–40).

10. Meister Eckhart, *German Sermons and Treatises*, transl. M. O'C. Walshe, London, 1981, vol. ii. p.13.

11. C.S. Lewis, *Spenser's Images of Life*, ed. A. Fowler, Cambridge, 1967, p.66.

12. Paul Ricoeur, in his brilliant gloss to Aristotle's *mimesis phuseos*, suggests that all metaphor involves vital movement: 'To present men *"as acting"* and all things *"as in act"*—such could well be the *ontological* function of metaphorical discourse, in which every dormant potentiality of existence appears *as* blossoming forth, every latent capacity for action *as* actualized.' (*The Rule of Metaphor*, p.43.)

13. Heather Asals writes illuminatingly and precisely about the poetic implications of the Anglican *via media* which argues the necessity of outward form. For Herbert, language is 'the ontological bridge to the divine' (*Equivocal Predication, George Herbert's Way to God*, Toronto, 1981, p.6).

14. Walter Benjamin writes thus about fragments: 'The value of fragments of thought is all the greater the less direct their relationship to the underlying idea, and the brilliance of the representation depends as much on this value as the brilliance of the mosaic does on the quality of the glass paste. The relationship between the minute precision of the work and the proportions of the sculptural or intellectual whole demonstrates that truth-content is only to be grasped through immersion in the most minute details of subject matter.' (*The Origin of German Tragic Drama*, transl. John Osborne, London, 1977, p.29.)

15. Philip Sidney, *A Defence of Poetry*, ed. Jan Van Dorsten, Oxford, 1973 (repr.), pp.72–3.

16. *Astrophil and Stella* 44: Bosola in the couplet with which he concludes act III, scene ii of *The Duchess of Malfi*, suggests an aesthetic of ill well done: 'Now, for this act I am certain to be rais'd,/ And men that paint weeds to the life are prais'd.'

17. *The Sermons of John Donne*, ed. Evelyn Simpson and George Potter, 10 volumes, Berkeley, 1962, vol. x, p.247.

18. William Empson, *Seven Types of Ambiguity*, Harmondsworth, 1972, p.260.

19. Helen Vendler, *The Poetry of George Herbert*, Cambridge, Mass., 1975, pp.59–60.

20. See Heather Asals' discussion of this poem: 'The uniqueness of "Providence" rests in its heroic attempt to relate oneness-in-language (equivocacy) to oneness-in-things (univocacy) and to offer this as the total *Oneness* of God' (*Equivocal Predication*, ed. cit., p.10.)

21. Martin Elsky, who relates Herbert's figured poems to a Christian cabbalist interest in letters as material things with symbolic significance, describes this poem as 'a linguistic hieroglyph, an *impresa*, whose picture is replaced by a word followed by a two-line motto' ('George Herbert's Pattern Poems and the Materiality of Language: a New Approach to Renaissance Hieroglyphics', *ELH*, 1, 1983, pp.245–60).

22. Walton reports the dying Herbert as requesting Mr Duncan to 'deliver this little Book to my dear brother Farrer, and tell him, he shall find in it a picture of the many spiritual Conflicts that have past betwixt God and my Soul, before I could subject mine to the will of Jesus my Master in whose service I have now found perfect freedom; desire him to read it: and then, if he can think it may turn to the advantage of any dejected poor Soul, let it be made publick: if not, let him burn it.' (Izaac Walton, *Lives*, Oxford, 1927, p.314.).

    In my opinion both Rosamond Tuve and Heather Asals assume too serene a harmony between Herbert's poetic and priestly vocations. Asals writes 'Language ... is the stuff of ontology for Herbert, and for this reason he writes poetry' (op. cit., p.15). This seems to me to be the wrong way round.

23. The same rhyme occurs in 'The Sacrifice' to characterise the stupid cruelty of Christ's tormentors: 'Servants and abjects flout me; they are wittie:/ *Now prophesie who strikes thee*, is their dittie.' (ll.141–2)

CHAPTER 4

1. See also III.i.289, and *King John*, III.i.180.

2. Cf. Janet Adelman, *The Common Liar, An Essay on Antony and Cleopatra*, New Haven, 1973, especially cap. I.

3. *Arte*, p.65.

4. *The Symposium*, transl. Walter Hamilton, Harmondsworth, 1951, 208c.

5. 'Shakespeare's Sonnets', 1934, in *Explorations*, London, 1958, pp.40–65.

6. Other examples are Samuel Daniel, *Delia* 45, and Philip Sidney, *Astrophil and Stella* 38.
7. For Elizabethan familiarity with the story of *Antony and Cleopatra* see Adelman, op. cit., cap. 2.
8. In *I Henry VI*, i.iv.107, Shakespeare plays on the acoustic similarity between 'pucelle' (virgin) and 'puzzel'; see Leslie A. Fiedler, *The Stranger in Shakespeare*, St Albans, 1974, p.45.
9. See Ridley's note to these lines in the New Arden edition; for anamorphic pictures in general see Jurgis Baltrusaitis, *Anamorphoses ou Magie artificielle des effect merveilleux*, Paris, 1969, trans. W.J. Strachan as *Anamorphic Art*, Cambridge, 1977; for their literary significance see Ernst B. Gilman, *The Curious Perspective: Literary and Pictorial Wit in the Seventeenth Century*, New Haven, 1978, and Alan Shickmann, 'Turning Pictures in Shakespeare's England', *Art Bulletin*, lix, 1977, pp.67–70.
10. 'The number of messengers in the play is symptomatic of [the] breakdown in direct and reliable communication...the audience is continually bombarded with messengers of one kind or another, not so much to convey information as to convey the sense that all information is unreliable, that it is message or rumor, not fact.' (Adelman, op. cit., pp.34–5.)
11. References to *A Midsummer Night's Dream* are to the New Arden edition, ed. Harold Brooks, London, 1979.
12. Mark Van Doren, *Shakespeare*, London, 1941, p.171.
13. Andrew Marvell, a poet whose imagination is engaged by processes of hardening and softening, writes of boiled sweets in 'Upon Appleton House', stanza XXII.
14. Shakespeare's Troilus and Cressida express a similar sense of their future statuses; see *Troilus and Cressida*, III.ii.172–205.
15. The contemporary belief that the eyes emitted light intensifies the uncertainty about what is being excluded from what.

CHAPTER 5

1. '...la mente humana partecipa della Diuina; che con la medesima Diuinità habita nelle paludi, & nelle Stelle: & del più sordido loto, fabricò la più Diuina delle Corporee Creature' (Tesauro, *Il Cannocchiale Aristotelico*, ed. cit., p.584; this passage is translated by S.L. Bethell, in 'Gracian, Tesauro and the nature of Metaphysical Wit', in *Northern Miscellany* i, 1953, p.33).

2. *Dialogue on the Great World Systems*, ed. cit., pp.116–17.
3. *EW*, vol. iv, p.449.
4. *On the Workmanship of God* in *The Works of Lactantius*, transl. W. Fletcher, Edinburgh, 1871, vol. xi, p.84: 'An potest aliquis non admirari, quod sensus ille vivus atque coelestis, qui mens, vel animus nuncupatur, tantae mobilitatis est, ut ne tum quidem, cum sopitus est, conquiescat; tantae celeritatis, ut uno temporis puncto coelum omne collustret, et si velit, maria pervolet, terras ac urbes peragret, omnia denique, quae libuerit, quamvis longe lateque summota sint, in conspectu sibi ipse constituat.' (*De Opificio Dei*, *PL*, vii, cols 9–77 (the passage quoted is in cols 65–6.)
5. Ambrose, *Hexaemeron*, Lib. VI, cap. viii, *PL*, xiv, col. 275; this passage is translated by Peter Clemoes in '*Mens absentia cogitans* in *The Seafarer* and *The Wanderer*', in *Medieval Literature and Civilisation, Studies in Memory of G.N. Garmonsway*, ed. D.A. Pearsall and R.A. Waldron, London, 1969, pp.66–7. *Wisdom*, 8.i. stands behind all these passages.
6. Augustine, *De Genesi ad Litteram*, lib. XII, cap. iv, *PL* xxxiv, col. 458. Aelfric, *Lives of the Saints*, ed. W.W. Skeat, London, 1881, p.19.
7. The reference is to the Revels edition of *Doctor Faustus*, ed. John D. Jump, London, 1962.
8. Boethius, *De Consolationae [sic] Philosophiae...translated out of Latin into the Englyshe tounge by George Colvile*, London, 1556, no page numbers. The translation expands into a gloss.
9. Svetlana Alpers' *The Art of Describing* (ed. cit.) contains much material along these lines. On p.9 she quotes Constantijn Huygens's response to the revelations of Cornelis Drebbel's magnifying lens where 'in the most minute and disdained of creatures [we] meet with the same careful labor of the Great Architect, everywhere an equally indescribable majesty'.
10. For an excellent survey of classical adoxography see Arthur Stanley Pease, 'Things without honor', *Classical Philology*, xxi, 1926, pp.27–42; the *encomia* on Helen are mentioned on p.29; see also Rosalie Colie, *Paradoxia Epidemica*, Princeton, 1966, especially the introduction: 'Problems of Paradoxes'.
11. This is Christopher Marlowe's translation of the lines.
12. *Metamorphoses*, ed. with a commentary by Raphael Regius, Venice, 1492.
13. Caroline Jameson, 'Ovid in the Sixteenth

Century', in *Ovid*, ed. J.W. Binns, London, 1973, pp.210–42, mentions a later development of the epyllion which involved a different and mystical form of moralising. Chapman's *Ovid's Banquet of Sense* (1595) is an example of this development; see also William Keach, *Elizabethan Erotic Narratives*, New Brunswick, 1977, p.13: 'Nothing could differ more from the rigid allegorical and moralizing impositions of so many of Ovid's medieval and Renaissance interpreters than the deftness and openness of his own handling of symbolic detail.'

14. See James Yoch, 'The Eye of Venus: Shakespeare's Erotic Landscape', *SEL*, xx, 1980, pp.59–71; he is mistaken, I think, in seeing Venus' conversion of the landscape wholly in terms of 'character' since her mythic status makes the conversion in some sense true.

15. In her essay, 'The Epyllion' in *English Poetry and Prose 1540–1674*, ed. Christopher Ricks, London, 1970, p.88.

16. A desire for incorporation with the beloved is expressed by Deloney's Sir Hugh: 'Oh how happie should I count my selfe, if those fishes which shall live on my bodies food, might bee meate for my Love!' (*The Novels of Thomas Deloney*, ed. M.E. Lawlis, Bloomington, 1961, p.102). Barnabe Barnes, in sonnet 63 of *Parthenophil and Parthenophe*, expresses a desire to enter his beloved as wine: 'To kisse her lippes, and lye next at her hart,/ Runne through her vaynes, and passe through pleasures part' in *Occasional Issues of Unique or Very Rare Books*, ed. A. Grosart, vol. I, Manchester, 1875.

17. Andrew Marvell, in stanza LXXVII of 'Upon Appleton House', imagines himself receiving such an embrace in a chaster fantasy: 'Bind me ye *Woodbines* in your 'twines,/ Curle me about ye gadding *Vines*,/ And Oh so close your Circles lace,/ That I may never leave this Place:/ But, lest your Fetters prove too weak,/ Ere I your Silken Bondage break,/ Do you, *O Brambles*, chain me too,/ And courteous *Briars* nail me through.'

18. *In Anguem, qui Lycorin dormientem amplexus est*; the title is given in Latin in the 1638 and subsequent editions of Randolph's poems.

19. The *OED* records Spenser's use of the verb in sense 7, 'To climb', in *FQ*, VII. vi. 8, as a Latinism in 1596.

20. Earl Miner, *The Cavalier Mode from Jonson to Cotton*, Princeton, 1971, p.237.

21. See also *Romeo and Juliet*, II.ii. 24–5: 'O that I were a glove upon that hand/ That I might touch that cheek!'

22. *The Harley Lyrics*, ed. G.L. Brook, Manchester, 1956, p.41; from 'A Wayl whyt ase Whalles Bon'.

23. James McPeek, *Catullus in Strange and Distant Britain*, Cambridge Mass., 1939, especially cap. iv, 'A Sparrow's flight'; Waller, in vol. 1 of *The Cambridge History of English Literature*, p.362, sees Catullus as behind the Harley lyric.

24. This is James Michie's translation (*The Poems of Catullus*, London, 1972).

25. John Skelton, *Poetical Works*, ed. A. Dyce, London, 1843, vol. i, p.56.

26. Sidney, *Poems*, ed. cit., p.244, l.85.

27. In a letter to Benjamin Bailey, 22 November 1817. *The Letters of John Keats*, ed. Hyder Rollins, Cambridge Mass., 1958, vol. i, p.186.

28. See Pease, art. cit., p.40.

29. It is thought that these were written by a certain Ofilius Sergianus and that the resemblance between Ofilius and Ovidius, along with the similarity of subject matter and treatment, prompted the confusion; see N.E. Lemaire, *Poetae Latinae Minores*, Paris, 1826, vol. vii, p.176 and Marcel Françon, 'Un Motif dans la Poésie Amoureuse au XVIe siècle', in *PMLA*, lvi, 1941, pp.307–36; Françon mentions the 'Carmen de Pulice' on p.313. The poem is headed 'P. Ovidii Nasonis De Pulice Opusculum incipit/ qq non putatur a quibusdam Ovidii opus', in *Publii Ovidii Nasonis Epistolarum Heroidum Liber Primus*, n.p., 1480, fol. gii.

30. The poem begins 'Enfant de quatre ans, combien,/ Ta petitesse a de bien'. See also Françon, art. cit., p.310.

31. Estienne Pasquier, *La Puce ou Ieus poetiques Francois & Latins Composez sur la Puce aux Grands Iours de Poictiers la'n MDLXXIX dont Pasquier feut le premier motif*, Paris, 1610, in *La Ieunesse d'Estienne Pasquier*, Paris, 1610, p.576. R.O. Jones traces the *topos* of this work back to a series of madrigals by Luigi Tansillo on the death of a butterfly entangled in a woman's hair ('Renaissance Butterfly, Mannerist Flea: Tradition and Change in Renaissance Poetry', *MLN*, lxxx, 1965, pp.166–84.

32. Pasquier, ed. cit., pp.571–2.

33. e.g. Juvenal, *Sat.*, ix.54ff.

34. See stanza XX of Donne's 'Progresse of the Soule'.

35. For a strenuous exercise in reading this poem see Don Cameron Allen, *Image and Meaning*, Baltimore, 1968, cap. 2., pp.20–41. He sees the butterfly as 'caught in the eternal struggle between reason and sensuality'.

36. Pease, art. cit., p.32.
37. *New Organon*, I, cxx, *Works*, ed. cit., vol. iv, pp.106–7.
38. *New Organon*, II, xxxix, ibid., p.192.
39. This is what Hooke has to say about the flea: 'The strength and beauty of this small creature, had it no other relation at all to man, would deserve a description ... as for the beauty of it, the *Microscope* manifests it to be all over adorn'd with a curiously polish'd suit of *sable* Armour, neatly jointed, and beset with multitudes of sharp pinns, shap'd almost like Porcupine's Quills, or bright conical Steel-bodkins; the head is on either side beautify'd with a quick and round black eye.' (Robert Hooke, *Micrographia: or some physiological Descriptions of Minute Bodies made by Magnifying Glasses with Observations and Inquiries thereupon*, London, 1665 (facsimile edition, R.T. Gunther, New York, 1961, Observ. LIII, p.210).)
40. There is a joke against James Howell here. Howell, in his *Epistolae Ho-Elianae*, writes of 'such glasses as anatomists use in the dissection of bodies, which can make a flea look like a cow'. John Carey unravels the two lines about the fleas thus: 'If fleas, when magnified, really look like cows ... then it follows that unmagnified fleas can't look like fleas at all but like very, very tiny cows. In other words, what Howell had at the end of his 'Multiplying Glasses' was a midget dairy herd, and that is why Marvell, seeing a midget dairy herd, likens it not just to fleas but to fleas waiting in Howell's multiplying glasses to be magnified and identified by him as cows.' (*Approaches to Marvell*, ed. C.A. Patrides, London, 1978, p.148.)

The expansive movement which takes place at the end of Randolph's poem 'Of a snake which embraced Lycoris' is very similar to that which occurs in stanza LVIII of 'UAH' but it uses, not modern optical glasses, but the ancient notion of stellification to move our eye from the minute animal to the heavens: 'And when, dear, snake, thou wilt no more renew/ Thy youthfull vigour, bid base earth adjew,/ Adde glory to the night, or from his spheare/ Huge *Python* pull, and fix thy torches there:/ Where like a river thou shalt bending go,/ And through the *Orbe* (a starry torrent) flow./ And thou, *Lycoris*, when th'art pleas'd to take/ No more of life, next thy beloved *Snake*/ Shine forth a constellation, full, and bright;/ Blesse the poor heavens with more majestick light./ Who in requitall shall present you there/ *Ariadnes Crown* and *Cassiopoeas Chayr*.'

41. St Augustine, *City of God*, ed. cit., pp.1071–2.
42. Sir John Davies writes that the soul 'is nigh, and farre, beneath, above,/ In point of time which thought can not devide./ Sh' is sent as soone to *China* as to *Spaine*,/ And thence returnes as soone as she is sent,/ She measures with one time, and with one paine/ An ell of Silke, and heavens wide-spreading Tent.' (*Nosce Teipsum*, ll.571–6.)
43. The nearest parallel to this is Spenser's description of the House of Alma in *FQ*, II. ix.

CHAPTER 6

1. Janel M. Mueller, 'Donne's Epic Venture in the *Metempsychosis*', *MP*, lxx, 1972, pp.109–37.
2. On the speed of fairy flight see William Empson, 'Fairy Flight in "A Midsummer Night's Dream"', *The London Review of Books*, I, i, 25 October 1979, pp.5–8.

Jan Kott also writes about Puck's speed, in *Shakespeare our Contemporary*, London, 1967, p.173.
3. Ibid., p.183.
4. Frank Kermode, 'Shakespeare's Mature Comedies', in *Renaissance Essays*, London, 1971, p.208.
5. This is Harold Brooks's phrase on p.cxix of his introduction to the New Arden edition.
6. Kott, op. cit., pp.184–8.
7. Cicero, *Tusculan Disputations*, I, xvii, 40–1; xviii, 42, trans. J.E. King, London, 1927 (Loeb edition), pp.47–51:

eam porro naturam esse quattuor omnia gignentium corporum, ut, quasi partita habeant inter se ac divisa momenta, terrena et humida suopte nutu et suo pondere ad pares angulos in terram et in mare ferantur, reliquae duae partes, una ignea, altera animalis, ut illae superiores in medium locum mundi gravitate ferantur et pondere, sic hae rursum rectis lineis in caelestem locum subvolent, sive ipsa natura superiora appetente sive quod a gravioribus leviora natura repellantur. Quae cum constent, perspicuum debet esse animos, cum e corpore excesserint, sive illi sint animales, id est, spirabiles, sive ignei, sublime ferri ... (Is autem animus ... ex inflammata anima constat ...) superiora capessat necesse est; nihil enim habent haec duo genera proni et supera semper petunt. Ita, sive dissipantur, procul a terris id evenit, sive permanent et conservant habitum suum, hoc etiam magis necesse est ferantur ad caelum et ab iis perrumpatur et dividatur crassus hic concretus aër, qui est terrae proximus, calidior est enim vel potius ardentior animus, quam est hic aër, quem modo dixi crassum atque concretum; quod ex eo sciri potest, quia corpora nostra terreno principiorum genere confecta, ardore animi concalescunt.

8. William Hazlitt, *Characters of Shakespeare's Plays*, Oxford, 1955, p.99.

9. References are to the New Arden edition of *The Tempest*, ed. Frank Kermode, London, 1962 (repr. with corrections).

10. See Peter Hulme, 'Hurricanes in the Caribbees: the Constitution of the Discourse of English Colonialism', in *1642: Literature and Power in the Seventeenth Century*, ed. F. Barker et al., Colchester, 1981, pp.55–83. Hulme argues that the word 'tempest' had specifically Providential associations which the word 'hurricane' had not.

11. See Appendix A of Kermode's edition, e.g. p.137: 'Yet it pleased our mercifull God, to make even this hideous and hated place, both the place of our safetie, and meanes of our deliverance' (from Strachey, *True Reportory of the Wracke*); p.141: 'All our men, being utterly spent, tyred, and disabled for longer labour, were even resolved, without any hope of their lives, to shut up the hatches, and to have committed themselves to the mercy of the sea ... when it pleased God out of his most gracious and mercifull providence, so to direct and guide our ship ... for her most advantage' (from Sylvester Jourdain, *A Discovery of the Barmudas*).

12. Jan Kott, 'La Tempête ou la répétition', *Tel Quel*, lxx, 1977, pp.136–162; this quotation is from page 136.

13. See Appendix B of Kermode's edition.

14. E.g. in I.ii.252ff; IV.i.175–84.

15. Leslie Fiedler notes the 'special ambiguity ... in the phrase "this thing of darkness I"', which seems for a moment completely to identify the ocultist Duke with the "savage and deformed slave".' (*The Stranger in Shakespeare*, ed. cit. pp.208–9.)

CHAPTER 7

1. See Richard Foster Jones, *The Triumph of the English Language*, Stanford, 1966, especially caps VII and VIII, 'The Ancient Language'.

2. Martial, *Epigrammata*, III.ii.3–5, IV, lxxxvi; Catullus, *Carmina*, xcv; see also Horace, *Epistulae*, II.i.269–70.

   E.g. Thomas Nashe, the first paragraph of 'The Introduction to the Dapper Monsieur Pages of the Court' in *The Unfortunate Traveller*; John Donne, 'Upon Mr.

Thomas Coryats Crudities', ll.34ff; Ben Jonson, *Epigrammes*, III; *The Underwood*, xliii, ll.51ff; Andrew Marvell, 'To His Worthy Friend Doctor Witty upon his Translation of the Popular Errors'; Laurence Sterne, *The Life and Opinions of Tristam Shandy* and *A Sentimental Journey*; Henry Mackenzie, *The Man of Feeling*; the last three prose fiction examples play with the idea of the literary fragment; see also Hugh Kenner, *The Stoic Comedians*, Los Angeles, 1962, cap. 2; Emrys Jones, 'Pope and Dullness', Chatterton Lecture, Oxford, 1968.

3. *Ben Jonson*, vol. viii, pp.581–2.

4. William Empson, *Seven Types of Ambiguity*, ed. cit., p.131.

5. William Empson, *Some Versions of the Pastoral*, Harmondsworth, 1966, pp.117–18.

6. Blair Worden writes: 'A book about Marvell which truly "united the disciplines of literature and history" might tell the parallel story of the damage to language, to literature, and to imagination' (*The London Review of Books*, V, vii, 21 April 1983, p.16.)

7. The corrupt and 'Suttle Nunns' in 'Upon Appleton House' attempt to lure the Virgin Thwates into their order by promises, not of austerity, but of softness: 'Nor is our *Order* yet so nice,/ Delight to banish as a Vice./ Here Pleasure Piety doth meet;/ One perfecting the other Sweet./ So through the mortal fruit we boyl/ The Sugars uncorrupting Oyl:/ And that which perisht while we pull,/ Is thus preserved clear and full.// For such indeed are all our Arts;/ Still handling Natures finest Parts./ Flow'rs dress the Altars; for the Clothes,/ The Sea-born Amber we compose;/ Balms for the griv'd we draw; and Pasts/ We mold, as Baits for curious tasts.' (ll.169–182).

   The molded sweet-meats, like the 'more luscious' kneaded earth in 'The Mower against Gardens', are the products of a false art which deviates from nature. The Nun's metaphor of firmness—that of the squashy fruit soul being crystallised into a boiled sweet—is conspicuously an image of illusory firmness. When, three stanzas later, we are told that 'The *Nuns* smooth Tongue has suckt [Isabel Thwates] in' (l.200), it is impossible not to recall the boiled sweet, and the soul it once was.

8. Thomas Sprat, *History of the Royal Society* (London, 1667), ed. Jackson I. Cope and Harold Whitmore Jones, Saint Louis 1958, p.113.

9. Jonathan Swift, *Gulliver's Travels*, ed.

10. Angus Ross, London, 1972, III, v, pp.167–8.

10. Walter Benjamin, in his work on the German *Trauerspiel* associates allegory with the Christian doctrine of the Fall (*Origin of German Tragic Drama*, ed. cit., p.224): 'The allegorically significant is prevented by guilt from finding fulfilment of its meaning in itself.'.

11. The rail cut down by the mower in 'Upon Appleton House' (ll.395–400) is both emblem and victim of that mower; similarly, the buds which little T.C. is asked to spare are representative of her as well as susceptible to her.

12. *The Tempest*, III.iii.2; V.i.242; 'amazement' I.ii.14; I.ii.198, V.i.104.

Index